A Creationist's Approach to

Organic Gardening

A Creationist's Approach to

Organic Gardening

James A. Eagle

TATE PUBLISHING & Enterprises

Published by Tate Publishing & Enterprises, LLC
127 E. Trade Center Terrace | Mustang, Oklahoma 73064 USA
1.888.361.9473 | www.tatepublishing.com

Tate Publishing is committed to excellence in the publishing industry. The company reflects the philosophy established by the founders, based on Psalm 68:11,
"The Lord gave the word and great was the company of those who published it."

Book design copyright © 2010 by Tate Publishing, LLC. All rights reserved.
Cover design by Amber Gulilat
Interior design by Joey Garrett

Published in the United States of America

ISBN: 978-1-61739-183-5
1. Gardening / Organic
2. Gardening / Vegetables
10.09.13

Dedication

This book is dedicated to Jesus Christ, the son of the living God and creator of all. The second dedication is to my wife of sixty-four years.

It is dedicated to Jesus Christ for His free gift of eternal life in Heaven, who died on the cross for my sins, which were many, and rose again on the third day. It would have been impossible for me to have written this book if it had not been for His gift of grace which was so great that it blotted out all my sins with His shed blood on the cross at Calvary. Today I have the assurance of a home in Heaven for eternity.

It is dedicated to my wife because of her patience and my absence from her presence, leaving her alone to read, perform needle-work, or watch TV. She also proofread each and every page of this book. Her love and support is greatly appreciated. She has been a great asset in my life. I owe much to her, and love her more today than the day we were married sixty-four years ago, if that is possible.

Acknowledgements

To Mr. Condrey, the FFA and Agriculture teacher at Rockwell High School, Rockwell, NC, from 1934 through 1938. He is now deceased, but he left a mark on me that endured for my life. With his prodding and encouragement, I won prizes at County and State levels in judging livestock, poultry, hogs, and seed. He left a desire for farming and gardening in me which never declined.

Miss Owens, my English teacher while in High School from 1934 to1938. With her encouragement and help, I was able to win speaking contests in High School and County level on Agriculture Subjects.

My wife, Maxine C. Eagle, has been my encouragement, help, and a real companion from September 8 1945 until now. Without her I don't know what I would have done.

My little sister, Mrs. Marjorie L. Eagle Miller, who has also encouraged me and had faith in everything I have accomplished. At the age of 86 she still encourages me. To our wonderful parents that brought us up in a Christian home, and taught us the morals taught in the Bible. They never let us go to bed, at night, without reading the Bible and having prayer. I have so much to be thankful to them for.

Contents

Introduction

When Adam and Eve sinned in the Garden of Eden, sin entered into this world. This perfect garden was to last for eternity. *No death.* But man polluted it with sin, so now we have to contend with weeds, thorns, diseases, and insects that destroy plants and produces death. Even with all of this, God left a way of escape whereby we can overcome these physical difficulties, by our *labor,* which God informed Adam after he sinned. *Labor* was one of the curses imposed on mankind for his sin (see Genesis 3:17-129). We all have inherited this sin nature. He also gave a way of escape from the punishment God provided for Satan and his angels. This shows how much God loves us regardless of our sin.

What are the established laws of God as related to gardening? The spiritual laws are given in the Bible, but there are many physical laws that relate to the growing of plants, which some will be covered in Chapter 1.

God thought of everything that could help us in our labors, after man sinned, to produce food. Beneficial insects were created to balance out the effects done by harmful insects in the destruction of plants. God's curse just made it hard, whereby we have to work and discover the many ways He provided to conquer the evil we have incurred upon ourselves.

Man, in his endeavors to restore the perfect garden, has destroyed it even more. Some of man's efforts have proven very detrimental to the life of our soil, as well as our own life. In Proverbs we read, *"There is a way that seems right to man, but it's end is the way of death."*

They have produced deadly poisons and carcinogenic solutions, which are causing thousands of deaths each year. Profit seems to be the main focus in the marketing of these deadly products. They insist that they are making life easier for us and that it is the only way we can provide enough food to feed the world. The fact is that they cause more trouble and provide food that is less palatable and nutritious. Even our government agencies and universities are promoting these methods because of the strong lobbying and support they give to our universities and politicians. The universities are even working to help produce new chemicals for the chemical companies, which, in turn, provide support for them.

We might as well get used to some imperfections in our fruit and vegetables. The perfections will not come until Jesus Christ returns to this earth. Then He will restore the perfect garden again.

Many tell me that they only purchase organic grown fruit and vegetables. How do you know it is organically grown? Too much produce is on the market that is falsely proclaimed to be organic.

This book is mainly written for the small, home gardener or small farmer, though much of the information can be used by commercial farmers. It can be amazing the amount of fruit and vegetables that can be grown and produced on a very small area. I doubt that there is any homeowner who doesn't do some form of gardening. Growing shrubs and flowers is gardening. Having houseplants to enrich the beauty of your home is also a form of gardening. We will cover as much of this type of gardening for you as possible.

There is an incident that happened during World War II that proves my point on the efficiency of small home gardens. Switzerland assigned small plots for all its citizens to raise their own food, then the government armed all citizens, closed its borders, and declared their neutrality. They survived without firing a shot during the war.

Gardening in accordance with the established laws of God is assisting your plants to grow and produce in the ways that have been established from the beginning of Creation. For life to be lived fully and in order for life to be reproduced, both animal and vegetable life, we must abide by the established laws God created in the beginning of time. As long ago as 70 years we did not have the amount of destructive insects and plant diseases as we have today. Man has upset this balance through his misuse of poisons and fungicides. The good insects and the good bacteria have been destroyed along with the bad. These issues will be covered in the main text of this book.

After World War II, the chemical companies started assuring the farmers that they would be able to produce massive crops on the same acreage by using chemical fertilizers, pesticides, fungicides, and herbicides. They intended to get rid of all harmful insects and eliminate disease. They failed to warn what the real outcome would be. They destroyed the beneficial along with the harmful. Not only that, but there are a number of untold deaths of humans and animals due to this use. More and more results of the health problems caused by these chemicals have been emerging. Also, many of the harmful insects built up resistance to their many poisons, making it necessary to seek stronger and more deadly ones.

Now scientists are proclaiming that genetic engineering will solve all our problems and feed the hungry of the world. This is one of the grandest myths ever to be perpetrated on mankind. This is due to Darwin's myth of evolution. After all, according to evolutionists, everything is here by chance. It takes time for evolution to establish the perfect earth, so their science will do it for us. The biotech people are building cartels and monopolies to make the world dependent on them in order to control the world. They will create the famines that will occur due to this type of science. If God had intended the different kinds of animals and plant life to cross breed, He would have created them that way at the very beginning of His creation. This technology is being driven by a mindset depleted and void of any moral values, and is contrary to God's laws.

When the Olympics were held in China, the Chinese claimed they were able to prevent rain during the Olympics. Is this claim true?

Anytime we violate a law of God's, we sin. In Romans 6:23, it tells us that the wages of sin is death. Therefore, when we sin, something or someone dies because of it. What has died? First of all, healthy soil is loaded with beneficial bacteria and insects that control disease, as well as insects that harm the plants. So, the soil has died when it is loaded with poisons and herbicides. It is dead soil and becomes just substance to plant seed in. Also, many people are dead or dying today because of cancer due to the carcinogenic fungicides, herbicides, and pesticides used. Exposure to some of these poisons can kill within minutes and hours. I am personally aware of instances of this happening.

All life, including animal and plant life, requires four main things to exist. They are water, light, food, and proper temperature. If you eliminated any one, life would cease to exist. One of the most important is light. Here is another proof that God created the universe, the earth, and everything in and on the earth in six twenty-four hour days. On the third day of creation God created all plant life (See Genesis 1:11-13). On the fourth day He created light (See Genesis 1:14-19). Since God created plants one day before he created light, this proved it was twenty-four hour days He created in. The plants could not have survived without light very long. Some theorize that a day could have been eons of time, since the Bible says that a thousand years is as a day with God. Before God created everything there was no time. He created time for us, not himself. Some ask, "Where did God come from?" The Bible tells us He was here from the beginning.

Gardening is an ideal way to have a close relationship with God. How can one work with plants and the soil and not realize that there was a Creator that did it *all*. Gardening also has a healing effect on those participating in it. In fact, many states have started gardening programs for the mentally ill and retarded, as therapy. Isn't it wonderful how God can use His creations to heal the mind? He can heal the body as well. Even writing about gardening is healing for me at the age of ninety. It is amazing how it has invigorated and recharged me.

You may think that Christianity is the main subject of this book instead of gardening. When God saved me for eternal life in Heaven, then Christianity became a very important part of my life. When one realizes that God loves us so much He sent His Son to live a perfect life then die on the cross for our redemption and rise again to eternal life. Salvation is a free gift of God. You must believe in your heart that Jesus Christ took your sins upon Himself to redeem you if you accept His free gift. We are saved by faith in Him and then His grace redeems us from eternal punishment in Hell. You too can have this assurance.

It is my firm belief that all who reads this book and practices the contents will have a beautiful, healthy, wonderful garden, and become acquainted with a wonderful Redeemer. May God bless you.

Chapter One

Five Laws of God Which Always Work

We will discuss five natural laws of God. These are laws I have named myself. Scientists may have a different name for them. The first is *The Law of Germination:* When you plant a good seed in the ground you know that it will sprout every time when the conditions are right. It bursts forth and comes to top of the soil. Why doesn't it sprout and go down? This principle has been tried over and over millions of times, but no seed sprouts down. It makes no difference as to what position it is planted. It will always come up through the soil and the roots go down into the soil. In most cases, when a seed is too deep in the soil it will lay dormant until the ground is stirred up, bringing it further to the top, then it germinates. Others will remain dormant until the right conditions, such as temperature and especially moisture, are present.

Let us consider the seed. It has a protective outer shell to protect it and it appears dead They can range in size from a tiny speck, like the seed of an African violet, and as large as the coconut. You can freeze most seed for years, and yet when you plant them in a moist, warm soil they will sprout with life, forming a plant that will bear fruit of its kind. How could this happen by chance? What gives it this life? God!

The *Law of Fertilization and Seed Production:* We know that when a flower of a plant has been fertilized by pollen, from the same kind of plant, it will produce seeds for reproduction. It does not change into a different species unless man changes it by genetic engineering. Genetic engineering is an unnatural method in which they are trying to change the way God created it. Many plants differ in their method of pollination, but it all boils down to the fact that two sexes are required in the reproduction that takes place. We refer to them as male and female. Some plants produce both male and female sections in the same flower. Some plants have both female and male flowers on the same plant. When this happens, there is a method the Creator provided for by using insects and birds to carry pollen from one flower to the other. There are some plants that produce only female flowers and separate plants produce the male flowers. Again, the insects and birds provide fertilization. I believe that God has a good sense of humor in creating the many different ways plants and animals reproduce, or else, He was proving his wisdom and power. Maybe these complex methods were created that way to make us realize there had to be a Designer and Creator.

The *Law of Need*: The Creator provided roots for the plant in order for it to have a method of taking nutrients and water from the soil to provide for the plant's needs. Those roots will grow towards any source where the moisture or nutrients are available. I have seen the roots of plants grow toward compost piles that were over thirty feet away, just to get the moisture and nutrients the compost provides. In our old age, my wife and I are using twenty-gallon tubs to garden in. They are set on timbers, and have one-half inch holes drilled in the bottom. We had roots from trees twenty feet away come up in the drain holes to get moisture and nutrients. It plugged the drain holes and there were so many fine feed roots in the tubs that it prevented anything else from growing in them. All plants require nutrients and water, but their needs vary as to the kind of plant. God has adapted them to grow in almost all climates. When either one of these needs are required by the plant, then you will see the Law of Need used by the plant. If you have a plant that requires full sun for maximum production, and it is planted in a shady area, then the cells in the stem on the shady side will start elongating and turning the plant toward the sun. I saw this demonstrated this past summer, when I planted some jalapeno peppers in some containers that were shaded by a very large holly tree, which was planted twenty-four years ago. This tree is now over thirty-five feet tall. These peppers grew about five feet tall and turned toward the sun so far that they had to be staked so as to hold them up.

The *Law of Seasons:* This law has demonstrated itself over and over, whereby we can depend on it for planting, harvesting, and many other things we do according to the season. It can be bitter cold in the winter, but we can always assure ourselves that warm weather is coming. We can always be certain that the seasons will occur.

In Daniel 6:20-21 it states, "Blessed be the name of God forever and ever, for wisdom and might are His. And He changes the times and the seasons."

The Creator has also given us events that happen pointing to things that will occur shortly. I can remember as a kid watching geese flying over going south in the early fall. My mother would say, "We are going to have an early and very cold winter." My dad would observe the maple trees in bloom in the spring, and he would comment, "It is time to plant corn." Another sign was when the oak tree's leaves were the size of a mouse's ear, he would plant corn. There are many other signs that have been used to judge as to when to perform certain jobs on the farm.

The fifth law is *The Law of Decomposition.* This is a law the Creator has devised to recycle vegetable waste into food for plants. Take a walk into a wooded area that has been there for some time, maybe forty or fifty years or longer. A forest not planted by man, but designed by the Creator. You will find that you will sink down into the soft, organic matter produced by the annual falling of the leaves. The top layer will be the last leaves to have fallen. The layer underneath them will be partially decomposed, but you will find the feeding roots all mingled in them already, obtaining the nutrients available. We call this layer *leaf mold.* Underneath this layer of leaf mold is soft soil that has been enriched over many years through this recycling program created by God. There is another thing you will notice in this forest: it will have practically no weeds. Here is another law of God's taking place. In the early stages of decomposition, plant material releases acids and chemicals that will restrain and inhibit the growth of many weeds.

Observe a field that has been tilled by man with machinery and where many chemicals have been used to grow crops. It becomes depleted of organic matter, and almost worthless for growing healthy crops. Leave it vacant, and in a year or two weeds will start growing and, in time, will cover the field. The weeds will die in winter and start the decaying process that will restore the field to a healthy field. In ten years or less, you will observe trees that will come up and start the restoring process all over again. The seeds of trees will be spread by many means, which God has established to restore the earth. Some seeds are equipped with a wing that can carry them long distances in the wind. Others have fruit which animals eat, consuming the fruit and seed. They in turn can carry them miles before depositing the seed, which then sprouts and germinates. Others have small fruit which the birds consume and deposit its seed long distances from where it was eaten. These methods were all established by God.

When observing the laws which have been listed here, and understanding how they work so perfectly, you have to realize that everything was designed. Therefore, if it was designed, then there had to be a designer. Gardening builds my faith in the Creator.

James A. Eagle

Many farmers today have discovered that the heavy equipment used in agriculture compacts the soil and makes it almost impossible for the plant roots to penetrate this compacted and dead soil. It is dead because it is lacking in humus and microorganisms that are needed for healthy soil. The microorganisms are needed to control disease organisms and to convert organic matter to rich humus. Many have started a method of no-till farming.

Recently, I heard a farmer state that he plowed a field that had been planted in wheat two years ago, and the stubble had been plowed under. The stubble was still about the same as it was when it was turned under two years ago. It could not start a decaying process because the microorganisms were destroyed by chemicals and improper farming methods.

God takes His time in restoring the soil, but, using His laws, we can restore it in a very short time when done properly. By taking a soil that is depleted in nutrients, it can be partially restored in one year. I say partially, because to make it completely whole it takes longer. Until the organisms that make a soil healthy are present, and the poisons, that are present in the soil, are leached out and depleted, then it is not completely restored.

You can start a program of no-till gardening and reduce your labor considerably. It is especially beneficial for senior citizens, like myself. This system will give you a healthy and productive garden with little labor. The food you harvest will be so much more nutritious and healthy than what you buy at the grocery stores. These methods will be discussed in another chapter.

Chapter Two

Preparing the Proper Habitat and Environment for Your Garden

So, you want a beautiful landscape, with flowers, flowering shrubs, vegetable garden, and even fruit trees, berries, and grapes. The best way to have all this is by using the established laws the Creator has given us, which we will cover in this book. If you come to some word or phrase you don't understand or know the meaning of, then go to Addendum I which is the dictionary of terms.

There are five very important fundamentals in making your backyard a bird sanctuary. They are food, water, shelter, nesting habitats and control of predators. Without these five fundamentals you will not have a thriving sanctuary for birds. We will cover them all here.

But first, I wish to cover some of the things my wife and I did when we retired. We bought seventeen acres in South Carolina to build our retirement home. It was nothing but a large weed field. The re-establishment by the Creator had already started to take place by all the weeds. Weeds are the first thing which God uses to re-establish dead soil. They grow during the spring and summer, then die and decay, reestablishing the nutrients that have been lost. Also, beneficial bacteria and insects start to emerge again. This was twenty-five years ago. Today it is a healthy natural habitat for many of God's creatures. My wife calls it our jungle. We planted many of the trees and shrubs, but being unable to maintain it properly in our old age, it now has many additional plants that established themselves naturally. My wife threatens to get a pair of monkeys.

It had been cultivated for many, many years using the chemical pesticides, fungicides, and herbicides. Around the edge of the place were many of the containers of the products that had been used, which we had to clean up.

After building our home, we started the clean-up. We didn't have the equipment we really needed to turn those weeds under, so we pulled weeds that were higher than we were. They were hauled to a place behind the house for composting (We will cover composting later in Chapter Four). It seemed that grasshoppers were everywhere. When you walked through the weeds they would take off in all directions. When we planted some hibiscus in our landscape, the leaves were stripped in two days. There were very few birds. About the only birds we saw were mocking birds, English sparrows, and crows.

Our first endeavor was to establish shrubs and trees to provide a home and nesting places for the birds. We set out a few pine trees, an ash, and two oaks, but the main thing was trees, shrubs and bushes that would provide food and nesting. We also constructed bird houses, especially for blue birds. We knew they were somewhere in the area.

Today about twelve acres are in woods, which many are self-seeded. Some of the trees are as large as twenty inches in diameter.

We also set out over eighty different plants of blueberries of 15 varieties. These were to be food for ourselves and the birds. Today those bushes are providing between thirty and fifty bushels of berries each season, even after the birds get their share. After gathering all we want, we give the rest to friends and neighbors. We also have Muscadine grapes

Since then, I have rooted more blueberries, which have been set out among the trees, especially for the birds. They do not bear as headily as they do in full sun, but bear enough to provide plenty of food for our feathered friends. Today it is rare if you see a grasshopper. There are many other insects that I never see any more.

We now had two of the very important items necessary to attract birds: that is, food provided by the fruit of the shrubs and trees, and the shrubs and trees that also provide the shelter. We sit on our deck, and if the dog next door comes over to visit, the birds will quickly head for some thick shrub or vine. This is their shelter. It provides roosting places for them. It also provides places for nesting for many species. For others, we have provided nest boxes. (See Nesting Habitat below.)

Other perennial shrubs, trees, ornamental plants, and perennials which can be planted to attract the birds are:

Amelanchier: (Service berries and Juneberry are common names) There are at least twenty-five genus of this plant, but only a few are sold by American nurserymen. All bear berries that are loved by many birds. Some of these are:

A. canadensis: It is known as the Shadblow or Downy Serviceberry. This is the tallest of the genus. It can grow as tall as 60 feet, but can be controlled by pruning. It is hardy to Zone Four. It has small white flowers in the early spring before the grayish, young foliage puts out. The foliage is also colorful in the fall of the year.

A. florida: It's common name is Pacific Serviceberry. It is one of the hardiest geniuses. It will grow as far north as Zone Two. It can also grow tall as much as 30 feet

A. x grandflora: It has a common name of Apple Serviceberry. This genus has the largest flowers of all. It can grow up to 25 feet tall. The flowers are 1-¼" in diameter and pure white. This is a hybrid and it has a variety named *Rubenscens* which has pinkish flower buds and opens to a light pink, but fades to a white shortly after opening.

A. laevis: This is called Allegany Serviceberry, and is another tall plant, growing from 15 to 36 feet There may be more varieties which are lower-growing.

Arctostaphylos: It has the common name of Bearberry. It has small white or pink urn-shaped flowers similar to blueberries. The fruits are red to brownish drupes. They are not as hardy as the Serviceberries, but most are lower-growing.

A. hookeri: With a common name of Hooker Manzanita, it's an evergreen and low-growing to only about 2 feet. It is sometimes used as a ground cover. The leaves are glossy and one inch long. It is hardy only to Zone Eight.

A. manzanita: It has a common name of Common Manzanita. It is hardy to Zone Seven. It has dense white or pink flower clusters in the spring, and grows up to twelve feet tall.

A. Stanfordiana: It's common name is Stanford Manzanita. It is hardy to Zone Seven and grows up to 6 feet It has lustrous evergreen leaves which are 1½ inches long and has brilliant pink flowers, born in dense panicles in March and April, which almost cover the plant. It is a well-rounded shrub with red bark.

A. tomentosa: It has the common name of Woolly Manzanita, and is hardy to Zone 7. It grows to 4 feet tall with oval leaves, 1 to 1½ inches long with wooly surface underneath. The flowers are white or pink from March to May.

A. uva-ursi: This is the hardiest of all, and one of the best ever-green ground covers. The foliage turns bronze in the fall, and has scarlet red berries. It thrives in poor, sandy soil in the hot sun. The leaves are small, ½ to ¾ inches long. It is ideal for planting on sandy banks along the highway.

Diospyros: This is the persimmon group of trees. The only native one is *D. Virginiana.* It can be found growing in the eastern and southeastern states. There are several on our place, and the fruit is relished by birds in the fall. They are also very tasty as food. When I was a kid, there were two large persimmon trees on our farm, which my dad really took care of. In the fall of the year, he would mulch a wide area with straw, about eight inches deep. When the persimmons fell, they would not mash and you could pick them up whole. The straw would then decompose and add nutrients to the soil. One summer a thunderstorm came and the lightening struck that tree and split it almost all the way to the ground. He refused to cut it, so he patched and pruned it. Several years later, lightening again struck the tree. They say lightening does not strike twice in the same place. This one finished the tree. My dad then surrendered it to the fireplace.

Empetrum: There is only one genus which I am familiar with, which is: *E. nigrum whose* common name is Black Crowberry. This grows to 10 feet, and is more of a plant to provide feed than it is be ornamental. The leaves are small, only about ½ inch in diameter. The flowers are purplish and small. The fruit is black and berrylike.

Fragaria: This is the botanical name for the many strawberries. The variety of strawberries you purchase in the grocery stores can be planted, but if you can find any of the wild varieties you will have better luck attracting the birds. The strawberries in the stores have been hybridized and developed for beauty and size, but so many are lacking in flavor. There are flavors in most of these wild strawberries that far surpass anything you can purchase in the grocery stores. When I was a kid, one of the greatest joys when spring came, was to search for wild strawberry patches.

These berries had more flavor and aroma than the many cultivated varieties. The sad part is that they are small, but this does not stop the birds.

Gaylussacia: It's common name is *Huckleberry,* and the only variety I recommend is *G. brachycranic.* It is a native of Pennsylvania, Kentucky, Tennessee, and Virginia. In time, it makes a beautiful ball of evergreen growth as much as 25 feet tall. In the fall the leaves can turn to a beautiful bronze color. It is slow growing, so be patient. It is hard to find in most nurseries because it is so slow-growing. It will take cold to Zone Five. It may be easier to obtain the seeds of this plant. Some have mistaken this plant for a blueberry, but they are not the same.

Ilex: This is the holly family and there are too many to list. The native holly in the United States is *I. Opaca,* also known as the American Holly. There are other varieties that have berries as well, and most have the female and male plants, requiring a male plant for about every six to eight female plants, in order for the female to bear fruit.

Juniperous: These are the junipers or, as some call them, cedars. There are many species of these, but the most common is the native tree, which covers over three-fourths of the United States. It is the *J. virginiana.* When I was a kid, this was the kind we hunted to cut as a Christmas tree. It seemed that we could always find one of just the right size and beautiful shape. The juniper berry is used in flavoring. It is a favorite of many birds in the winter. The seeds need stratification before germination, but when the birds eat them, the stratification takes place and they then deposit the seed where you can find them coming up.

Malus: Trees of this group are the apples. It is the crab apples which you would be interested in for the birds, but I see a lot of bird damage in our apples as well. There are many species of crab

James A. Eagle

apple, so pick one for its beauty when in bloom, as well for the smaller size crab apple.

Morus: This is the mulberry group. Some varieties grow into very large trees, and many people use them for eating and making jams and jelly. I wouldn't plant them in your yard, because they really cause a mess in summer when they start dropping. My favorite for the birds is the *Russian Mulberry.* or *M. alba 'Tatarica.'* The fruit is smaller than many varieties and the birds clean them as fast as they ripen in late summer. They root easily by cuttings.

Myrica: There are four species of this plant which are native of U.S. *M. californica* has the common name of California Bayberry. This is an evergreen, upright-growing shrub, growing to 36 feet tall. It is a native of California, and hardy to Zone Seven. It has purple berries in the fall of the year. *M. cerifera* is known as the Wax-myrtle and can be seen growing in the eastern part of the U.S. Traveling along I-95, you can observe many along the highway through the Carolinas, Georgia, and Florida. It has waxy leaves and evergreen. It is hardy to Zone Six. The gray, waxy fruit appear in clusters, and remain on the plant into the heart of winter, providing feed for the birds when it is scarce. This species is extremely aromatic, including the berries, leaves and twigs. This species makes an excellent landscape plant. *M. gale* has a common name of Sweetgale. This species is hardy throughout the colder parts of the U.S., and growing in moist peaty sections of the country. It is hardy to Zone Four. The flowers are in the form of catkins, and sexes are on separate plants. It's fruit is very small, and not used much for ornamental purposes.

M. pennsylyvanica is just called Bayberry. It grows to 9 feet tall, and is semi-evergreen. It is found along the coastal sections of Maryland to Newfoundland, Canada, and is hardy to Zone Two, and the hardest of all. This species will survive saltwater spray. It can be grown in poor sandy soils. All parts of the plant are aromatic.

Here, we have four species of the Wax-myrtle or Bayberry adapted to four widely different areas, which God provides in all of His creations:

Nyssa: This tree has several common names. It may be called even different names in other areas. They are: Sour Gum, Black Gum, and Black Tupelo. These trees are deciduous (shed leaves in the fall). They produce fruits that are small blue drupes in the fall of the year. *N. sinensis:* The common name is Chinese Sour Gum, and is a native of China. This tree has beautiful yellow leaves, combined with red in the fall of the year. It makes a fine specimen tree in the landscape. It can grow as tall as 60 feet in time. If you purchase one, get a small one in a container, because it is difficult to transplant bare-root. *N. sylvatica:* This species is known as Black Gum and Black Tupelo. You can find this tree in the woodlands of the eastern United States along streams, rivers and in swampland. As a kid, I can remember an old German lady who lived on a farm next to us. She would get a twig of this tree and cut a piece about six inches long, remove the bark for about an inch on one end, chew on it until it was in fine bristles. She then used it to dip snuff. My mother said she use it as a child to brush her teeth, because her family couldn't afford tooth brushes. The leaves appear from orange in color to a dark purple. The fruit is a small drupe appearing in late summer. Grow this in a moist place.

Rhus: These are the sumacs and have spread from underground roots. There are many different species. I do not recommend these for the small landscape because of their underground roots. Neither are they very decorative, but they do bear clusters of berries which are consumed by the birds. They are ideal for naturalizing for the large landscape. There are many species of these, including the Poison Oak. Here will be only the species best recommended.

James A. Eagle

R. aromatica: This species was formerly called *R. Canadensis.* You may find some nurseries still selling it by this name. The common name is *Fragrant Sumac.* It can be found growing over much of the eastern part of North America. It is hardy to Zone Three. It is eye-catching when its small yellow flowers appear before the three leaflet leaves appear. The fruit turns red in the early summer, and starts providing food for the birds. Then the foliage turns a brilliant scarlet to orange. This species is good for planting on sunny dry banks

R. glabra: Has the common name of Smooth Sumac. I would not recommend this for small spaces, but is good for larger landscapes. There is some located on our place. Not all of these plants have fruit, because they have no pistil. The mature plant of this species grows to 9 or more feet tall.

Rosa: This is the rose that we are so familiar with, but we are interested in the ones that is so good at providing food for the birds. It is *R. rugosa,* and the common name is the same 'Rugosa Rose'. It is one of the most famous because of its flowers, which come in several colors, because it is vary adaptable and can even stand salt water spray. For the habitat we chose it because of its red fruit which is rich in vitamins, especially C. The birds love it. You can eat these as well. There are excellent recipes for rose hip jelly. Yes, the fruit is called rose hips.

Rubus: This is the berry group of fruit such as blackberries, raspberry, dewberry, etc. There is quite a list of the species, and many, many varieties. Purchase the ones you like, and I would recommend the thornless varieties. You can share these with the birds.

Sorbus: This is known as Mountain Ashes. There are species that are native to the northern temperate regions of the world. Only what I consider the best as a habitat for wildlife will be listed.

S. Americana: This is a native of northeastern North America. It is hardy to Zone Two. Horticulturists claim that this tree will not survive in Zone 8, which we live in, but we have one over twenty-four years old and about fifty or sixty feed tall. It is suppose to be too hot in our area. Again do not listen to what is always touted as fact.

Water for the Habitat: Birds need water just as we do. A good source of fresh water should be provided for drinking and taking baths. It can be as simple as a plastic birdbath, or an elaborate fountain or pool. The extent you wish to go to in establishing this is your choice. There are many sources where you can obtain this equipment. There are stores that cater only to bird lovers, which carry all kinds of watering, nesting, and feed for the many different kinds of birds.

Nesting for the Habitat: Many birds nest in hollow trees and stumps, but since man has destroyed many of these natural nesting areas, we must provide substitutes. These are in the form of different kinds of bird houses to meet the need of the different species of birds. The Purple Martin is one of our favorite birds, but if you have large trees in your back yard, then there is no need to try and attract them. They like an open area with multiple houses or sections to build in. The gourd is a favorite nesting site for the martin. There should be a dozen or more gourds on a single pole. Martins are colony birds, and enjoy others around the site they select.

Here is a story about martins we experienced about ten years after moving where we live today. We had about twenty gourds up for martins, and had them build in them every year until 1995. My wife was setting on the deck one afternoon watching them when she started screaming for me. I went out on the deck and a black rat snake was climbing the pole. Before I could get to him he had crawled into a gourd where there were baby martins. We had a telescoped pole, so I lowered it and burst the gourd open. He had already eaten the birds, but I killed him. The martins continued to finish raising their young, but no martins would ever build nests in these gourds again. I even moved the post about 150 yards in a different location, but no martins. I have heard that they have a way of comminuting information to others as to where danger lurks.

The Blue Bird also likes an open area away from dense growth of trees or shrubs. The Blue Bird house should be in the open section of your garden. The opening in the box should be 1½" inches diameter. This will prevent many unwanted birds, such as starlings, from entering the box. The starlings will eat the eggs and small birds of other birds. An opening of one inch is large enough for the Carolina Wren. The wren house can be attached to a storage building or garage. They will go inside the building if they can find an opening. I have seen them build inside of a tin can inside of a building. I have also known them to build in the top of a butane-gas bottle. If you live near a forest, or where there are many trees, then you may have woodpeckers building in your bird houses. The Downy Woodpecker will quite often go into a house that is put into a tree. I had a Red Headed Woodpecker to open the hole of a Blue Bird house and build in it. He had a hole as large as three inches in diameter. There has been a family of Flickers that cut out a hole in the top of the electric light pole next to the house and built their nest in it for the last several years.

Protecting the Habitat from Predators: We have one predator that is not natural to America. It has been multiplied by man and has assumed an undesirable role in reducing our bird populations. That predator is the common house cat. The house cat is not even a native of this continent. It was imported from Europe and Asia and then to the Americas. I have no objections to people owning cats, but when they let them run loose and use no control over them, they become an enemy to our birds.

What I have to say about cats will offend many people that love them, but I have more love for my birds than I do for stray cats. We have many species of cats in the wild, but they have not exceeded uncontrollable populations as the house cat has, because they have natural predators in the wild. Every year there are millions of house cats put to sleep at animal shelters because we do not have them spayed or neutered. I have known female cats to drop a litter in the shrubs or planted areas of my place. These are stray cats that have become wild in nature. I have seen them climb the pole where I had a Blue Bird house and reach inside with their paws to remove the birds. There was a mockingbird nest in a large tomato vine, and the baby birds were almost large enough to leave the nest. The next morning there were cat tracks and baby bird feathers over the ground. The evidence spoke for itself.

If you have cats, please bring them in at night, or have some kind of enclosure to put them in for the night. I have been told that cats could be trained not to eat birds, but I do not believe it. Maybe some cat lovers can provide this information. If your neighbor has cats, then ask them to cooperate and confine their cat at night. If you do not know who the stray cat belongs to, then here is an alternative method. There are available live traps on the market for raccoons, opossums, and other wild animals. Get one of these, bait it, and when you have caught the cat, inquire of your neighbors if they are missing one. If they are not, take the cat to the animal shelter.

Other predators, especially if you live in a rural area, are hawks, owls, and foxes. There are very few birds destroyed by the hawks and owls, because the bird will dart into a dense shrub or thicket which the hawk or owl cannot penetrate. I have bushes and shrubs that have thorns which provide excellent shelter. The fox is the enemy to birds that nest and roost on the ground, like our Bobwhite, Whip-Poor-Will, Chuck-Will's-Widow, and towhees. You can use the trap I mentioned above for the fox.

Once you have established a rather ideal habitat for the birds, you will find that they will congregate at your place, finding it an ideal home. You will start seeing species of birds you have never seen before. Now you will need a bird guide. See your book store for one that appeals to you.

James A. Eagle

Have you ever realized that the majority of birds and insects which are our worst enemies were imported intentionally or unintentionally? Their natural enemies are not present here to keep them in balance, therefore they become a real nuisance and menace. The point I am trying to establish is that once we institute a natural environment for the birds and animals, we will be able to control the harmful and undesirable insects and birds. It is rare for us to see an English sparrow or starling today. It seems when the native birds are present, they seem to leave.

With the proper environment, we will encourage the presence of the beneficial insects and birds. Not only that, but there are other predators of insects and rodents which we will attract when things are in balance. Some of these are toads, lizards, snakes. Oh! Did this offend someone? I know that many think of these as enemies, but they are very valuable in keeping things in balance. You would be amazed at how many insects and rodents these animal forms eliminate from our garden area. As far as I am concerned, my place is a good example. I do not mean that I am not troubled by any insects or rodents, but it is nothing compared to what it was before we started restoring the natural conditions.

Plant food bearing plants that provide food, especially for winter food. Even the annuals' you plant in your garden will provide seed for them in the winter if you do not cut the flowering heads off or destroy the plant. To leave those dry, dead plants may not be your idea of a well-groomed garden, but the birds will love them. Some of my favorite flowers that provide food are the Mexican Sunflower, Bee Balm and the Black-Seeded Sunflower. In the summer they provide food for the Humming birds, then in the winter, the seeds provide food for the Cardinals, Towhees, Thrasher and many other birds.

In our own garden we have blueberries, blackberries, strawberries, and grapes. We enjoy them, and are willing to share them with the birds, because they do more good in controlling the insects than the few berries they take. Birds can be wonderful friends.

Establishing a Habitat for Beneficial Insects: Why do we want to establish a habitat for insects? We do not wish to establish a habitat for all insects, but just the beneficial. Before the proliferation of the petro-chemical attack to destroy all of our insects through chemistry, 98 percent of all insects were beneficial. Through their attempt to solve man's insect problems, they have destroyed a large percentage of our beneficial insects that gave us a balance in nature, and kept the destructive insects in check.

There are two main types of beneficial insects that destroy the destructive ones. These are the predators and the parasites. The predators will attack the insect and eat it, while the parasite type will usually attach itself to the body and enter it Or it will enter the body by laying eggs inside, and then feed on its host, while it is in the larva stage.

One of the most popular kinds of parasitic insects is the trichogramma wasp. This is a very small wasp, and the adult can be found feeding on the nectar in small flowers. They are harmless to humans. They lay their eggs in the eggs of moths and other insects, therefore destroying the insect before it has a chance to harm your garden.

How do you establish a habitat suitable for these insects? First of all, you must stop using pesticides. The poisonous pesticides not only kill the destructive insects, but most likely will kill more beneficial insects. Even biological controls such as pyrethrum and rotenone, although they will break down and leave no residue, still kill all insects, both beneficial and destructive, when they are exposed to it. No pesticides of any kind that destroys the beneficial insects can be used.

Next, attract them by food sources. The adult, parasitic, beneficial insects feed on nectar, and so plants which provide nectar for them must be provided if you wish to attract them to your garden. Even the ladybug, which is a predator, still needs nectar or pollen to be able to mature and lay eggs. Many weeds that have small daisy-like flowers provide nectar. Some other plants are the different varieties of clover, tansy, lovage, caraway, scented geraniums, fennel, buckwheat, Queen Anne's Lace and many others. There is one other type of plant you can put in your border of flowering plants, which will provide nectar, and that is the carrot. If you do not have carrots which you have wintered over, then buy some carrots at the grocery store and set them into the soil in late winter, or early spring. It will not be long until they will emerge new growth from the top of the carrot. It will put up beautiful flowering heads, resembling Queen Anne's Lace. All of the different small insects you see all over the flower heads are beneficial insects. Queen Anne's Lace is the wild carrot, so that is why the two look alike.

There is one thing you should never do, and that is to kill any insect, unless you know what kind it is. If the balance in nature can be reestablished, then 98 percent of the insects you see will be beneficial. Even the large wasps are predator insects.

Those of you who grow tomatoes, I know you have no doubt seen one of the large tomato hornworms with rows of white little cocoons on the back of the worm. Do not mash the worm at this stage. If you do, you will be destroying many of the cocoons of the Braconid wasp. These wasps lay their eggs directly into the body of the worm. The larva feeds on the worm, then emerge and go into the cocoon stage. They will eventually emerge as the Braconid wasp, so there will be more next year to control your tomato hornworms. The hornworm has already quit eating at this stage, so it cannot do your plant any more damage.

There is one beneficial insect which I must write about, and that is what most of us call "ladybug." How often have you watched these little bugs hustle about over your plants eating and destroy the aphids, scale, mealybugs, and many of the other insects which eat our plants? The more proper name for this insect is "Lady Bird Beetle," but most of us know it as the "Ladybug." There are several hundred kinds of these beetles in North America, and they all are beneficial. They range in color from red, orange, yellow, gray and black, but the most common is orange with black spots on their back. This past summer I observed more of the black variety. All of these small insects have an almost round body about 1/8" to 5/8" long. The adult ladybugs can eat more than 200 aphids, their favorite food, each day. The little alligator-shaped larva ranges in length from about 3/16" to 1/2" long. These little creatures really look destructive, but protect them. They can consume fifty to one hundred aphids each day.

The larva has black with orange markings. The ladybug lays her eggs on the under side of plant leaves, so unless you know for sure what kind of eggs they are, do not destroy them. The eggs are all in a little cluster and have a yellowish-orange color. If you are not sure as to what kind of eggs they are, try removing the leaf and placing it in a jar with a lid. Watch the jar daily, and if those little weird-looking doohickeys hatch out, try placing part of a plant loaded with aphids in the jar. You will soon find out what they are. Then release them in the garden where you see aphids.

The life span of the larva is approximately twenty-eight days before developing into the adult beetle stage. The life span of the adult is around eleven months. Weather conditions can change this to shorter or longer periods. Cool weather will slow down their reproduction as well. To attract them to your garden, try planting tansy, angelica and scented geraniums. These are by no means the only plants which provide nectar for the adult lady-bugs, but are some of their favorites. As I stated before, they must have nectar to be able to complete their life cycle and lay eggs. During the winter you can find them in clusters under leaves, bark and weeds. We have had them get in our home this winter. They are trying to find a warm place to spend the winter. I pick them up when I can reach them, and put them outside. They will usually die in a day or so inside because of the low humidity and lack of moisture.

Now, if you do not see any ladybugs in your garden, but have plants infested with aphids, then you can get supplies of them from many companies that ship them all over the country. There is one bad fault when releasing ladybugs in your garden; they have a tendency to flay away to your neighbor's garden, especially if you have no insects on your plants which they feed on.

James A. Eagle

They are cheap enough that you can afford to lose from 90 to 95 percent. Yes! That is correct. Releasing them properly, you will probably lose 90 to 95 percent. If you purchase a unit of approximately 5,000 bugs, you can expect to keep from 250 to 500 in your garden. This amount can really do a good job for a fairly large garden. They will naturalize as long as there is food for them. Many of the companies that sell the ladybug beetles also sell a flowering mix or a special bait for them to keep them around until they get settled.

My advice is to get plants, seeds, or bait in advance before releasing them. These plants will be established to provide the nectar that the ladybugs need. Ladybugs can be stored in your refrigerator for several months, if done properly. This will give you time to order and receive them in advance if you are expecting an infestation of aphids. Some order them as soon as they see aphids. Most companies will ship immediately when receiving your order, or ship whenever you wish. Once you decide you want to release them in your garden, do the following after receiving them: Store in the refrigerator until the day you intend to release them. Release them at night. Water the plants so they will have plenty of moisture on the leaves. This will entice them to stay. Then release them after dark. Companies which sell beneficial insects will give you complete instructions.

There is another beneficial insect. It is not a predator, but is absolutely necessary for pollination of our plants. According to scientists, the bumblebee is not supposed to fly, in accordance to the laws of aerodynamics. These insects certainly do a good job of doing something it is not suppose to be able to do. What are God's laws concerning its ability to fly? Is it possible that we, as individuals, have missed something that gives them such ability to fly? Man does not know all of the laws of God concerning this earth. There are many things we can learn just by observation. Actually, he is one of our best flyers. He can shoot off at a moment's notice, and then maintain himself in the air at one position. In the early spring, when walking through the blueberry bushes, I will see many bumble bees, but no honey bees. It is a native of this country, and there are quite a few species of this insect. They are actually better pollinators than the honey bee, which is not a native of this country. The honey bee was brought here by the Europeans in the early history of our country.

Only the queen will winter over. She mates with a male in the fall and then he dies. In the spring she will find an opening in the ground and begin laying her eggs, starting a new colony. Female workers will be the first to hatch, and they take over the duties of maintaining the colony. Later in the season, the males will start to hatch. They will mate with new queens which are produced to start new colonies the following year.

There is at least one species which starts their colonies by boring holes in wood. You have probably seen them in your storage houses.

Since the bumble bee is our best pollinator, and especially of clovers and alfalfa, and with their long tongue, they can pollinate flowers which have deep throats, which the honey bee is incapable of reaching with their short tongue. Actually the bumble bee is the perfect pollinating machine. It has the ability to pollinate the very small flowers to the large deep throated flowers, like daylilies.

Unfortunately many of these bees have been destroyed with pesticides. The morning I started this chapter, the paper had a news item for farmers to register to take a refresher course on the use of restricted pesticides so they could renew their licenses. Another news item from the same day was encouraging those who did not have a license to take a beginner course to get a license. We are destroying the balance of nature so that we will never be able to control anything. We are killing most of our beneficial insects, along with ourselves by eating the produce. These pesticides are so dangerous that you, as a homeowner, are not allowed to use them. Of course I do not want to use them, neither do I want them used on fields close to me, but this is one thing I do not have the power to control. We, as a nation, must decide which way we are going to proceed. Will it be self-destruction or will we try to restore our environment? The choice

James A. Eagle

is ours. We must start one person at a time. If we sit back and tell ourselves, "What's the use, nobody else has stopped using poisons?" then there will be no change in conditions.

The bumble bee has predators in nature, but the bees' greatest enemy is man. When the spray tanks start spitting out their poison, man destroys the lowly bumble bee, which is busy pollinating his crops, along with the insects he tries to get rid of. The tragedy is that more of the farmer's friends are destroyed than his enemies. Will we never learn?

Many people are afraid of the bumble bee. I can remember being stung only once by one, but I have been stung many times by the honey bee. The bumble bee will not bother you, unless you plow up their home, or slap at them while they are gathering the pollen you wish them to carry to another flower, in order to pollinate that crop you need pollinated. I have actually picked them up by placing my index finger and thumb on each side of their body, then released them and they would continue to go about their busy duty of pollinating my flowers on the plants. There is one company that I am sure of which sell bumble bees for restocking your area. If you are interested in reestablishing them in your area, then write or call: The Green Spot, Ltd., 93 Priest Rd., Nottingham, NH 03290-6204, Phone (603)-942-8925.

Soil Health for the Habitat: When soil has been polluted with pesticides, herbicides, and fungicides, it will take time to heal the soil to the point where it will not carry these pollutants into the fruit and vegetables you grow. God has a healing process He will use to restore it back to a healthy soil. But He will do this at His own time and pace. We can help by the adding of compost annually or even more often. Decaying compost is the only thing that will feed the earthworms and beneficial microorganisms which help to restore the soil to a healthy state. Earthworms are the best measurement of a soil's health. When they start returning, then you will know your soil is restoring itself, because the beneficial microorganisms will have also returned. Aristotle called earthworms the "Intestines of the Earth." Leaching is another natural process that will carry chemicals down into the lower layers of soil, but the bad part of this is that it then pollutes our water supply when it feeds into the underground aquifer. There have been many cases, which have made the news, to confirm this, but the sad part is that much of it never reaches the news media, or else they suppress it. The leaching process also takes time. This is why it takes earthworms so long to return to the soil once they have been destroyed by chemicals. But they will return in time. You may try speeding this process by adding some earthworms, providing you have enriched your soil with compost.

Activated charcoal is another method that can be used to help restore soil in a small plot. The charcoal will absorb the chemicals, thereby obstructing the roots from taking them up into the plant. If these pollutants are taken up in the roots of the plant, then it will then pollute your food supply. A limited method of control is to mix three tablespoons of activated charcoal to one gallon of water and water the plants you are transplanting. Of course, this is a limited method. The feed roots of the plant can grow out beyond from where the soil has been treated. A better method is to apply 6-1/2 to 7 pounds of activated charcoal to each 1,000 sq. feet of garden space and work it into the soil. This would allow the roots a wider range of growing without having the plants absorb the chemicals through their roots.

If you are wondering what activated charcoal is, the briquette you use for your barbecue grill is not the kind of charcoal to use. Activated charcoal is highly porous charcoal which can absorb the pollutants in your soil. I remember my father would construct a pit to make this charcoal, using hard wood. He would start a fire and build up a large pile of wood and get it smoldering. If I remember correctly, he had a small flue coming out the center of the pile of wood. He then would cover the wood with soil and let it smolder for days. When no smoke came out the top, it would be broken down, and there would be large lumps of activated charcoal. I was very small when this was done, so I am not sure what it was used for. It seems that one use was to add it to the hot water used for scalding hogs at hog-killing time. It was also fed to hogs in small quantities. I am only ninety, so maybe some of you older youngsters remember what all this charcoal was used for.

If you want to try the charcoal from your fireplace after using hardwood to burn, then take the larger pieces of charcoal, *not the ashes,* and crush them into a powder. This can be done in a blender or food processor, or placed in a cloth bag and crushed with a hammer, and applied to your soil, using the amount outlined above.

Activated charcoal can be bought at some drug stores in small quantities, but this can be expensive for our purpose. Maybe some enterprising company will stock it locally for gardeners in your area.

I believe it is better to have some vegetables damaged by some insects, than to be consuming these chemicals into my system. Remember, you are not only contaminating your food when you use poisons, but also your water supply, or maybe the water supply of someone else as well. Polluted water can be carried for miles underground through the underground aquifer.

Words of Wisdom: "Listen to counsel and receive instruction, that you may be wise in your latter days. (Proverbs 19:20)

Chapter Three

Methods and Types of Gardening

This will be a discussion of methods or types of gardening, especially for the small gardener. There is no need to have an acre of land to grow vegetables for a family. It can be done in a small area, using different methods. Methods depend on you and if you are hampered in any way, such as age (like myself), physical disability. Methods can be altered to reduce the labor and make it easier to garden.

I have often wondered how much of these gardening methods, using a very limited space, came from soldiers returning from World War II. I'm sure it had an effect on many of those who returned. I know it did on me. The Europeans were using what little space they had to grow food. and Many used their front yards. I saw it in England, Sicily, Corsica, Italy, and Germany. They also composted any type of vegetable or animal matter, including human feces. They produced their food on very small spaces. You are not only able to produce your food in a small space, but you will be amazed at the wonderful improvement in taste and nutrition using these methods. There have been many tests conducted on fruit and vegetables comparing organic grown with the chemical grown. The organic grown always come out way ahead in flavor, taste and nutrition. Prove these methods to yourself.

Row Gardening: Row Gardening is the form most use, or have used in the past. We make rows and plant where we can cultivate between the rows. This is the most laborious form for me. It requires a tiller, or some other method of working the soil. In some cases it is more difficult to control some soil born diseases and insects. If I choose this type of gardening, I would put a deep mulch over whole garden to keep from having to till or hoe. This would reduce the work considerably. It would also promote better growth of the plants, because the mulch would preserve moisture, reduce weed growth, and, best of all, as the mulch decays it will add nutrients to the soil. By mulching every year you can reduce the need to add any nutrients at all. Each year the soil will continue to increase in fertility. When you are ready to plant, all you need to do would be to pull the mulch back, plant the seed, and let it germinate and grow in that soft moist soil. As the plants grow, pull the mulch back around the plants.

Wide Row Gardening: This form is similar to the form above, only in this form, you have wide rows, instead of single rows, and can sow seed or plant spacing the plants as you desire. To accomplish this method of gardening, first till or dig an area 15 to 36 inches wide or wider. It's your choice. You want to be able to reach and harvest from either side without stepping on the loose soil. Leave a space between this tilled area about 18 to 24 inches wide. This space will be your walk and harvesting area. You will never have to step on the area your plants are growing in. This serves a great benefit in that you do not pack the soil to prevent the circulation of oxygen to the plants' roots. Packed soil will also inhibit the growth of the roots.

The distance between the plants will depend on the type of vegetable you are growing. For lettuce, carrots, beets, onions, kohlrabi, turnips, mustard, and many other small plants, a dis-

James A. Eagle

tance 3 to 6 inches apart is ideal. For larger plants such as peas, southern peas, cabbage, broccoli, green beans, and sweet corn, space them 6 inches to 12 inches apart. It is still easy enough to harvest without stepping on the space where the plants are growing. You can also intermix different vegetables, herbs, or even flowers in the garden. This will confuse insects and even repel some.

Most of the vegetable seeds you plant in a wide row can be broadcast, rather than planted in hills. When they come up, they can be thinned as needed. For small plants such as lettuce, radishes, etc., the seed can be sowed thicker than the peas, beans and other larger plants. If seeds of cabbage, broccoli, etc., are being planted, they can be scattered where they are only six or eight inches apart. Corn can be planted in hills, staggered to get maximum use of the bed. Sweet corn can be planted as close as 8 to 10 inches apart, even closer in good fertile soil.

When the plants germinate, it does not take long for them to cover the row with their foliage. The foliage acts as mulch, shading the ground, therefore keeping the ground cool and preventing the loss of moisture. This shading of the area can also reduce weed growth. The middle of the row, your walk space, can be mulched. This will help to control packing the soil in this area that you walk on. Much of the time, I use a black woven polypropylene fabric in the middle of the rows. You can find this locally in the stores and garden centers. It allows the water to pass through, but inhibits the growth of weeds. You can place a light mulch on top to hold it in place. In the fall you can take up the fabric and till in the mulch. Mulch can also be applied to plants in the wide rows.

This method of gardening also provides assistance in having cool weather crops into the warmer weather. The plants keep each other cool, which discourages bolting. This is especially true of lettuce and spinach. By the plants keeping the soil temperature cooler and more constant, they are less likely to be attacked by root knot nematodes. For a definition of nematodes see Addendum I. Nematodes prefer a warm dry area. Plants are not isolated in this method, therefore less prone to attacks by flying insects and their larva. This method is more like how things grow in nature. This method will keep the fruit of the harvest cleaner. You will not have sand and mud splashing on the plants as you do in single row planting.

When preparing my rows, I drive a stake at each end of the row, then till on one side. The side tilled will become the wide row. For small plants a single tilling space is adequate, for larger plants, a double or triple tilled space is needed. This gives me about 18 inches for the single tilled row, 36 inches for the double tilled row, and 48 inches or more for a triple tilled row. A layer of compost, about two to three inches thick, is applied. This is then tilled into the soil. My bed is then ready to plant. (Sentence deleted here.)

Container Gardening: There is no reason whatsoever for anyone who wishes to garden to be denied this wonderful hobby. Americans are quickly adopting the Europeans love of gardening. You cannot go anywhere in Europe without seeing every space possible utilized in some way so they can grow plants of some description. The balconies of large, multi-story apartment buildings are filled with growing container plants. The small back yards, and even the front yards are filled with plants of all descriptions. If you love plants, then there is no reason not to grow some container plants around your own residence.

A raised planter can be made from lumber, brick, or stone, and can grow more plants than you can imagine when established correctly. Raised planters are an especially ideal way for those in a wheel chair, or the old and impaired, like myself. If planters are built with brick or stone, then you will need to choose plants that love an alkaline, neutral, or slightly acid soil. The mortar used in the brick will raise the pH of the soil, unless you use special methods to lower the pH. I would never advise anyone putting azaleas, gardenias, camellias, blueberries or other acid-loving plants in a planter where cement was used, unless special care was taken to lower the pH. Concrete will raise the soil pH,

James A. Eagle

and you can see the leaves of acid loving plants turning yellow because they cannot utilize the minor nutrients, such as iron and magnesium, even though there may be a sufficient supply in the soil.

If you wish to grow acid loving plants in a planter constructed with any amount of cement, then the best way to prepare the planter would be to add oak leave or pine straw compost to the potting soil you use. One-fourth to one-third of the potting soil should consist of oak leaves or pine straw compost. Using cottonseed meal as a nutrient will also lower the pH.

Smaller containers can be of all kinds and descriptions, plastic, terracotta, clay, cement, and wood. Wood makes a beautiful planter when some design effort goes into them, but they will not last as long as others. I still prefer them to most for their beauty. The best wood to use is cypress, black locust, or cedar wood. The black locust is one of the best if you can find the lumber. There have been cases where fences were made out of black locusts that were more than one hundred years old, and never had any finish put on them to preserve the wood. If there is someone that wishes to grow the black locust for its lumber, there are places you can obtain the seed. It is a fast growing tree, and also makes a good hedge to keep out animals of all kind, including the two legged ones. For this purpose you will need to keep them pruned to form the hedge. This plant does have thorns which make it ideal for this purpose.

Planters can be used to plant vegetables, herbs, flowers, or a mixture of them all. You can grow tomatoes, cabbage, collards, kale, broccoli, cauliflower, beans, and many other kinds of vegetables in a planter like this, along with the smaller growing plants, such as lettuce, turnips, beets, etc. Also, you can add some nasturtiums and mint to repel insects.

All containers should have drain holes. This is necessary in order to have adequate drainage to prevent diseases which can rot the roots of plants. When you find a plant that is wilting, but still has adequate moisture, then you can almost be certain the roots have rotted and are not able to take up the necessary water to maintain life.

The types of containers used for growing vegetables, fruits, and flowers can only be limited by the imagination. Anything that will hold soil and provide drainage can be used. Most plants need good drainage. Everything from baskets to garbage cans have been used for containers. There are many beautiful pots on the market that are ideally suited for container growing, but going this route can be expensive. Some containers that I started our container garden with were some of my wife's discarded plastic storage containers. Two measured 20 x 14" with a depth of 8-1/2". In these were planted carrots and beets. Two other plastic storage bins measured 12 x 10" and a depth of 6". These were planted with lettuce and radishes. I had an old twenty gallon plastic pot that was planted with parsnips, and an old planter which was planted with corn salad.

Today we are using shipping containers and the twenty-gallon plastic tubs with rope handles. The shipping crates are the best and last longer. Holes were drilled in these for drainage.

Baskets can be used. One person took wooden baskets and painted them with a water resistant paint and used them. They can be very colorful.

If you go in for collectable items, then why not look for such items as old coal buckets, wash pots, and other containers that are in great demand today? These items will need to have a drainage hole in the bottom to provide drainage.

One of the most unique container gardens I have ever seen was a three-foot wire ring used as a composter. After the vegetable matter had partially broken down, the individual made a hole in the middle of the pile and placed some garden soil in the hole. Into this soil he planted cantaloupes. As they grew, the roots extended into the rotting compost. He had some of the best cantaloupes you would ever hope to sink your teeth into. The vines ran down the sides of the wire composter so that you would never know what was under the growing cantaloupes...

James A. Eagle

all types of veining plants can be planted in this manner, such as cucumbers, ice box watermelons, and others.

The smaller containers can be placed on a patio, deck, or porch, and planted with flowers, herbs, and small growing vegetables. This is a great place to have herbs. You can harvest a few fresh herbs or lettuce, onions, or radishes right before a meal. How much fresher can it be?

There are potting mixes on the market, but I do not have much enthusiasm for them. Many of them have been blackened with burnt wood chips to make them look dark and fertile. You can find some with chemical nutrients added. These commercial potting soils do contain organic materials which will completely decay adding nutrients. They are better than no organic material at all. Sometimes you may have to resort to them if you are not able to make compost, or cannot find compost to purchase. Some cities have started composting vegetable waste. The city of Columbia, SC does this. At one time they were selling it for $15.00 a pick-up load.

I made my own potting mix. The formula usually consists of equal amounts good garden soil, compost, and peat moss. Since you have a large amount of vegetable matter, it will decay more quickly and it will be necessary to add more potting soil as it settles. If the plants show signs of needing additional nutrients later, then water with a solution of fish emulsion and liquid kelp, compost tea, or you may add more compost, or any of the seed meals given in Chapter Four.

Chapter Four

Providing Nutrients for the Garden

A plant is a living organism. It doesn't have the ability to move around like animals do, but it does have the ability to synthesize food from carbon dioxide. Plants have specialized sense organs, digestive, nervous, and circulatory systems. So, when you look at a plant, realize it is a living thing. God created the plants as well as all other living organisms on this planet. Do you realize scientists do not have an answer as to what *Life* is, and where it goes? Who gives life to us, animals, and plants? The answer is quite obvious to those with open eyes: *God.*

Plants require food, which we call nutrients or fertilizer, water, light, and proper temperature to survive and grow. First we will discuss the food we provide our plants. The food we provide can come in many different forms. The Creator provides nutrients by recycling dead organisms, such as leaves, wood, weeds, and other vegetable matter. Even the bodies and the waste of animals are recycled by nature. As a plant removes these nutrients from the soil, then we must provide additional nutrients. We can do this in many different ways, such as commercial fertilizers, or organic fertilizers. If we garden in accordance with the established laws that have been created by our Creator, then we will use organic or natural means.

As an organic gardener, the things I use to make corrections in the soil, when it is lacking nutrients for maximum production, I refer to as *amendments*. I like to avoid using the word fertilizer. Most think of fertilizer as the chemicals that are used to grow flowers and vegetables. To avoid any confusion, amendments will be used, and the word fertilizer will be used when speaking of the chemical commercial fertilizers. In fact, most commercial fertilizers only provide the three major nutrients that are most likely to be lacking in the soil. These are nitrogen, phosphorus, and potassium. Calcium is another major chemical element that is lacking in some soils, and some may even have an abundance. There are many more minerals and chemical elements which occur naturally in nature and are necessary for proper plant growth.

There is an enormous difference in commercial fertilizers and organic amendments. Most commercial fertilizers are available immediately to the plant. Excessive use of them can do more harm than good when used excessively. They can burn the foliage or roots of the plant, and even kill it when too much is applied. If dry weather occurs, then expect more damage than you would have when using organic amendments. More of the chemical fertilizers are lost by run-off to our streams, ponds, and lakes, or by seeping down into the water aquifer, than are used by the plants. About thirty years ago, there was a large lake in Florida that became so polluted from run-off from the orange groves surrounding it that it was closed for fishing for years.

Organic amendments are slow in releasing their nutrients, preventing damage. The natural soil microorganisms convert them to a useable form, and the plant uses them as they are needed. These beneficial organisms can also help to prevent diseases and control many pests.

Chemical fertilizers are taboo and unthinkable for me. Very few of the minor nutrients are provided by chemical fertilizers. These are just as important as the others, but in less amounts. Neither do chemical fertilizers provide fruit and vegetables that are rich in the nutrients the body needs for good health. The natural plant nutrients, which are recommended, will provide these. These nutrients are transferred from the plant to our bodies when we consume them. When you garden in accordance with the established laws of God you are accomplishing the ideal method of recycling much of the items that many consider waste.

Natural nutrients come from animals, animal waste, such as manure and urine, and vegetable matter and everything manufactured from plant material. We will try and cover all methods of natural methods of obtaining good nutrients that provide healthy fruit and vegetables for your table. Using natural ingredients is recycling what we take from the earth. What God has made is good, indeed.

First, I wish to cover an episode that was on ABC on *20/20* in February 2000. Part of the show was an effort to discredit the healthfulness of foods grown organically. I consider it one of the most outstanding hoaxes ever perpetrated on the public. This is just another example how the liberal press tries to control the truth, along with the full cooperation of the United States government and the large agriculture industries, which try to convince you of the safety of pesticides, fungicides, herbicides, and the genetic engineering of our foods today.

The test they performed was on foods taken from grocery stores and then tested for Ecoli, which is a common intestinal bacterium. There are several strains of this bacterium, which occupies the intestinal tract of many animals, and some can cause serious illness. The most amazing thing was that they used alfalfa sprouts and chopped salad greens. Foods that have been handled by individuals are not usually washed in any manner. Many of these foods came from Mexico and Central American countries, which use raw human feces to fertilize their crops. Human feces is OK to use when it has been composted properly. The good bacteria that breaks it down into compost will destroy Ecoli and other dangerous bacteria. This is not the method of organic gardening I advocate.

The individuals they were interviewing were from the U. S. Department of Agriculture and the Food and Drug Administration. There were other individuals they interviewed from industries that very much wish you didn't know the truth. They claimed that foods taken from plants, where pesticides and fungicides were used, were healthier than organic grown foods. That is one of the greatest deceptions I have ever heard. Most of this data had been taken from a book written by Dennis T. Avery, titled *Saving the Planet with Pesticides and Plastics*. Do you want people like this making decisions for you?

There is one main purpose of feeding the public with this kind of falsehood, and that is whereby the Mega Corporations can take control of all farming. They can use their poisons and biotechnology without any consideration for the health of the public. The family farm is out, and the mega farm is in. In 1978 there were 1,269,305 independent family farmers that said that farming was their chief occupation. But the 1992 Census figures indicated that there were only 961,560 that indicated that farming was their chief occupation. The figure is much lower today. The Mega Corporations claim that they can produce food cheaper than the smaller farmer, which is true. But is this food good for you?

Many of the universities in this country are also involved in this scheming policy that is going on. Even the *Washington Post* reported that university laboratories are enmeshed in contractual deals that guarantee that industry partners get the first look at laboratory findings and get exclusive rights in many cases. We have known for some time how the agriculture and chemistry interest finance these many research labs. If the result of their work does not conform to their desires, it is never published. If it was published, then the universities could lose their funding from these industries.

Back about the turn of the century, the U. S. Centers for Disease Control issued the following statement, "...People who eat organic grown foods are eight times more likely to get infection from E.coli bacteria." Such a statement made by a U.S.

Government agency can be truly alarming, but it is also completely false. The CDC had never conducted a study, up to this time, that compared organic produced foods to the customary method of production. The statement was taken from Avery's book.

Since Avery wrote the book, *Saving the Planet with Pesticides and Plastics,* he has appeared on numerous TV shows and has been quoted in many publications, giving credibility to his statements.

When the Centers for Disease Control was confronted with their false statement, they recounted and issued the following statement,

> The Centers for Disease Control has not conducted any study that compares or quantitates the specific risk for infection with Escherichia coli 0157:H7 and eating either conventionally grown or organic natural foods.

Here is a quote from my Bible on this, which I consider very appropriate at this point:

> "For My thoughts are not your thoughts, nor your ways My ways," says the Lord. "For as the Heavens are higher than the earth, so are My ways higher than your ways, and My thoughts your thoughts. "
>
> Isaiah 55:8-9 (NKJV)

Man will never know all the ways and knowledge of God, but we learn His ways when we observe the miraculous way he has designed things. Just observe what happens when man tries his ways. It usually leads to ruin. I was just watching individuals removing dead birds and animals from the oil spill in the Gulf of Mexico the first of June 2010. This a good example of why God's ways are not like mankind's ways. Man's ways, so many times. lead to destruction.

The methods that will be recommended in this book will accomplish one thing that the many pesticides and especially the fungicides will not do. They will strengthen the immune system of the plants, and of those who eat them. I wonder how many of you take supplements to strengthen your immune system. I know my wife and I do. Our doctor tells us as we age our body does not absorb the nutrients as well as when we were young, so we supplement with extra nutrients. The plants' health will greatly improve to ward off disease when it is in the best of health. Also, insects will attack a plant in poor health quicker than one in good health. The same happens in the wild. A predator animal will attack the weakest animal in a herd.

Some years ago I tested four organic fertilizers in my lawn. I had a plastic ring about four feet in diameter. I laid the ring down and applied one pint of alfalfa meal inside the ring. The ring was moved and one pint of fish meal was applied. This was repeated until I had made five rings of nutrients consisting of alfalfa meal, fish meal, cottonseed meal, soybean meal, and 10-10-10 of a chemical fertilizer.

Markers were put up, indicating the type of nutrients that were added at each place. Within one month, all showed some sign of new growth (more than the rest of the lawn,) but the alfalfa meal and 10-10-10- fertilizer showed the most growth. They were faster acting. Within two months all showed much improvement. Within three months the 10-10-10- fertilizer showed signs of declining or waning. All others were more lush with growth than ever. The following June, the organic fertilizers were still showing more lush growth than the rest of the lawn, but you couldn't observe any difference where the 10-10-10 was applied from the rest of the lawn. The point I am trying to make is that organic fertilizers last longer than chemical, and provide nutrients the chemical fertilizers do not.

Composting should be your main method of providing nutrients your plants need. Not only will it provide nutrients, but compost holds and retains moisture, reducing the need for watering so often. Compost acts like a sponge. It absorbs and retains water, letting the plants use it as they require it. It is also a

James A. Eagle

recycling program, returning to the earth much of what we have taken from it.

I have discovered that when I add adequate compost it is not necessary to add additional supplements except in rare cases when the compost was made by others, such as the mushroom compost. It is rare that the soil will need any other nutrients. There may be a shortage of some nutrients when you use material to make the compost that has been grown by farmers that use the chemicals. I have discovered when I purchased hay or straw grown through the use of chemicals, that I needed to add other nutrients. The plants were lacking in the minerals they needed for good health.

Composting the Speedy Method: This is a method of composting that can provide excellent compost within several weeks to a couple of months. It is important to note here that the proper ingredients, and where they are obtained, are the most important factor.

The unit you use to make the quick compost can be made or purchased. The ones available on the market are of many forms. I have several units made out of heavy duty plastic. The top cover can be removed, and the ingredients inserted from the top. There is a sliding door at the bottom that can be opened to remove compost that has completed composting. These types of units are not the best on the market. There are others which rotate, and you can turn them by hand daily, or every couple of days, in order to speed the composting process. I also have one of these. When I am not composting, then I use it to mix potting soils for my containers that I use for gardening. It is about thirty years old and still working.

It is much cheaper to make your own composter. I started out this way. You can purchase wire about three to four feet high and with a mesh of about three to four inches, and about ten feet in length, it will make a ring about three feet in diameter. Lap it over about a foot and tie it with nylon cord or other strong cord that will not rot. It can also be tied with one strand of flexible wire. Another method is to build a bin out of wood with a gate in one side to open to remove the compost.

You are now ready to get the ingredients needed to start composting quickly. First you need a good source of nitrogen and other minerals for the composter unit. This feeds the bacteria which produces the decomposition process of the material. This can be supplied by several methods. Animal manure is one of the best sources. It can be from a horse, cow, sheep, goat, rabbit, or chicken and other poultry. *Warning:* Fresh manure, when used on the garden, can cause burning of the roots because of the high nitrogen content in it, such as poultry and cow. Therefore, it is always best to compost it for a couple of weeks, which will then eliminate this.

The nitrogen can also be provided by green plants, especially grass cuttings, leaves of vegetables, flowers, and weeds. The finer they are cut, the quicker they will decay. Another source is the seed of some plants such as cottonseed meal and soybean meal. Alfalfa meal is one of the best sources of nitrogen. Fish meal is also a good source. I used it once in a closed composter, and the next day buzzards were flying overhead. My wife noticed them first, and we started wondering what was dead around our place. When they returned the next several days, some even lit on the roof of the house. This is when we were able to figure it out. They were after our fish meal.

If you have a milling company in your area that grinds grains for feed then you will probably be able to purchase these materials much cheaper by the bag. I am able to get mine in fifty lb. bags. They usually sell fish meal also, which is used in feed for animals. Kelp meal in small amounts should always be added to the compost pile. It not only provides for any minor nutrients that may be missing, but activates microbes that break down the other material.

Now we come to the dry plant material you are going to need. This can be leaves, straw, hay, etc. Wood chips can be used, but it takes much longer for them to break down. Personally, I do not recommend them if you are wanting fast compost, but they are wonderful for making slow compost.

There is one ingredient, when available, which I use from cotton gins. This is the moats cleaned from cotton when it is ginned. It is very fast in decaying, and adds nutrients in a hurry. The objection I have is the chemical defoliant they use before harvesting the cotton (See Moats in Addendum II). The piles which the gin blows these moats onto will have places where the moats have already broken down. When I find an earthworm in them, then I use it.

There is one more item I use in small amounts. Although it is organic, there are some chemicals in it. This item is paper. We shred all documents and medical records after so long, and this is what we use, plus any other paper items, such as newspapers. When we started using twenty-gallon tubs to garden in, we still had trouble with fire ants invading our tubs. They were after the earthworms. We discovered that when we used paper they would leave. I figure it must be the chemicals used in the manufacture of paper. I do not recommend using very much. About 10 percent or less of your material should be paper. I feel the same way about the use of paper as I do about what the doctor tells me about some of the drugs he prescribes. The benefits outweigh the side effects. The paper not only repels the ants, but it provides nutrients. After all, it is a wood product. It is the chemicals used in its manufacture that are undesirable.

If you are using a rotary composter, the material can be inserted in any manner, because you have an easy system of mixing, just by turning the unit. Insert the following material by measurement: Five parts dry material such as the leaves, straw, hay, etc, two parts of manure or green material for the nitrogen. If you are using any of the seed meals, then use only one part for the nitrogen content. Wet this thoroughly and turn the composter several times. Within twenty- four hours the temperature should have reached 120 to 140 degrees. If not, add a little more of the nitrogen material. Keep turning the composter every day or two for the next several weeks, and if it starts drying out, add more water. By this time you should have nice, crumbly compost ready to use on your garden.

If you are using wire rings or bins to compost, then you make layers in the containers. First put down a layer of dry material, then a layer of manure or whatever you use to start it heating up, and keep repeating this action. If you turn and mix this twice each week it will compost much faster.

As a kid on our small farm in North Carolina, I recall how we farmed during the depression. One job my brother and I had was the cleaning out the cow and horse stables and making a very large compost pile. We laid down a layer of straw about a foot deep and twenty feet in diameter, and then put a layer of manure out of the barn about four inches deep. Then this was repeated until the pile was higher than I could fork hay or manure. We would load it on a wagon and unload it onto the pile. That pile must have been eight to twelve feet high. Naturally, it would start settling before spring.

I remember a cold morning when it had snowed, I looked and saw smoke, at least what I thought was smoke, coming from behind the barn. I hollered to my dad that the barn was on fire. We all headed out and when we got to the compost pile, we realized it was just steam coming from the compost pile, as the snow was melted on top of the compost pile. That is an example of how hot it can become. In the spring, that compost went on the fields. We didn't know that was called *organic farming* back then.

Composting, the Slow Method: This will be our main method of providing nutrients our plants need.

There are many ways composting can be accomplished. We will try and cover most of them. But first, I wish to outline the methods we used at the last home we owned in Florida before retiring and moving to South Carolina.

Our house was on a lot that measured 65 x 110 feet. It was sandy soil down as far as three feet. That is as deep as I ever dug. There was no sub-soil worth mentioning. I wondered if I would ever be able to grow anything on this sandy soil. We had

James A. Eagle

the backyard fenced, then built beds 3 feet wide and 24 feet long out of timbers 2" x 8" x 12'. This gave us sides 8 inches high. The sandy soil was removed from the beds to a depth of approximately 10 inches.

Leaves and some partially rotted wood chips were put in the bottom of the beds to a depth of about four inches. Then a layer of green grass clippings were added, then a layer of the sandy soil which had been removed, and after that, a light sprinkling of alfalfa meal. This was added to provide nitrogen and other nutrients for the bacteria that would aid the decaying of the leaves and grass clippings (see alfalfa meal in this chapter). This was repeated until the soil was about 4 inches above the edges of the bed. After watering this down and starting the composting process of the material, it settled in a couple weeks below the edges of the beds.

In the meantime, we started compost rings made out of ½ inch mesh wire. These rings were about 3 feet in diameter. I started compost in these rings the same way I started my beds. By turning this and mixing it ever few days, I had compost in a several weeks which was ready to add to our beds to bring the soil level back up to the top of the beds. This method of composting is a slow natural method.

Our neighbors kept making comments as to all the effort we were putting forth to have a garden, but their tune changed when we started harvesting.

In addition, we set out two peach trees on one side of the back yard, put in two muscadine grape vines and four fig bushes. It wasn't long until we were freezing, canning, and making jams and jellies from our harvest. The peach trees were bearing approximately fifteen bushes of peaches, even after the kids and squirrels got their share. It wasn't long until we were sharing our produce with our neighbors. I recall one neighbor telling me that the tomatoes he received were the best he had ever eaten.

I use a similar method for the site where we intend to set out trees, shrubs etc. Dig the hole where you intend to plant the shrub or tree, about two feet deep. Insert about 6 or 8 inches of leaves, hay, straw, or grass clippings in the hole. Put about 4 inches of soil back in the hole, and repeat this until it is full and heaping up above the soil line. It will settle in several weeks. Then insert more hay, straw, etc., and another layer of soil. Let this set for several months and you will have a perfect place to give your tree or shrub a good healthy start. Remove enough of this soil and compost to insert the plant in and cover the roots with the soil you removed. Leave a slight indentation to water the plant and keep the water from running off. I have done this for some vegetables as well, such as tomatoes, peppers, etc.

Mulching Organically: This is a method of covering the soil with organic material, such as leaves, straw, hay, wood chips, etc. This covering can be only a couple of inches deep, or very deep, such as 12 inches or more, as long as you don't cover the plants growth tips. You can start mulching seedlings with a thin mulch and add more as the plants grow. Trees and shrubs can be mulched very deep. Some like to mulch with rocks, and that is satisfactory, as long as you do not want to add nutrients. The mulches listed above will add many nutrients, preserve moisture, and keep the soil cool.

One of the main advantages of mulching is that it will retain moisture under the mulch much longer during dry spells. About twenty-four years ago we had some peach trees, but we had no way to water them during a very dry period. Some of the trees I mulched with moats. Moats are the hulls of cotton boles and leaves, which are cleaned when they gin cotton. The ones we failed to mulch started dying, but the others seemed to be okay. I dug down under the mulch and there was moisture and cool soil, even though it had not rained for about two months. Digging down around the trees that had not been mulched, I could not find any moisture and the soil was very hot and dry.

Another observation I had was about two rows of tomatoes we had about four feet apart. One we mulched, and the other we never got around to mulching. There didn't seem to be much difference in the two rows. Both had good crops. That fall when

I started taking the plants up to dispose of them, I discovered that the roots of the un-mulched row were going to the mulched row. There were only a few small roots on the opposite side of the un-mulched row. Here you see God's natural *Law of Need* demonstrated (see Chapter One).

Another great benefit of mulching is you are using one of the methods of composting, the slow way. Mulch will be breaking down in less than one year, depending on the type of mulch. This is when you will see plants reacting to the nutrients the mulch is starting to release

Using organic mulch reduces the need for other amendments. As the mulch decays, it will provide these nutrients. Mulching helps protect plant roots in the winter from severe freezing cold when it occurs. It will provide warmth and will help to hold in the earth's own natural heat.

When mulching in the vegetable garden, I like a mulch of hay, straw, or leaves with a depth of 4 to 6 inches, or even more. It will settle as it starts breaking down. At the end of the season turn the mulch under for a complete breakdown, and mulch again. If it is a winter garden, then I leave the mulch on until early spring, and then turn it under.

If you have a large garden area to mulch, then it is well worth the price to purchase one of the many models of shredders that are available. Many come with a combination of a shredder and chipper. You can shred your leaves to a fine consistency for mulching, and even chip up your brush and limbs when pruning your plants. A shredder/chipper will make excellent mulch material and speeds the composting process. A shredder is also good for shredding newspapers for mulching or composting. When leaves and newspapers are shredded together, they make excellent mulch without the wind blowing paper to other parts of the yard. They will stay where you put them when performed in this manner.

How many times have you seen a plot of poor ground that people made statements that it would not grow anything except weeds? They are wrong. It can be made into a profitable garden. I don't care how poor it is, it can be changed.

Seventy-eight years ago I remember when the county changed the dirt road that ran by my father's property. The county straightened the road and left an old, hard road-bed, which they filled with old clay subsoil. We had about one-fourth of an acre that no one thought we would ever be able to grow anything in again. My dad first tried planting field peas to improve the soil. They came up, but never reached over a few inches high, never producing anything. That fall, he had my brother and me haul wheat straw and cover the place about fifteen inches deep or more. That stayed there until the next summer. We put another layer of straw on it then. That stayed there until the following spring when it was plowed into the clay subsoil. The clay subsoil was already soft and moist from the deep mulch, but after mixing all that straw compost, it became a black fertile soil. Our neighbors could not believe the difference it made. We were able to grow anything we desired.

Heavy mulching can change the hardest soil into soft pliable soil in time. I can remember converting another dirt road at the facility I worked before retiring. I had the men haul wood-chips and leaves and covered the place with deep mulch. My men thought I was crazy, but after a couple years we were able to disc that soft soil and landscape it.

If you have that plot that you think nothing will grow in, I challenge you to try this method. Cut the weeds first and let them stay where you cut them, then put a thick layer of straw, hay, leaves, grass, or a combination of these items on it. Let it decay until next spring. Dig down into that mulch and take a view of what you have underneath. If you plow or till the soil before you mulch, you won't even have to till it next spring before planting. Just scratch the mulch back, plant your seed, and wait for them to come up. After they get a good start, pull the mulch back around the plants. There will be very little weeding you will need to do. To give the plants a good start, water them with a liquid fish emulsion and seaweed mix, or use the compost tea

James A. Eagle

mentioned below. Later, you can apply any of the nutrients listed below.

Providing Additional Nutrients: There are many elements a plant needs. Some are in large amounts, which are called *major elements*. Others are in smaller amounts, which are referred to as *minor* or *trace elements*. The ones which we consider major are: nitrogen, phosphorus, potassium, calcium, manganese, and sulfur. The minor or trace elements are: zinc, copper, boron, and molybdenum. There are other elements that don't seem to have much effect on plant growth such as sodium, chlorine, aluminum, and silicon. Most soils usually have sufficient amounts of the trace elements. Sometimes it may be necessary to add some. The best method of adding these minor nutrients is by adding fish emulsion and liquid seaweed. Both of these are available in garden centers and on the internet.

Sometimes, when you are just starting a garden, you may need some of the following nutrients to get your plants off to a good start, especially if you wish to get started in a hurry, before you have time to compost. These are the ones which are some of the best and natural.

Alfalfa Meal: Alfalfa meal is a good source of nitrogen and potassium, about 2 percent is immediately available. It also contains a small source of phosphorus, approximately 0.2 percent. It also has many trace minerals and one important element is the growth stimulant, *triaconatol.* This chemical stimulates the growth of plant roots, but stimulates the increase of beneficial microbes which suppresses many soil-borne diseases. It is made from grinding cured alfalfa hay into a fine meal.

Bat Guano: This is one not readily available, and it is expensive when it is. This is the manure of bats, and it is harvested from caves where many bats spend the day sleeping. Its nutrient value depends on the age. It is very dusty, and I would advise you to use a mask when using it. It has fungicide qualities and can prevent some soil born fungal diseases. It is not likely to be contaminated with pesticides or other chemicals. Remember this is a potent manure and use it lightly.

Blood Meal: Blood meal contains approximately 11 percent nitrogen. There are some trace minerals. It is extra fast-acting, especially for fast-growing plants such as corn, and the cole crops. A small amount is recommended in order to get a crop off to a quick start. Overuse can burn a plant just like chemical fertilizers.

Bone Meal: Bone meal is another source of phosphate and calcium. Bone meal is more readily released to the plants than colloidal phosphate or rock phosphate. It contains more calcium than the other phosphates, and more suitable for acid soils when you wish to raise the pH.

There are two kinds of bone meal on the market. One is raw bone meal with 20-24 percent of phosphorus and about 3-4 percent nitrogen. The finer it is ground, the quicker it is available to the plants. Use approximately 2-3/4 to 5-1/2 lbs. for each 100 square feet of garden space, or 4 to 8 ounces per square yard.

The other bone meal is the steamed bone meal, which is more readily available. It has slightly more phosphate, but less nitrogen: approximately 1 percent. Use about half the amount of the steamed bone meal as you would the raw. Applying bone meal each year may not be necessary when compost is added regularly.

Colloidal Phosphate is usually sold as lonfosco, a soft phosphate. It is a natural untreated clay formation whose main ingredients are phosphate and calcium. Two percent of the phosphate is available immediately, but it has 18 to 20 percent total phosphate. It also contains calcium and minor and trace elements as well. In most cases, I have a preference of this phosphate over the rock phosphate. Apply at the same rate as the rock phosphate. The colloidal phosphate is the wash from the rock phosphate after being mined. It has a white or cream color. Colloidal phosphate is used in Florida, where it is mined, as a road base before paving.

Compost Tea: Compost tea can be made out of your own compost or you can use cow or horse manure. I like to use the manure in my compost pile when it is available. You will need a five-gallon plastic bucket, or a plastic garbage can or some other suitable container. It depends on the amount of tea you wish to make at one time. Use one part compost or manure for five parts of water. Put the compost in a cloth bag. Using an old pillow case works really well. Put the cloth bag into your container and put five times the water as you did compost. Stir it several times for the next twenty-four hours. At this time, you have a dark liquid ready to spray or sprinkle on your plants. Dilute the mixture until it appears as a weak tea. This can be used on your plants about every ten days or two weeks. After emptying the liquid in the can, refill the can with water for another batch. Let it soak for twenty-four hours again. After the second soaking, remove the compost and refill the bag with fresh compost. Use the old compost you take from the bag on your garden or compost pile. To really make a potent tea, mix a cup of fish emulsion and one-half cup of liquid seaweed to this mixture for every twenty gallons of manure tea. This mixture will help repel insects, control disease, and put health and vigor into your plants. Use on vegetables, flowers, or shrubs.

Cottonseed Meal: Contains approximately 6 percent nitrogen, 2 percent phosphorus, 1 percent potassium. This is slower acting than alfalfa meal. It will acidify the soil, unless some alkaline agent is added such as bone meal, lime, or rock phosphate. Only use an alkaline agent if you are using it on plants that love a more neutral pH. Cottonseed meal is an excellent fertilizer for acid-loving plants, such as camellias, azaleas, gardenias, and centipede lawns.

Fish Meal: This is one of my favorite source of nitrogen and phosphorus. It contains approximately 10 percent to 11 percent nitrogen, and 6 percent phosphorus. It also contains many trace minerals, and releases slowly, lasting over a six to eight month period. There is one disadvantage in using it. It will attract animals, such as cats, dogs, and wild animals.

Granite Meal: This is a source of potassium that releases slowly over several years. Granite meal contains 67 percent silica, which aids soil fertility and structure. It also contains 19 trace minerals needed by plants, and from 1.0 to 4 percent potassium.

If adding granite meal, for the first time, add approximately 10 pounds for each 100 square feet of garden space the first year, reducing half this amount the next two years. Your soil should not need it after that.

Greensand or *Glauconite* is a green colored mineral that looks like very small grains of mica or sand, from which it receives its name. Deposits of this mineral are located in Wisconsin, New Jersey, and Colorado. It is a silicate of potassium and iron, with some phosphorus and other trace minerals. It contains 6.7 percent potassium. Greensand is slow in releasing the potassium, so it is better to apply it very early in the spring or fall. Apply at the rate of 7 pounds, if your soil is very lacking it potassium, to each 100 square feet of garden space. The following year it can be reduced to 4 or 5 pounds, and 2 pounds after that. Greensand is one of my favorite sources of potassium

Gypsum (land plaster) will provide calcium to the soil without raising the pH. If your pH is below 5.8, then do not apply gypsum, use lime instead. Gypsum also supplies 17 percent sulfur.

Hoof and Horn Meal: I'll list this one, but it may be hard to find. It may be that you can grind or get a source to grind this meal. This is a slow releasing amendment that starts releasing it's nutrients about four to six weeks after applying it, and lasts one year or more. It contains approximately 12 percent nitrogen and 0.5 percent phosphorus, and some minor nutrients.

James A. Eagle

Kelp Meal Is one of the most amazing plants that God has established on this earth. It comes from the sea, and it is loaded with nutrients and contains about every element on earth. Besides providing nutrients, it simulates microbes to break down other organic material. It is great to add to the compost pile. (See Addendum II for more information.)

Langbeinite (sold as Sol-Po-Mag) is a natural source of potassium, sulfur, and magnesium. It is named after the person who first discovered it, Langbein. Langbeinite contains 22 percent potassium, 22 percent sulfur, and 11 percent magnesium. It is an excellent source of potassium when there is also a shortage of sulfur or magnesium. Only apply one pound for each 100 feet of garden space, and after the second year, reduce to one-half of this amount.

Rock Phosphate in its natural state is slow releasing. It depends on where it is mined as to the color. It can be white or cream colored or black. After applying, you will get some benefit in a short period of time, but it will continually release over a period of several years. Soil testing for phosphates may show erroneous results, because bacteria must work on the rock for the phosphorus to be available. Apply approximately 10 pounds for each 100 square feet of garden space the first year, if your soil is very lacking in phosphate. The second year, apply 2-1/2 pounds, and the third year 1 pound. If you have been applying compost to your garden, then you can dispense with applications after the first year in most cases. The compost will provide the needed phosphate.

Soybean Meal: Soybean meal is another slow-releasing amendment. It starts releasing it's nutrients about three months after applying, and lasts for one year or more. It contains 7 percent nitrogen, 0.5 percent phosphorus, and 2.3 percent potassium.

Wood Ash: You may have been throwing out and disposing of one of the best organic potash fertilizers there is, each time you clean out your fireplace or wood stove. Wood ash is an excellent source of potash. It is immediately available to your plants, but will not last as long as some other sources of potash. Never put it on your garden or flower beds, unless you dig it into the soil at the time of applying. Rain will leach it out quickly. The best thing to do is store in a dry container where it will stay dry until you are ready to apply it on your garden. Never exceed approximately one gallon per fifty sq. feet Excess use can damage your plants.

Chapter Five

Diagnosing
Plant Problems

One of the best ways to prevent diseases or excess damage by insects is to have healthy soil that produces healthy plants. Plants are like our own bodies. If they are lacking in the proper nutrients, they will get diseases and sometimes die, the same as our bodies do. Keep your plants healthy and you will prevent many diseases. Even insects usually will attack a sick plant first.

You will find that this chapter does not list the name of diseases or the insects, but the symptoms, damages, and conditions are listed instead. This is necessary because the average gardener is not familiar with the many diseases, or insect problems, but sees the damages that are indicated. I hope this will aid you in discovering your problem.

Wilted Leaves: There are many ways to diagnose plant problems, and one of the first will be to observe your plant with wilted leaves. When you see the leaves wilting, what is the first thing you think the plant needs? If you answer was water, then you are like most of us, but it could be some other problems.

The plant could have diseased roots, whereby the plant is unable to take up moisture to supply its needs. Dig down and expose the roots on one side of the plant without disturbing the rest. Are the roots black and the outside layer of the roots easily removed, exposing dark tissue inside the root? You could have bacterial root-rot due to excessive watering. Yes, you can water many plants to death. Or the roots may have some other disease.

The plant may be saved, provided it has some parts of the roots still healthy. Since it has rotted roots, remove the plant completely. Remove all the soil. Prune off all damaged roots and soak the roots in a solution of equal parts of 3 percent hydrogen peroxide and water. The hydrogen peroxide in the grocery stores is 3 percent (a solution of water and 10 percent bleach can be used instead). Reset the plant in another pot or area of the garden. Mix cornmeal with the soil wherever you are resetting the plant (see cornmeal in Addendum. II). It has been proven that corn meal destroys many harmful bacteria and virus. The cornmeal also provides nutrients. Also apply the most efficient multiplier of beneficial bacteria you can get. It is in your grocery store. Get a bottle or jar of molasses. Mix one-half of a cup to a gallon of very warm water. Mix well and let cool to room temperature. Soak the soil where you intend to reset the plant. Good bacteria can multiply many times in twenty-four hours by feeding on this, and will destroy disease bacteria.

Another time you may see plants wilting, when not due to lack of moisture in the soil, is on very hot summer days. It can be seen especially with corn. I have seen corn wilt right after a heavy rain on a very hot day because it wasn't able to take up enough moisture fast enough through the transpiration process to keep it cool. The hot sun was causing it to give off more moisture than normal, causing wilting. This is only a short-term problem. The wilting will vanish at night.

Ensuring you have enough moisture in the soil can be accomplished by adding plenty organic matter and mulch.

Sunken Spots on Leaves and Fruit: When you observe small sunken spots in the leaves, and sometimes the fruit, of a plant it could be a disease known as *Anthracnose*. In rainy or damp weather, the

James A. Eagle

plant can have dark, shriveled leaves. There are several kinds of fungi that cause this disease. This is especially noted in beans. It appears as small, sunken, and darkened places on the pods, leaves, and stems. There are some varieties of beans that are resistant to it. This is also observed on other plants as well, such as oaks, sweet peas, and other plants. The effects on some of these plants may appear differently. Dusting with cornmeal or spraying with hydrogen peroxide and neem can control this problem (see cornmeal, neem, and hydrogen peroxide in Addendum II).

Dark Spots on Leaves: Dark spots are fairly common on many plants. We have roses that get *Black Spot,* and this same fungus that causes it can produce it on other plants, such as strawberries. There are several fungus diseases that cause dark spots on the leaves, fruit, flowers, etc. Use the fungicides that are natural, such as *baking soda, cornmeal, neem, and Hydrogen Peroxide.* These can be sprayed, dusted or sprinkled on the leaves and stems of the plant. The cornmeal can also be mixed with the soil to control soil borne diseases.

Seedlings Falling Over and Dying: If you will inspect the stem of seedlings of plants near ground level, you will notice that it is very weak at this point and falls over. At this stage it cannot supply the upper part of the plant with moisture and nutrients necessary for growth. This is known as *"Damping-off Disease."* Here is a good use for the cornmeal again. Dust the cornmeal all around your plants on the ground. It has been about ten years since I first heard of this treatment for fungal disease. The A & M University in Texas had a field of peanuts that were dying and with all the fungicides they used, nothing was stopping the disease. Why they came up with this treatment I do not know, but someone recommended the dusting of the field with cornmeal. It stopped it over night.

The day I read this, my wife came in the house and said our okra seedlings were just coming up, but were falling over and dying. I asked her where the cornmeal was. She got it for me and wanted to know what I was going to do with it. I replied, "Dust the okra." The next morning all the plants were upright and looking perky, except two. This disease is very fast-acting and can destroy a crop in a short time. You may also try the molasses treatment above.

Mounds or Tunneling in garden or yard: There are several things that produce mounds. One that is causing lots of trouble in the South is the invasion of fire ants from South America. When we first moved back to South Carolina, we had quail feeding on our blueberries shortly after they started bearing fruit. It was a pleasure to hear the male calling his mate, or run across a pair with a covey of babies.

The last five years we seldom see any or hear them calling their mate. The South Carolina Wildlife Department released a warning that they believed it was due to the fire ant infestation. When the fire ants attack it is quick and deadly. I read of a case where a senior citizen in a Nursing Home was attacked while sitting in her wheel-chair, and was bit and stung so severely that she died.

We had them so bad at our place that I finally used poisons to try and eliminate them. No success. The reason they are such a problem is that they have come here without their predators. One of their predators is a small type of flying insect that invades their mounds and tunnels. Yes! They have tunnels that can extend for fifteen to thirty feet from the mound. That is the reason poison is not successful. You may kill a few at the mouth of the mound, but within in a few days, you will see one or two mounds pop up fifteen feet or more from the old mound.

I have discovered two things that have worked for me. I first heard of using grits to kill them from the Internet. But it didn't mention the fact it had to be instant grits. I tried regular grits and the five-minute grits, but those didn't work. It was supposed to swell inside the ant, whereby it wouldn't be able to pass through their digestive tract. Then I began to think that it would have to swell really quickly to do that, because it is a very short time that food would remain in an insect.

At this point, I started looking for instant grits. All I could find was instant grits in little packets. I wanted it in bulk. I finally found it at Wal-Mart. We started dusting the mounds, and it worked. If they clean it up, just dust some more. The colony will finally disappear. The worker ants are not the only ones eating it; it is also fed to the queens and babies. This past summer we only saw one mound, and I heard quail again in the blueberries.

There are not only imported fire ants, but there are native fire ants as well, located in Texas. But do not try to eliminate the native fire ants. They actually help retard the imported fire ants. Both will immediately mobilize and sting quickly when their mounds are disturbed.

There are also imported black fire ants that came from Argentina. They were hardly settled and were spreading fast until the red fire ant arrived and they started pushing the black fire ants aside and to dominate and take over the areas they were in.

There is another kind of mound made by a rodent. This pesky little animal is known as a *vole*. This is an English name for what they consider is a wild or field mouse. About the only cure for these is a good dog, such as a Beagle, trapping, or using rat poison, and I do not like using the latter.

Leaves with White Powdery Appearance: This is called *Powdery Mildew* and is caused by parasites that thrive in damp, but not rainy, weather,. The parasites live in the tissue of the leaves and stem of the plant, producing a white powdery substance. Plants most commonly affective are: squash, cucumber, peach, apple, and others. This can be prevented by dusting with cornmeal or spraying with hydrogen peroxide or baking soda Two tablespoons of baking soda to a gallon of water will kill it. The damage that has been done will not disappear. Neem-oil spray will also control it.

White, Pinkish, or Black Substances on Leaves: These are usually molds that can be caused by aphids on the plant. The aphids excrete a sweet substance that feeds the mildew spores. This is the reason ants gather and take care of the aphids. They feed on this aphid excretion. Apples can get a black fungus on the leaves and fruit, and crape myrtles can also. Use the same controls listed for powdery mildew. You want to kill the aphids and the fungus, so add neem to the above spray.

Yellow Spots on Leaves: If you have yellow spots in the leaves, you may assume it has some form of disease or nutrient deficiency, but it could be due to spider mites, scale, white flies, or aphids. If the veins of the leaves are still green, most likely it is due to a nutrient deficiency. To diagnose the problem correctly there are several things you must do to try and determine the cause. You must carefully examine the plant. Look at the undersides of leaves and the top. Most small insects, such as aphids, spider mites, scale, and white flies will be located under the leaves of the plant. A good magnifying glass is good to use to observe some of these small insects.

Aphids can infest many species of plants. There are many species of these little insects, which vary from 1/32" to 1/8". They can vary in color as well. They are soft-bodied insects that suck the plant juices. The leaves will become discolored and twisted, usually falling from the plant in badly infested cases. These small, pear-shaped insects will cluster on the leaves and stems usually near the growing tip of the plant. Their choice of the plant is the tender parts, such as new growth. These pests will cover the stems and leaves, even the newly-set, young, tender buds and fruit.

If you grow roses, then you no doubt have had these light-colored aphids on the new growth and buds of the rose plant. If they are not destroyed, then they will disfigure the buds and the rose will be disfigured when it opens. All of these aphids can be destroyed with the vegetable-oil spray listed above, or Neem. Also check Addendum II for additional formulas for spraying.

James A. Eagle

If just one or two aphids are left, then you must spray several times every few days to get rid of them all. They can multiply extremely fast.

I have discovered that many think they have some form of disease when they have scale-insects. This is one of the hardest types of insect to identify for many. You may find a small bump on the underside of a leaf, or on a limb or trunk of the bush or tree, and think it may be some form of disease, but it could be one of the many forms of female scale-insects. They are legless and wingless. Some stay in the same position without any movement. Some attach themselves to the plant and remain there, forming a hard scale over their body to protect themselves. The young will appear as very tiny crawling insects. You may never see a male, but they are around. They are very small flying-insects with yellow wings. The spray above will control them. The oil will close the pores on the body of the insect, and it then dies. Insects breathe through their outer covering. This is the way an oil spray will destroy all insects

If you find any type of small insect such as mentioned above, then spray with a solution of two tablespoons of vegetable oil to one gallon of water during the growing season. Use three tablespoons of oil during the dormant season. To obtain a good mixture in the water, add one tablespoon of Murphy's Oil Soap for each gallon of mixture. If you think it may be some fungus disease, add two tablespoons of baking soda to the above mixture. Other sprays suitable for aphids are the insecticidal soaps and the new light oil sprays, which are available at good gardening centers and many seed and plant catalogs.

Nutrient Problem: This is a subject that can be difficult to diagnose in many cases because some forms of nutrient deficiencies look much like disease, environmental, or insect problems. I will do my best to diagnose the most common nutrient deficiencies. Many of these symptoms will look very much like some types of insect as it appears on some plants, such as scale insects. But scale infestations can be ruled out when you know how to identify them.

Most all of us think we can identify a plant that has a nitrogen deficiency, but can you tell if there is too much nitrogen in the soil? I have received calls that someone has some plant that looks beautiful, but it will not set fruit. This, in many cases, can be caused by an excess of nitrogen. Over-fertilization of nitrogen with chemical fertilizers can cause a flush of luxurious growth, but little or no flowering. This is one of the reasons I use organic fertilizers. If the plant is deficient in nitrogen, the foliage will become a light green or yellow. Not just the bottom leaves, but all leaves. Some of the best sources of organic fertilizers are compost, blood meal, fish meal, alfalfa meal, soybean meal, fish emulsion, or cotton seed meal. Cotton seed meal should be used with acid-loving plants, such as azaleas, blueberries, and camellias.

If a plant is deficient in phosphorus, the leaves will be very dark green, or even purplish or reddish in color. The growth will also be stunted, and you may notice a light set of fruit also. The best source for phosphorus is rock phosphate or bone meal. Do not use bone meal around acid-loving plants. The bone meal will raise the soil pH.

When a plant has a deficiency of potassium, the tips and edges of the plant turns yellow and then brown. The stems will become limp and weak. This is mistaken as some form of disease, in many cases. This condition can be corrected by using greensand or wood ashes. There are two other sources of potassium, but they are not available locally, in most cases. They are granite meal and langbeinite. Langbeinite is sold under the trade name of Sul-Po-Mag.

Magnesium and zinc deficiencies are very similar in the way they are detected. The leaves of the plant will turn yellow, but the veins in the leaf will remain green. If there is a zinc deficiency, the leaf will have a tendency to thicken and become fleshy. Growth will be stunted with both of these deficiencies. If the deficiency is magnesium, then here is where a dose of Epson salts is needed. Mix two tablespoons for each gallon of water and water the plant

James A. Eagle

with this solution. For a zinc deficiency, spray the foliage every two weeks for several applications, with liquid seaweed (Kelp). This will also help correct a magnesium deficiency. Kelp meal may also be used by applying it directly to the soil at the rate of one pound for every 100 square feet of garden area.

A calcium deficiency first shows up on the new growth of the buds and young leaves of the plant. The buds and leaf tips will turn brown and die. The fruit of the tomato will show up as rot on the blossom end of the tomato. Lime and gypsum (land plaster) is good organic means to correct this deficiency, but it can be corrected by spraying skim milk on the foliage of the plant several times at two week intervals, or water the plant with milk.

An iron deficiency will show up similarly to magnesium and zinc deficiencies. The leaves turn yellow, but the veins remain green. Use the liquid kelp (seaweed) or the kelp meal for this deficiency also.

When young leaves on a plant turn yellow all over, and growth is stunted, then it may be a sulfur deficiency. This can best be corrected with gypsum (land plaster) or sulfur powder. A light application of the powder is all that is needed. It does not take much sulfur to correct this deficiency. Excess sulfur can also cause troubles. Spraying with a sulfur-spray would be the best way to correct this deficiency, and the sulfur can control or cure some diseases. Sulfur is also a fungicide.

Boron is a minor nutrient that is required very little for a plant's health, but if the soil is deficient it will show up by the young leaves turning pale green at the base and with twisted leaves. New buds will usually die, preventing new growth. This sometimes will show up in the soil over a long period of time where pecan trees are growing. The pecan trees will deplete the boron over a long period of time if organic fertilizers are not used. The kelp meal is a good way to correct this deficiency. Applying Borax powder will also correct this deficiency. A foliar spray may be made of the Borax and sprayed on the foliage.

There are other minor nutrients which can cause trouble, but all of them can be corrected by using organic fertilizers, especially kelp meal.

Holes in Leaves: If there are large holes from one-fourth to an inch or more, then it is probably snails or slugs. The snails have a shell they carry with them, and the slugs do not have a shell. You are not likely to see them during the day, because they hide. They are night feeders. They may be hiding in the leaves of cabbage, or under mulch during the day. Check your plants about an hour after dark. This is when you will find them. One of the best treatments is a slug and snail bait that works very well. It will kill them, and it is safe and harmless to you and beneficial insects. Another method is using diatomaceous earth, Oyster shells, or crushed eggshells, applying them on top of the soil. The sharp edges on these items will cut their soft bodies.

If the holes are small it can be flea-beetles. They are small beetles and quick moving. By shaking the plant you will see them hopping away. Spraying with neem will control them.

Other Information for Your Excellent Enjoyment: Is there a purpose for insects? Yes! There are good and bad insects. Let us try to understand how insects help and destroy the plants we try to grow. When God cursed the earth He didn't destroy all the good He created. Most of the marvelous creation was maintained, but the curse was used so we would have to labor and toil to supply the food we needed.

The beneficial insects we still have, but some were equipped with stingers and jaws to bite, after mankind sinned. The bee, for instance, still pollinates the flowers, but if you hassle it, it will sting. The wasp now eats other insects for its food, and will also sting. I could fill pages on different insects and how they were changed, but I think you get the idea. There are many insects that help to control the bad, such as the ladybug.

Many insects, when observed closely, seem to be all bad. The Japanese beetle, for instance, does. In the stage of a grub, it eats the roots of plants and destroys their ability to take up nutrients and moisture. If the damage is too severe, the plant will die. When they emerge as beetles from the soil, they can strip a plant in one day of its foliage.

There are insects so small that you need to put them under a microscope to observe them. They are the nematodes. There are good and bad nematodes. One known as the *root-knot nematode* attacks the roots of plants and can even cause a plant to die or not produce as it should. Then there are good nematodes that attack grubs and worms in the soil and even attack the root knot nematodes.

At this point I wish to inject another thought into your mind. There is an all-out effort to start restricting carbon dioxide in the air. Carbon dioxide is a natural-occurring compound that is needed to maintain life on this planet. Our food source is the plants and the fruit of plants that God has established on this planet. Plants take in carbon dioxide in order that they may convert nutrients into energy to promote growth and production. Without carbon dioxide, there would not be any plants on this earth, and we would die. Plants, in turn, give off oxygen for us to breathe in that we are able to maintain life. This is the way God has established the system. Destroy carbon dioxide and we die. Take the oxygen away and we die.

Chapter Six

Controlling Insects
and Diseases

"Can anyone teach God knowledge, since He judges those on high?"

Job 21:22, NKJV

"Go to the ant you sluggard! Consider her ways and be wise, which having no captain, overseer or ruler, provides her supplies in the summer, and gathers her food in the harvest"

Proverbs 8:6, NKJV

Have you ever watched ants at work? When I was a kid, I would get down on my knees and watch them going to food sources in long lines. The food source might be a worm that was still alive and squirming as the ants were biting and attacking it. You could see them carrying large pieces of food, even larger than they were, back to their underground home. As they were heading back to their home, you could see them stop as they met other ants coming their way. They would put their heads together as though they were communicating and telling the other ants where the food source was.

Scientist confirmed that they do communicate with each other, and let other ants know where the food source is located. Bees communicate also. I have watched bees come to a hive loaded with pollen and nectar. They would stop at the hive entrance and start fluttering and turning, with the other bees crowded around them. These bees would then take off to the new source of nectar.

The workings of the Creator are marvelous and a wonder to behold. Anyone who observes their surroundings must realize the miracles that God has established for our good and pleasure.

Many have the idea that all bugs, insects, and worms, in all of their many stages of development, are harmful or a pest. This is one of the greatest misunderstandings of all. There are more beneficial insects to assist us in growing our crops.

The solution to insect problems is not in a tank of poison, but understanding God's laws and the ability to work with those laws.

One of the first of these laws is "the survival of the fittest," as the evolutionists call it. This law was established after the fall of man in the Garden of Eden. Death did not exist before this. Because of sin, everything now deteriorates and dies. This applies to mankind, animals, and plants. The life span is long on some forms of life, and very short on others. The decay and returning to the earth is God's way of replenishing the soil of its nutrients, which we took from it. Animals and humans with the highest degree of health, strength, and vigor will survive longer. This same principal applies to plants. The more healthy and vigorous they are, the longer they will live and bear fruit.

As an animal predator seeks out the sick and infirm in a herd, so will the insects which feed on plants. They will seek the weak, stressed, and infirm plant to attack, so it is our goal to have healthy plants. This was also covered in a prior chapter.

In the world of insects there are predator insects that attack other insects, as well as it is in the animal kingdom.

How many of you that use poison pesticides or herbicides have you ever read all the *Warnings* and *Environmental Hazards*

James A. Eagle

that are listed on the container? This should be enough to cause you to stop *now* in exposing your family to them.

Let us take one pesticide that the EPA has classified as safe for the homeowner when used according to instructions. It is sold over the counter and can be purchased at any store that sells pesticides. I will not name the brand.

On the front of the label it states in large letters, "This product must not be used on golf courses and sod farms." On the back, in very small letters, it gives instructions for using on your lawns. Is it okay for your children to play where you use it, but not for golfers?

Above the instructions, for using on your lawns is the "Warning" in small letters.

"Causes eye injury. Harmful if swallowed or absorbed through the skin. Do not get in the eyes. Wear goggles or face-shield when handling. Avoid contact with skin or clothing. Do not use on household pets or humans. Keep children and pets away from treated area until completely dry. Keep out of reach of domestic animals."

I didn't see anything where it should be stored out of reach of children. It goes on, giving the lengthy methods of treatment when exposed. The treatment method alone should be enough warning not to use it.

One of the most startling things is the instructions for using on your vegetables and fruit. Does this sound reasonable? If it is this dangerous, I certainly have no desire to consume it.

There is one thing that those who use these poisons should be aware of. The EPA approves or disapproves a pesticide or herbicide on the grounds of tests conducted by the manufacturer and the claims they make in most cases. This is like the tobacco companies telling you that tobacco is safe for use. This is another reason why they go on the market and cause untold deaths before the EPA will ban them. Hardly any of the chemicals in use today have been tested thoroughly for chronic effects on our health, especially cancer and the ability to cause mutations

There is another notice that you should be aware of that is in small letters on the back of the container. It states:

> "*Notice*: Buyer assumes all responsibility for safety and use not in accordance with instructions."

This puts the liability for its use right back to the buyer. It is imperative that you read all instructions given on the container. If you cause damage to your neighbor in any form, then you are liable. This includes any damage to children, pets, birds, or anything your neighbor may conceive of. With the suing craze we have today, there is no limit to what they will conceive of to obtain damages from you.

Scientists have discovered that many of the supposedly "inert" ingredients have the potential to do enormous amounts of harm in the long run. Inert ingredients like vinyl chloride and formaldehyde were used at one time until they discovered the dangers they can incur.

What makes this such a serious problem is the fact that many gardeners will use these sprays prior to ever seeing any insect damage. They seem to think it is a must to protect their plants. In most cases, the insects would have never developed to the stage that they would have done any serious harm.

Some time ago, a scientist with the National Cancer Institute suggested that 30 to 40 percent of all cancer deaths could be avoided if people took heed of the knowledge we now have on environmental carcinogens. Rare and new types of cancer keep showing up, especially some of the liver cancers, which they have no cure for.

Some time back, there were three EPA attorneys that quit working for the EPA, and issued a warning that stated,

> "It is clear from recent actions that the Environmental Protection Agency intends to restrain from vigorous enforcement of available toxic substances controls and to entrench

from the few legal precedents which it has set for evaluating the cancer hazards posed by chemicals."

If you have been depending on the government to protect you, then *don't*.

Our obligation now is to return to the God-made laws of control and strive to recover the balance we once had. When we let God's laws prevail, a beautiful method of checks and balances occurs. In the 1930's the destructive insects were beneficial in one function: they destroyed the weak plants.

There are three main classifications of beneficial insects: predators, parasites and pollinators. There are some that pollinate as adults and feed on other insects in their larva stage. A predator will attack and eat other insects or parts of it. The parasite usually lays eggs where the hatched larva will eat on the destructive insect, its larva, or its eggs. The pollinators feed on the nectar of flowers thereby pollinating as they satisfy their food needs.

Encouraging Native Beneficial Insects: Even though a plant may not deter insects, it may be used to attract beneficial insects. Most beneficial insects require plant nectar and pollen to complete their life cycle. So, by providing flowering plants the benefits will be attracted. Insects also need water, so it may be necessary to sprinkle an area in your garden each day to supply their water needs, or buy clay pottery saucers that will hold an inch or two of water. Place these around in the garden. By putting a few small stones in the water, it will provide an area where they can land and sip the water. Most of the plants that attract the beneficial insects are small flowering plants such as daisy type flowers, mint, carrot, and mustard families. There are flowers of some weeds that attract beneficial insects.

Insects Traps and Barriers: Another good way to control insects is to use traps and barriers, which are easy to use. One of the most popular is the floating row-covers that are available. These can be cut in squares for individual plants, or you can cover a whole row or small garden. These covers will allow light and water to pass through, but will keep out the insects. Sometimes it may be necessary to only use them during a critical stage in the plants' life. These barriers will also protect plants from birds as well. These are the same covers used to protect plants from cold.

Another barrier, which is one of my favorites, is diatomaceous earth. It feels like powder to the touch, but it is very abrasive to the bodies of soft-bodied insects. It can be dusted on the ground or the foliage of the plant. *Do not use diatomaceous earth that has been processed for the use of swimming pool filters. It has been processed where it no longer has the sharp edges.*

Copper strips to prevent snails and slugs from entering the garden are available from many sources that sell organic pest controls. These pests will not pass a copper barrier.

One of the most widely used traps is the *Pheromone* traps. They are used to attract the male insect to the female insect and trap them. When a large number of the traps are located in an orchard, it confuses the male so that he can no longer locate the female insect. These traps are not advised for the small gardener.

Tanglefoot is a sticky, nontoxic substance made of vegetable-based oils and resins that can be painted on trunks and limbs of trees to trap insects. I would advise putting duct tape on the bark of trees first, then applying the tanglefoot on the tape.

Micro-controls: Micro-controls are microorganisms that are used to eradicate certain pests. These may kill insects by infecting them with a fatal disease, or kill them with a toxin the microorganism carries. In other cases a microorganism is used to colonize a plant surface so a disease organism cannot get established. For the home-gardener these controls are more feasible than using beneficial insects in cases where you must order them. The microorganisms will stay where they are applied, but the insects you release may decide to go to your neighbor's garden instead. These are better than sprays or dusts in that they will not harm humans, pets, and wildlife, or even beneficial insects, in most cases.

Bacillus thuringiensis, most commonly called Bt comes in several trade names, such as Dipel and Thuricide. When the worm eats a sprayed leaf, they stop eating, become dark in color and soon die. This is especially good for many caterpillar pests, including cabbage worms, corn earworms, gypsy moth larvae, tomato horn worms, and many more. Bt. variety *San Diego* controls some beetles such as Colorado potato beetles, elm leaf beetles, and black vine weevils. They are now making baits of Bt. which are available from some sources. Be forewarned, do not overuse. Only use when you notice the insect's presence on the plant. Already there are cases where the insect has been able to build a resistance to it.

Beneficial Nematodes are very small nematodes that eat insects in the soil instead of the roots of plants. They are mixed with water and sprinkled on the soil. They may come dehydrated or suspended in a sponge or other moist substance. They are most effective when applied to moist soil. Follow the instructions that come with them.

Milky spore disease is an excellent way to get rid of the Japanese or June beetle grubs in your lawn or garden. It contains two kinds of bacteria, *Bacillus popilliae* and *Bacillus lentimorbus*. The grubs that are infected will die and inoculate the soil with more bacteria. (See Lawn care in Chapter 7.)

Nosema Locustae is a protozoan that infects small grasshoppers. It should be applied in the early spring when grasshoppers are less than one-half inch in length. It comes in several different trade names such as *Semaspore*, and *Nolo Bait*.

Sprays and Dusts: Insecticidal soap is a very safe spray available today. It must be sprayed directly on the insect to be effective. It is especially good for the following insects: aphids, scale insects, white fly, and many other soft-bodied insects. It contains fatty acids that are toxic to insects and harmless to plants.

Oil sprays have been used for many years to control disease spores and the eggs on deciduous trees and shrubs during the dormant season. Now oil sprays have been developed that can be used during the active growing season. Always use according to directions. Now they are starting combining the summer oil sprays with baking soda to prevent powdery mildew and black spots on plants. Cornell University found that one tablespoon of baking soda and two and a half teaspoons of summer oil mixed with one gallon of water sprayed once each week will control both of these diseases.

Neem is fairly new in this country, but has been used in India for hundreds of years. They not only use it to protect their plants, but take it internally to cure illnesses. It is the oil that is extracted from the *Azadirachia Indica tree,* more commonly called the neem tree. It is a tropical tree, but is now being grown in the lower part of Florida, and many other countries. It is unique in the many ways it acts on insects. It acts as a contact poison, stomach poison, repellant, anti-feedant (causing an insect to lose their appetite), growth retardant, and egg-laying deterrent. Many studies are still being conducted here in this country. You can apply it as a spray or drench. Neem kills at least seventy-five kinds of pests, yet it is relatively safe for humans and animals. Preliminary studies have shown that parasitic wasps and predatory mites are not poisoned by it.

Hydrogen peroxide is very safe and effective in controlling many diseases. Mix 50 percent water and 50 percent hydrogen Peroxide. Spraying about every seven days prevents and stops many diseases.

Some safe and excellent fungus fighting teas can be prepared by mixing one pint of good rotted manure or compost in one gallon of water and let set for twenty-four hours or more. Apply this weekly to your tomato and other plants that are subject to fungal diseases. (This was discussed earlier.)

An even better control is using earthworm castings to make a spray or water plants with.. Take fresh earthworm castings (These are available on the internet.) using one quart castings to four quarts of water. Put castings in a cloth bag and soak in the water for 24 hours. Spray or water your plant with this.

James A. Eagle

By the earthworms digesting waste and compost, beneficial bacteria multiply much faster than normal. I have read about this for years, but never put it to a test until this year, 2010.

A friend gave me two large pots a nursery used to put trees in for landscaping. They measured four feet in diameter and three feet deep. My wife and I put a layer of leaves, then a layer of shredded paper, then a layer of garden soil. This was soaked good with water. This was repeated until about four inches from the top. At this point we added a little ground limestone. We let the containers set for about ten days, and the tubs settled down about a foot. We then put a mixture of garden soil and compost to fill it to the top. Corn is a heavy feeder. We added about a quart of alfalfa meal to each tub.

The tubs were planted on March 23, 2010, with Golden Bantam Sweet corn. The plants were thinned to twelve (12) plants in each tub. On the 10th of April one pound of Red Wiggler earthworms were added to one tub, none were put in the control tub. On June 8, 2010, we harvested our first corn, and it was delicious.

On the control tub (the tub no earthworms were inserted) there were ten full long ears, two shorter ears, and six nubbins. On the tub with the earthworms there were twelve large ears, four almost as long as the large ears, four a little shorter, and four nubbins. The stalks, on the tub with the earthworms, were much larger and sturdier than on the control tub.

This was our first really true testing with the use of earthworms. We are using earthworm castings in the tubs we grow tomatoes, beans, cabbage, etc. It amazes me the difference a double handful of worm castings can make to eliminate most diseases and repel insects, and plants are much healthier.

Another control method for diseases is crushing about twenty-five cloves of garlic and adding a pint of water and letting it set for three days or more. Strain and add an additional gallon of water and apply. To make it easier to prepare garlic, you can order garlic oils from many herb supply companies, and some are now offering sprays made from garlic.

Here is a wonderful cure for many fungal diseases. Some years ago the Experiment Station at Texas A & M University in Texas had a field of peanuts that were dying from a fungus. They tried several fungicides, but nothing seemed to help. Someone came up with the idea to dust them with a product sold in your grocery store, *corn meal*. Yes, regular corn meal. It stopped the fungus within twenty-four hours. At first they believed that the cornmeal was probably feeding bacteria that was destroying the fungus, but later they realized that in a part of the peanut field where they grew corn the year before, there was no fungus. It was determined that the corn contained a chemical that destroyed the fungus.

The following controls are not recommended unless in an extreme emergency: Pyrethrums are organic controls made from the pyrethrum flower. (Do not confuse pyrethrums with pyrethroids, which are synthetic compounds that resemble pyrethrums, but are more toxic and longer-lasting in the environment). Pyrethrums cause the insect to become instantly paralyzed. This may kill them by starvation or leave them vulnerable to predators. Pyrethrums will kill beneficial insects, as well as the bad.

Here are three more that I do not recommend: *nicotine, rotenone, and sadadilla*. At one time, these were used quite extensively by organic gardeners, but they are no longer recommended by many because of their toxic effects on wildlife and beneficial insects. They will break down and eventually become harmless, but in the meantime, they would also damage your environmental structure, which you are trying to establish.

Building a Healthy Soil: Building a healthy soil is the first priority in insuring you have disease-free plants. Organic matter is a must-have requirement for a healthy soil. As it decays, it releases nutrients into the soil. It produces a sponge-like structure that increases the soil's ability to hold moisture and provide proper air circulation in the soil. As organic matter continues to break down in the soil, it is converted to humus that continues to release

James A. Eagle

nutrients and keeps working for you. Organic matter should be added at least once each year, and more often, if you have heavy clay or silt soil. Organic matter can be animal manures (except dog and cat), composted leaves, hay, straw, garden waste, wood chips, or sawdust. In applying poultry manures, mix them with the garden soil and let them compost naturally for two weeks before planting. This manure will burn the roots with its high nitrogen content until it has composted.

I must tell of a bad experience I had with poultry manure. Since then, I have learned much. In 1960 we had purchased thirteen acres near Shaw Air Force Base new Sumter, SC. I was making preparations to retire from the military, so we purchased 100 peach trees to start a small peach orchard. This soil was poor and I wanted something to give them a good start. One of the owners of the Palmetto Pigeon Plant in Sumter was a reserved officer, and he came in our office quite often. I asked him if pigeon manure would burn like poultry. He assured me it would not. I hauled a pick-up load and applied to those peach trees. Every last one died.

When you have a healthy soil, it will support helpful bacteria, earthworms, and other beneficial insects. If additional nutrients are needed, they can be added by adding amendments and minerals, which have been mentioned in detail in Chapter 4.

The benefits of the earthworm have been mentioned several times, but I want to extol some more benefits here. Emphasis is being given to the earthworm and its wonderful benefits even by large industrial farmers. The vermicompost that they produce has proven so beneficial that many have gone into the business of raising earthworms just to sell vermicompost and make a tea from it to spray on plants for the nutrients, disease control, and even to repel some insects. In fact, the earthworm is so beneficial that I think the president should declare an "Earthworm Awareness Week."

Start with Healthy Plants: When buying plants for your garden or orchard, they are required to be inspected and certified pest- and disease-free by the government before shipping across state lines. This does not mean that they have all been inspected. Only a sampling is done at certain times. It is like your meat. It is spot-checked at certain times and then all the rest is stamped. It is up to you to be sure they are pest- and disease-free. When buying plants locally, it is your responsibility to be certain they are healthy and pest-free. Starting with a diseased plant, or one that has not had the nourishment it needs, is asking for trouble later.

Choose Resistant Varieties: Most seed catalogs will indicate when certain varieties are resistant to diseases that may be a problem in our area. For example, the cantaloupe "Scoop II Hybrid" is listed as a highly disease-resistant variety in seed catalogs. The tomato variety "Celebrity" has the letters VFFNT after its name in seed catalogs. This means that it is resistant to Verticillium Wilt, Race 1 and Race 2 Fusarium Wilt, nematodes, and Tobacco Mosaic.

One of our favorite flowering trees in the south is the flowering dogwood (Botanical Name: *Cornus florida*). It is bothered by several diseases that the Japanese dogwood has a resistance against (Botanical Name: *Cornus kousa*). If you have been bothered with these diseases, then you may want to switch to the Japanese Dogwood.

Rotate Crops: Planting the same crop in the same spot year after year is only inviting trouble. Soil-borne bacteria that cause many diseases on one plant will die out when that plant is not put in the same area again and again. Not all plants will contact the same type of diseases. Even in animals this is true.

The tomatoes is one plant of which we certainly should be careful of repeat plantings in the same area year after year. You should wait three or more years before planting them in the same area. Tomatoes are of the nightshade family, and this applies to any plant of the nightshade family, such as eggplant, peppers, and Irish potatoes. *Do not* put tomatoes in any area where any nightshade plants have been grown in for the last two or three years. There are some methods you can use to kill these disease organisms. You can till grass clippings into the soil. They will

James A. Eagle

decay within about two weeks. The methanol gas put off during this period will kill many of the harmful organisms. You can also mix cornmeal with the soil to prevent many diseases

Companion Planting: For centuries gardeners have noticed that some plants seem to thrive and do better when planted with others. Some combinations have been said to protect plants from insect pests. Many tests are being conducted today by researchers in order to better understand the possibility of repelling pests by inter-planting with others. Something that we know already is that pest outbreaks are less likely when we have a number of the different kinds of plants planted together. Many insects will seek out specific plants, and when they find a large planting of one kind that they desire, they can then quickly multiply and create an outbreak of that one specific kind of insect.

Insects primarily seek their food first by smell, next by taste, and last by sight. It is believed that mixed crops confuse them when they are seeking their favorite crops. If you have mixed crops with strong smells, which they dislike, then it may be possible to protect the plants you like. Some combinations that have proven to have beneficial effects are:

- Southernwood with cabbage-family crops, to repel the cabbage butterfly.
- Catnip or tansy with squash, to repel squash bugs.
- Catnip or nasturtiums with peppers, to repel the green peach aphids.
- Nasturtiums with any plant, where white flies are a problem.
- Potatoes with beans, to repel the Mexican bean beetle.
- Peanuts with corn, to reduce the corn borer damage.
- Radishes with cucumbers, to reduce the stripped cucumber beetle damage.

- Marigolds (such as Nemagold or Queen Sophis varieties) with any crop, to repel cabbage worms and nematodes.

- Garlic, to repel many insects on many different plants, especially the peach borer. Onions are also effective in controlling insects.

Chapter Seven

Growing of Specific Plants

This chapter will be devoted to growing specific vegetables, flowers, fruit, lawns, etc. It is hoped your favorite plant is covered. Some plants that seldom get attention by other writers are covered here. Or they are covered because they are plants that I have received many questions about regarding their culture, and readers said others did not cover them sufficiently.

The number of different plants God has created is beyond the imagination, and all were for food and our enjoyment. After Adam and Eve sinned, God changed the nature of some plants and animals.

Tomatoes: The tomato has come from a position where it was once thought of as a deadly poison to being the most sought-after and grown vegetable in America. If you eliminated the tomato from all recipes and cookbooks, it would leave a hole large enough to drive a bulldozer through. It can be used in so many ways, from eating fresh right from the garden, frying them green, to making preserves and mincemeat, pasta, stew, soups, salads and as sliced tomato on a sandwich. No other vegetable is as versatile.

There are two types of tomato plants. They are determinate and indeterminate. The determinate stops growing after it blooms and starts setting fruit. All the fruit usually will ripen in several weeks. The indeterminate will continue growing and setting fruit until frost, if not damaged by diseases. The indeterminate tomatoes will need staking. There are rings that can be used.

Your selection for a growing site should be where they will have full sunlight and the soil is well-drained. If your soil is lacking in nutrients or drainage, it can be corrected. Nutrients can be added as composted animal manure or other composted vegetable matter such as leaves, grass clippings, hay, and other waste that we usually throw away. Add about three inches over your garden area and dig into the soil.

If you have a drainage problem, then I would advise you make a raised bed for growing your tomatoes. The height depends on how bad a drainage problem you have, and what causes it. If poor drainage is caused by a heavy clay soil, then adding compost or peat moss will aid in this. If the garden spot is low land and just lacks drainage, then the beds should be anywhere from 6 to 12 inches high, or higher.

If your soil has a pH below 6.5, then add lime or bonemeal to raise it to 6.5 or above. They will grow in a soil with a pH of 5.5 to 7.5, but naturally you desire the ideal conditions. If your soil is lacking in magnesium, then you should use dolomite instead of ground limestone. Dolomite contains up to 40 percent magnesium carbonate, which is an essential minor nutrient.

If your soil test indicates that you do not have a magnesium shortage, then bone meal will be the best source of raising your pH. It is also an excellent source of phosphate for your tomatoes. If you didn't have a soil test performed, then I would advise you add approximately three pounds of bone meal and four pounds of dolomite per 100 sq. ft of garden space. This should provide the magnesium, calcium, and phosphate needed by the tomatoes with the addition of the compost mentioned above.

If you wish to get an early start, then cover the soil with black plastic before planting. This will warm the soil. Do this about two weeks before you plan to set out your plants. Punch holes in the plastic and set out your tomatoes. To protect the plants from cold snaps, I use the unit known as *"Wall-O-Water." The patent on this has expired, and others have started manufacturing it. One new name is 'Insulating Teepee.'* I have protected plants when temperatures were in the middle twenties and icicles were hanging on the outside of the unit.

Plants can be purchased, but if you like variety, then start your own from seed. Some of the best tasting tomatoes I have ever eaten are varieties that you cannot find plants of on the market. Tomatoes come in many colors, from red, the standard color, to white, yellow, orange, purple, and black. Try some in all sizes and shapes as well.

One of the biggest problems for the home gardener is not being able to rotate his tomatoes to help prevent diseases. To help overcome this, use disease resistant varieties, such as Better Boy, Celebrity, Quick Pick, Beefmaster, Pilgrim and Big Beef. There are others, so if you buy seed, look for the capital letters after the name in the seed catalogs. The more letters there are, the more things they are resistant to. Also, you can kill many disease organisms where you have had tomatoes by burying green material, such as grass clippings. As it decays, the menthol gas it releases will kill many of the disease organisms.

Sweet Potatoes: Are you as tired as I am of the media and the cooks that appear on those morning shows calling sweet potatoes *yams?* It is doubtful if any of these people have ever seen a yam. The companies that can the sweet potatoes, and the grocery stores that sell the fresh ones, call them yams, in most cases. Folks, they are not yams; these delicious roots are sweet potatoes.

The yam belongs to the genus *Dioscorea.* There are several species of the yam, but they are a tropical plant grown in the tropics for their edible tubers. One called the "air-potato yam" is a climbing plant and the tubers are formed in the leaf axils. It is another one with tuberous roots, two to three feet long, that is also edible.

The sweet potato belongs to the genus *Ipomoea.* There are several species of this plant as well, but the sweet potato is *Ipomoea batatas.* It is nothing like the yam, so let us stop calling it a yam.

Many small gardeners would like to grow a few potatoes in their home garden, but have trouble finding plants or *slips* as they are called, in small amounts. For the small home gardener, here are several ways you can start your own plants.

It is best to get sweet potatoes grown locally if possible, if not, then purchase a nice, unblemished one in the grocery store. Get a vase, jar, or some other type of container that the potato will fit into where one-fourth of the potato can be emerged in water. Keep the water level up as it evaporates where one-fourth of the potato is covered. The lower end will take root and potato slips will start growing on the top portion. When the slips get about four or five inches long, you can remove them and place them in small pots with a potting soil mix. When all danger of frost is past and the soil temperature is seventy degrees or more you may set them out in your garden.

Another way to start your plants early is to take a hanging basket eight to ten inches in diameter. Fill it with a potting soil. Take a medium sized potato and cut lengthwise in half. Place the halves of the potato in the hanging basket with the cut sides down, and cover with about one to two inches of soil. This will give you a lovely hanging basket of sweet potato plants as they put out and grow. Let them grow one to two feet long, and then cut off about four to six inches of the tip. Place these tips in small containers with your potting mix. These will readily root if the medium is kept moist.

Sweet potatoes prefer a light sandy and slightly acidic soil, but will grow in other soils as well. Apply approximately ten to twenty pounds of compost for each 100 square feet and work into the soil. Avoid fresh manures or fertilizers with a high nitrogen content. The nitrogen will produce plenty of nice foliage, but small and few potatoes. They also like a slightly acidic soil. One that has a pH of 5.5 to 6.0 is ideal.

If your soil is heavy or poorly drained, then it is best to build up a ridge to plant them on. This will provide better drainage and let oxygen get to the roots of the plant.

James A. Eagle

Each plant should produce two to three pounds of potatoes. You can judge by this how many you should plant to supply the needs of your family.

The plants can be planted in rows or in beds. They should be twelve inches apart in all directions in the bed. If you plant in rows, then place the rows approximately three feet apart, and the plants twelve inches apart in the row.

Keep the soil moist all summer during the growing period. They will continue to grow up to first frost, but you will want to harvest before they have frost. The sweet potato is very tender, and the cold will give them a bitter, unsavory taste. It will also cause the potato to rot. Storage should be in a cool, dry place and protected from cold.

Irish Potatoes: The Irish potato comes to us from South America, where it is still highly valued by the Indians. It is a member of the nightshade family. Its botanical name is *Solanum tuberosum*.

The potato is a cool-season crop, which is why it is very important to get them planted as early as possible. The highest yields are produced during short days and when the temperature is below sixty-five degrees. When the days are hot and long, as in the summer, the material produced by the leaves is used to produce vegetative growth, but when the days are shorter and cool, vegetative growth is reduced and the excess food produced by the leaves moves down and forms the tubers. This is what we want, so cool short days are the ideal situations for potatoes.

There is a disadvantage growing potatoes here in South Carolina, where I live, but if we get them out early we can have a decent harvest. Most books or instructions will tell you to plant two to three weeks before the last killing frost. If we have a mild February, then it makes for an ideal season for us. The potatoes will take light frost without too much harm. Covering them with the white row covers that are available today will also help when that frost does come.

You should get your seed potatoes by the first two weeks in February in Zone Eight, or better yet in January, so they will have time to sprout before planting. They should be disease-free certified potatoes. Disease can be carried by the tuber from one year to the next. Large potatoes can be cut into pieces weighing one and one-half to two ounces. Make sure you have at least one eye on each cut piece. Place them in boxes with only one layer with the cut surface down. Place in a warm room with plenty of light so they can sprout. A sprouted potato will produce more and come up quicker than a dormant potato. Plenty of light will produce a nice green sprout, which is the most desirable. If you have a green house that is heated, then they can be put there to sprout. During this time the cut sides will have callused, preventing bacteria attacking the potato, causing it to decay. As soon as they have sprouted about one inch long, then they are ready to plant.

A sandy loam is the ideal soil for potatoes, although they will grow on most soils. They prefer an acid soil with a pH of 5.0 to 6.0. If your pH is lower than this, then add ground limestone where the magnesium is adequate. Dolomite should be used if a soil test indicates that you have a magnesium deficiency. A liberal amount of compost should be applied and tilled into the soil.

There are many different ways to plant potatoes, and each person thinks his is the best. I think mine is the best. I plant my potatoes only about an inch deep, then add mulch with leaves, grass clippings, or hay. This first mulch will be about four inches, but as the young shoots start coming through the mulch, apply more, just leaving the tip of the shoots showing. This will also protect the young potatoes from any late frosts. You can keep adding mulch until it is eight to twelve inches deep. This will control the weeds and keep the soil cool and moist.

New potatoes can be harvested as soon as they are large enough to use. This is usually about the time the blooms appear. You can easily check for new potatoes by pulling back the mulch. You will usually find them in the mulch or around ground level. These will serve for your early treats. The main harvest can be harvested when the tops start wilting and dying. By planting in

James A. Eagle

this manner, you can easily harvest by pulling off the mulch and digging a few inches in the soft moist soil.

One of my favorite varieties is the Yukon Gold. It is a nice butter-yellow and makes wonderful mashed potatoes and potato salads. It is a mid-early variety. You will find that the early and mid-early will be better producers in the warmer areas than the late varieties. Long-season varieties are more suitable for the colder Zones.

If you would like to try varieties that you cannot find locally, then here is a source for many different varieties, all organically grown: Wood Prairie Farm, 49 Kinney Rd., Bridgewater, Maine 04735. Phone (207) 429-9765.

Peppers, Hot & Sweet: The peppers we grow in our vegetable garden are members of the Capsicum family of plants. There are species that include the Bell Peppers (Capsicum grossum), Tabasco Pepper (C. frutescens), the Red Cluster Peppers, which grow their fruit erect and very pungent, (C. fasciculatum), and the Chili, Cayenne, and other strains of C. longum. There are other species, but these listed are the most common kinds grown in our gardens. The pepper plants are native American plants, most coming from Central or South America. Many will grow as perennial plants in a tropical zone. We had hot pepper plants in our landscape in Florida that were as many as twelve years old. They were kept pruned to three or four feet high. Many of the employees where I was employed enjoyed the bountiful harvest during the summer.

We have divided the pepper plants in two main groups, the sweet or mild flavored peppers, and the hot peppers. The sweet peppers are used for stuffing, salads, and garnishing. The hot peppers are used in sauces and for flavoring where one enjoys the pungent flavor.

Peppers belong to the Nightshade family, the Solanaceae. Therefore, they are closely related to the tomato, potato, and eggplant, and their culture is about the same as the other Nightshade members.

Peppers can be started from seed. It takes from sixteen to twenty days for pepper seeds to germinate. If the seeds are old, it can take even longer. They can be started indoors six to eight weeks before the last frost. Now you are wondering when we will have the last frost. For this you can let a zone map be your guide. These are available on line or many seed and nursery cataloga.

Should you set them out and have a late frost, the plant can be protected by covering them with buckets, boxes, or using the Wall-O-Water (trade name) or one of the hot caps that are now on the market.

Plants are also readily available in Garden Centers, especially the bell peppers. Plants of the hot peppers are not as readily available. If they are available it probably will be one of the jalapeno varieties. We purchase our seed from either Tomato Growers Supply Company, Fort Myers, FL., or Totally Tomatoes, Randolph WI. Both specialize in peppers and tomatoes. The last several years they have expanded and carrying some other vegetable seed.

You should have a well-drained soil. They do not like an area that stays excessively moist. Provide plenty of good compost for the nutrients and increase the soil's ability to hold moisture during dry periods. Excessive nitrogen can produce a beautiful green bush, but with few peppers. Do not over-fertilize with nitrogen. They also need an area that has full sun for maximum production. Mulching the plants with several inches of hay, straw, or leaves will help maintain moisture and provide a cool soil during the hot summer days

Spacing of the plants should be fifteen to eighteen inches apart in rows or in wide row beds. My plants were planted in a three-foot wide raised bed with three rows in the bed. In the middle row, the plants were spaced alternately from the outside two rows. This gave me fourteen plants in a twelve-foot, three-foot wide bed. The two outside rows have five plants in each row, and the middle row has four plants. Last year we dried, froze, and gave away many peppers to friends and family members.

To anyone growing any vegetable or fruit with the intention of preserving their harvest for the fall and winter months, I would advise the purchase of a dehydrator. Peppers are delicious when dried. They can be dried whole or chopped and then dried. One of my favorite condiments was a blend of several hot peppers that had been chopped in the blender, then put on wax paper on trays and dried. They were ready in eighteen hours. I could not keep my three sons and their families supplied with enough of this combination. They wanted me to commercialize it and put it on the market. No thank you, not at my age. I will provide methods I use.

Some peppers have much more flavor, which is pleasing to the appetite. Some of the varieties I use for flavor is the Jalapeno varieties. There has been a lot of crossing these peppers with others to produce larger and in some cases hotter peppers. One of my favorite is Chicimeca hybrid. Now to add hotness and more flavor I use one called Peter Pepper. Seed of this pepper can be found on the internet. It has excellent flavor that adds much to your favorite dishes. For even more hotness add a few of the habanero varieties. These also have a wonderful flavor. There are quite a few of these. There are other peppers that can be used to suit the taste of about any individual. If you prefer your mix to be milder, then use more of the milder peppers.

When you discover the mix you prefer, then dry your peppers. If you don't have a dehydrator, you can string the peppers up with a string, put them in a large paper bag, and store in a warm dry place until they will readily crumble. Blend to a powder and use some old spice jars to sprinkle the mix on your food.

Winter Squash: Squash belongs to the cucurbit family, which includes some of our most popular and colorful vegetables. These include the cucumber, cantaloupe, watermelon, pumpkins, and summer and winter squashes. Culture requirements are about the same for all of these. Most have trailing and winding vines that can cover a large area, but many bush varieties have been developed for some members of the cucurbit family, especially the squash.

In most cases winter squash is grown for their ability to have a long storage period, providing us with food throughout the winter. The flesh of the squash is not the only edible part; the seed also makes a tasty treat when roasted. No doubt many of you have eaten pumpkin seed, but the squash can be just as tasty.

Successful squash growing requires a good fertile soil with plenty of humus (organic matter) and good drainage. Although adequate moisture is very important, proper drainage is necessary for proper growth and disease prevention.

Winter squash takes much longer to mature than summer squash. There are some varieties that mature quicker than others, but all require a longer growing period than summer squash.

Space is an important consideration in selecting a variety to grow, and there are many. If you have a small area, then you should probably select one of the bush varieties. The varieties of that vine can be grown in a small area by using a trellis. Even the large varieties like the Hubbard can be grown on a trellis, but you will need the support a fruit sling. The slings can be made out of old bed sheets, or panty-hose, and then tied to the trellis.

If you have unsightly areas on your place, get those vineing varieties. These can be planted in those areas and allowed to run over the area and turn an unsightly area into a lovely landscape. The areas can be rocks, bushes, or weeds you want covered, and these vines can change the landscape completely. Just be sure that a good place is provided for the vines to grow their roots for proper nutrients. A three-foot diameter area is sufficient when enriched with compost and the proper nutrients. After the seeds germinate, mulch this area immediate with hay, straw, or leaves to hold and maintain moisture. Seed should not be planted until all danger of frost is past, usually two weeks after your last frost.

Squash can be easily crossed with each other, and with pumpkins, and some species of gourds. If you plan on saving seed, then you should hand-pollinate the one that you intend to save seed from. If the fruit on your vine shows signs that it may be mixed and is not true to the kind you planted, then it was probably mixed the year before. Seed should not be saved from any plants showing signs that it may have been crossed. If you wish it to remain true to the variety you planted, crossing may be an improvement over the variety you planted. You may produce a variety that has better flavor, which you may like more than the original variety. God provided this system of pollination for our benefit. This is demonstrated in the Canine family of animals. From one variety we have wolves, coyotes, foxes, and the many dog varieties. From one human species we get may kinds of colors and kinds of humans. The same thing happens with plants.

To hand-pollinate one for seed, select a bud that has not opened, but has a small, bulbous swelling on the stem. This is the bloom that will develop into a squash when pollinated. Cover the bud with a small bag to protect it from being pollinated by insects prior to you pollinating it. The next day, or maybe two days afterwards, the bud should be open. The male flowers will be those that do not have a bulbous swelling on the stem. Take a cotton swab and rub it on the anthers of the male flower, collecting the small grains of yellow pollen. Take the cotton swab containing the pollen and rub it on the stigma of the female flower. Cover the flower again for two more days in order to prevent it from being pollinated again. Be sure you marked the flower you pollinated in order to save the seed from the correct squash.

Winter squash should fully ripen on the vine before harvesting. The skin should be hard enough that you cannot pierce it with a fingernail, and the stem should be tough and woody. The stem should be cut with a sharp instrument. Leave as much of the stem on it as possible. Do not handle or carry the squash by the stem. If it breaks off, it will leave an area that is subject to infection causing rot.

If they are to be stored in an area where the humidity is not controlled, the squash should be cured for approximately ten days prior to storing. Cure them in a shady area, either by hanging them or placing on a table, so they will not be exposed to the moisture from rain or the ground. Store then in a cool area, such as a basement, or under your home.

Summer Squash: The word squash comes from the North American Indian word *asquash*. This means to eat foods when immature, as we do with the summer squash, including the zucchini and pattypan varieties. The yellow squash, which we know mostly as the crookneck, and the above-mentioned varieties are all from the same species. They can mix easily.

Growing summer squash is easier than growing the winter squash because they are the bush-type and the maturity time is much shorter. It is a very popular vegetable crop because it grows quickly and produces an abundance of fruit. Most of us are inclined to plant more than we actually need, and end up giving them away to our neighbors until they close their doors when they see us coming.

The type of soil is the same as for the winter squash. It just takes less area to grow them in than the winter squash. Mulching is important to preserve the moisture they need.

Summer squash come in many varieties, shapes, and colors, with new varieties appearing almost every year. There are some quick-maturing varieties of winter squash that can be used in their immature state like the summer squash, such as Jersey Golden Acorn, Table Queen, or Kuta. These squash can be used as summer squash, or they may be left to mature and used as winter squash. Zucchini is one of the largest summer varieties. It is green in color, but today we have varieties that have been crossed with yellow squash, which are yellow and almost as large as the green Zucchini.

Summer squash can be planted as close as three feet apart. Enough room should be provided to allow good air circulation to help prevent diseases. Give them enough moisture and sunshine, and you will have squash to harvest within about two months.

Planting should be staggered by planting a few hills each month. Most varieties can be planted up to five or six weeks

James A. Eagle

before the average frost date for your area, and still harvest a crop before frost.

The most predominate pests we have on the squash are the vine-borer and powdery mildew. The larvae or pupae rest over winter in the soil. The adults, which are narrow wing moths, emerge just as the squash vines are starting to lengthen or right before they start blooming. She will lay her eggs at the base of the squash vine. When the egg hatches, the larvae start eating their way into the base of the vine. You can tell when the vine is infected by shiny white castings at the base of the plant. It will work upwards in the stem and the vines will wilt and die.

If you find an infected vine, you may be able to remove the white grub by carefully slitting the vine until you find it. The best way is to prevent them from attacking your vines is to apply mentholated petroleum jelly at the base of the plant before it starts blooming. This can be purchased at almost any drug store. Another way is to place a piece of aluminum foil around the plant. The moth will be distracted by it and will fly on to the next squash vine it can find. You can also cover the plants with floating row-covers, but if you do this, you will have to hand-pollinate the female flowers each day, or else remove the covers in the morning for several hours so the insects can do the job for you.

Powdery mildew is a fungal infection, and the first symptoms are white or gray spots on the leaves. They will enlarge quickly if not controlled. One way to control it is by selecting resistant varieties. The catalogs will give this information. My favorite spray for powdery mildew is made using two tablespoon of baking soda, one tablespoon of vegetable oil, and two tablespoons of Murphy's Oil Soap, or one teaspoon of dishwashing detergent to a gallon of water. To make it more effective, try mixing these ingredients with cold, leftover coffee instead of water. Instant coffee is satisfactory. This solution should control the mildew. This is good for blackspot on roses and other plants as well. Spraying should be done every five to seven days. Dusting with cornmeal should also control it.

Stressed plants are more subject to insect and disease attacks than healthy plants. To insure your plants are healthy, be sure you have good, fertile soil and plenty of moisture, but with good drainage. If you do have an attack of mildew, then be sure and remove all leaves and vines and destroy them.

Brassicaceae Family of Plants: Many of our favorite vegetables are in this family. The largest genus of this family is the *brassica,* and the largest species is *oleracea.* This species includes cabbage, broccoli, Brussels sprouts, cauliflower, collards, kale, and kohlrabi, and they all will cross with each other. All plants in the same species can or will cross with each other. So, we have to deal with the problem of saving seeds without our favorite cabbage crossing with our kohlrabi. Will your broccoli mix with your collards? Yes, they certainly will! The *Brassicaceae* family was formerly known as the *Cruciferae* family. Some botanists still refer to this family when speaking of the *Brassicaceae* family of plants. Some refer to the *Brassicaeae* family as the mustard family or cole crops. I have referred to this family of plants as the cole crops. At times, the different terms can be confusing for many, and sometimes it can be difficult to interpret what one is really referring to.

Members of the *Brassicaceae family* can make it difficult for the average gardener to be able to save seed without crossing. There are wild species of this family that can cross with the garden varieties. In the beginning after creation, we probably had only one variety, and all the others may have come from it by cross pollination.

Most members of this family have flowers that are perfect, which is when the flower contains both male and female organs. But some genera are unable to pollinate with themselves, and are considered self-incompatible. They are like some fruit trees. They require another plant to cross-pollinate, so insects must carry pollen from one plant to another. This is where we run into difficulty in preventing cross pollination with other varieties, or maybe some wild variety. Plants of the same species should be separated by one-half mile in order to insure purity of the variety.

James A. Eagle

This is almost impossible, because of what others may be growing in their garden.

If you are planning on letting a variety bolt and put out flowering heads, then it is best to select only one variety at a time to let it go to seed. If it was possible to space the flowering of any of the varieties, then this could prevent cross pollination. But this also is hard to accomplish. I use a policy of saving one variety each year. For example, I will let a variety of collards go to seed one year, and cabbage the next.

Cabbage is a biennial. Therefore, it is necessary to start it one year and let it go over winter before it will bolt to flower the following spring. It is possible to have cabbage flower early, and prevent it from mixing with collards by starting collards in the spring. The collards will usually bloom later than the cabbage by doing it in this manner.

The best-looking plants should be selected for seed. More than one plant should be selected to insure genetic diversity. Here again, you want to prevent too much inbreeding.

Remember that you can have plants from different species flowering side by side without mixing, such as mustard and collards, or turnips and mustard, or even cabbage and Chinese cabbage. These all are of different species.

When seed pods form, and start drying, it is best to place a clear plastic bag over the seed-head and tie it to the stalk of the plant. This will prevent you from losing many seeds from the pods popping open before they are harvested. The pods should dry completely on the plant before harvesting. After the majority of the seed is dry, cut the seed stalk and turn the bag upside down before opening the bag. This will prevent the loss of the seeds that are in the bag.

Seeds of the *Brassicaceae* family have a shorter viable life-span than the seed of many other species, but they can be kept for several years when stored properly. After the seeds are shelled, let them cure in a warm area out of the sunlight, for a week or two. For proper storage, as much of the moisture should be removed as possible before storing. When ready to store, put seed in a glass container that can be sealed, such as a baby-food jar. Place some silica gel in the jar. This can be obtained from most drug stores. This will draw additional moisture from the seed. Now place them in a refrigerator or freezer to keep until ready to plant. I have also used plastic zip-lock bags to store seed in, but I prefer glass containers

The Brassicaceae family is one of the most prolific family of plants which is so easily crossed. Why God made it this way I do not know, but he had a purpose. We do know that many of the vegetables we grow today are varieties that did not exist after the flood. By crossing we have many varieties of plants, such as cabbage, broccoli, cauliflower, Brussels sprouts and others.

If the reader likes to experiment, then I urge them to let plants cross and save seed from them and discover what kind of plant they will get.

Beans: Let us analyze as to what is the ideal temperature for the best germination of bean seed, and what is the ideal air temperature for maximum production. The ideal soil temperature for seed to germinate quickly is eighty degrees. We do not get soil temperatures that high until late spring or early summer during a normal season. Some will germinate when the soil temperature reaches sixty-five degrees. The ideal air temperature for the plant to produce is sixty to seventy degrees. This certainly does not fit the ninety and ninety-five degree temperatures we get in July and August here in the South. When you look at these figures, it is easy to determine the ideal time to plant and grow snap, dry, and lima beans. Since we need warm soil for good germination, our soil is right for planting in July and August. Then by the time they obtain enough maturity to bloom, the air temperature is already cooling to the ideal temperature for good production.

During the years I've written gardening columns, I have received so many letters and phone calls as to why people's beans are dropping or why their plants were not setting fruit. The excessive air temperature is causing the problem. We must change our planting times to meet the needs of the vegetables we wish to grow.

How many times have you had failures with your beans by planting in early spring, then having a cold snap, which caused either the seed to rot before they germinated, or the plants to be killed by a frost if they were already up? If you wait until it gets warmer, and then plant again, this time it gets too hot for them to set fruit. Do you feel like quitting in exasperation?

I want to tell about the success we had by planting as late as September one year. We still harvested beans before frost. Of course, we have a lot of variation in our weather patterns these days, so the weather does not always cooperate, but we had an ideal temperature for good production in the fall in 1998.

I challenge you to try planting some of your favorite snap and lima-bush beans in July and August. Then you determine which proves more successful for you.

It is best to plant quick-maturing varieties in the area I live, regardless of whether you are planting for fall harvest or planting in the spring. You want them to be able to set fruit before adverse weather conditions began. It can be frost in the fall and excessive heat in the spring.

Some early varieties are Earliserve bush, Contender bush, Bountiful stringless, Burpee's Stringless Green Pod, and Venture Green Bush, which is one of our favorites.

Beans are not heavy feeders, and they are also a legume, which means that they have the ability to draw nitrogen from the air and store in their root tubercles for use. If you have been adding compost at regular intervals, then it may not be necessary to add any soil amendment. Only a soil test could satisfactorily determine that. If you have not been using compost, or do not have any to add, then apply an application of fish meal, bone meal, and greensand.

Do not soak dry beans before planting. This will cause many to split and you will lose viable seed. Plant in moist soil, and they will germinate just as fast as if you soaked them in water.

After the beans germinate, if they show signs of slow growth and pale-green leaves, then make applications of fish emulsion about every two weeks for three applications. Use three tablespoons per gallon of water for this blend.

Here is a tip for next spring to help you get an early start. Cover the area you plan on seeding in beans with black plastic about four weeks before you plan on planting. After the plastic has been installed for two weeks, punch holes in the plastic and plant your favorite bean seed. The black plastic will heat up the soil, allowing the beans to sprout earlier than normal. Leave the plastic on until after harvesting the beans, but cover the plastic with a couple inches of straw or leaves after the beans come up. This is to keep the soil from heating up too high for ideal production, and will actually keep the soil cool.

Cucumbers: Wouldn't it be wonderful if we had the power to establish our own weather patterns? If we did, I am afraid we would screw things up. Maybe that is what the government is doing now. Have any of you ever read about this highly secret government project called "High-frequency Active Auroral Research Project," named H.A.A.R.P? If not, then you need to read the book, *Angels Don't Play This HAARP,* by Jeane Manning and Dr. Nick Begich. Reading this book can be a very enlightening experience.

When man comes to the point that he thinks his wisdom is greater than God's, he becomes a fool according to the Bible.

The cucumber is a hot weather crop, which requires warm soil for good germination and cooler air temperatures for maximum production. The ideal soil temperature for cucumbers to germinate more quickly is between eighty-five and ninety-five degrees, but the ideal air temperature is seventy to eighty-five degrees for maximum production. You need warmer temperatures for planting and then cooler temperatures for getting the best harvest.

Which to plant first depends of the type of cucumber. The vine types should be planted first. The bush and pickling types can be planted as late as two months before your first average frost date for your zone, in most cases. The variable weather patterns are what hamper our efforts many times.

All open-pollinated varieties have both male and female blooms, and I have been stressing the urgency of the fact that you should start selecting open-pollinated varieties to insure you have proper pollination. At least plant several among the hybrid cucumbers, if you plant hybrids. Many of the hybrid varieties now have mostly female flowers. They can set fruit about one-third of its yield without a male flower, but after that it, will require male flowers to set fruit. This is why I prefer open-pollinated varieties. I can also save my own seed this way. Mixing hybrid varieties with open pollinated varieties will help solve this problem of pollination.

The open-pollinated varieties will have all male flowers for the first six or more flowers before the female flowers start showing up. This is God's way of insuring pollination. You can identify the female by a small, bulbous growth at the bud before it opens. If this is not pollinated at opening time, the small bulbous cucumber will stop growing and drop off.

Cucumbers love a sandy loam soil with plenty of compost for good growth. This insures good nutrition for the plant and the ability of the soil to maintain proper moisture. They also prefer a slightly acidic soil to neutral with a pH of 6.0 to 7.0, but they will grow in almost all types of soil, with lower and higher pH readings. We seek the perfection for best production and taste.

Vine types of cucumbers can be grown in a wire ring. This protects the fruit from the soil and some insects that invade underneath the cucumber as it lies on the ground. Cucumbers grown in this manner will have nice green color all over, without the bleached look on the bottom where it touches the ground.

Mulch around the plants to maintain moisture and keep the soil cool. This also adds nutrients to the soil as it decays.

Next spring, you can follow the guideline I gave for starting beans early. Prepare the soil early, turning under any mulch on the garden area. Smooth the soil and put down black plastic to help heat the soil for early planting about four weeks before your last average frost date. After about two weeks, punch holes in the plastic and plant your seed. Leave the black plastic on until harvest is over. After it warms to summer-type weather, then add mulch of hay, straw, leaves, or grass clippings, over the black plastic to maintain a cool soil.

I have spoken of soil temperatures and I recommend all gardeners should have a soil thermometer. They are very reasonable in price. When taking your soil's temperature, take it one to two inches below the depth you will be planting the seed. If you plant at one-half inch depth, then take the temperature about two inches deep.

Sugar Snap Pea: If you have never grown the sugar snap pea, then you are missing out on one of the most delicious and nutritious vegetables that can be grown in the garden. Eating this tasty morsel fresh will be one of the most enjoyable treats you have ever had the pleasure of savoring. It has the sweetest, crunchiest texture when eaten fresh and raw. Eaten cooked, it has the representation of the delicious snow pea, only it has the delicious peas inside the hull. One of my favorite moments is pulling some off the vine, stringing them like you would string beans, and popping the delicious morsel into my mouth, while working in the garden. The hull stays tender and crisp until it is well matured.

This delicious pea is very versatile, in that it can be used raw for salads or used as an addition to your favorite sandwich. They are excellent in stir-fries or used as the only ingredient for stir-frying. It also can be cooked as a complementary vegetable dish, and is delicious.

Growing this enjoyable pea requires cool weather, so plant them six to eight weeks before the average frost date for your zone. They will withstand light frost. If you are expecting cold below twenty-five degrees, then cover the plants with a row-cover.

To have a good fall harvest, plant fifteen weeks before your first average frost date. You can plant again in two weeks to insure you of a longer harvest. You should continue planting until the daytime temperature drops below eighty degrees for several days.

James A. Eagle

Since we cannot predict the weather, we must try to out-guess it. They may be slow developing seed pods if temperatures remain high. They produce best when daytime temperatures remain in the sixties.

This pea will take temperatures down into the twenties. Some have reported having it survive temperatures as low as twenty degrees. Maturity time is about the same as other sugar peas.

Since the first sugar snap pea was introduced, there have been several varieties introduced since then. One, called the Sugar Daddy, grows only about twenty-four to thirty inches tall. The original sugar snap grows as high as eight feet tall. Another one on the market is called Super Sugar Snap, which is also a tall growing variety. There is one called Mammoth Melting Sugar which grows four to four and one-half feet tall. All varieties need some kind of support. I grow mine around the rings that I make for my tomatoes. They are made out of concrete reinforcement wire and put together with hog rings. If you don't know what a hog ring is, then ask some old farmer, like myself. If you cannot find them at a modern hardware store, then find an old country hardware store. You will need the hog ring pliers to press the rings together. Other supports or trellises can be used as well.

A soil rich in organic matter will produce many luscious peas for the table or snacks. If you have been adding organic matter to your soil, then adding an inch more will provide all the nutrients you will need. The sugar snap is a legume, having the ability to fix nitrogen from the air and store in its roots.

Asparagus: Years ago, recommendations for preparing an asparagus bed were so demanding that I think the preparation part was what discouraged many from trying asparagus in the garden. Today, due to many tests that have been conducted, it has been proven that asparagus does not require planting at depths such as twelve inches, as was previously advocated. Tests conducted have established the fact that the crowns will establish their own level. Tests indicated that crowns planted ten and twelve inches deep had established levels of approximately four inches within five years, so now the soil is prepared and the crowns are planted at a depth of four inches, and the results obtained are as good as when planted much deeper.

Many perennial plants have what is referred to as *crowns*. That is the point where the stem and root of the plant meet. It is from this base where new growth stems are sprouted from. This is a simple definition, but adequate for understanding what is meant by a crown.

Plants can be started from seed. Some seed houses do sell the seed. If you wish to be able to harvest spears sooner, then it will be a better alternative to buy the crowns (plants).

If started from seed, then the seed should be sowed in early spring, but crowns should be planted in the fall or early winter.

Asparagus is a heavy feeder. Therefore, it is important that the soil be prepared properly before planting. Asparagus does best in a sandy loam soil, but if your soil is very sandy it can be improved with compost. They do not do well in a heavy clay soil.

Apply approximately a pickup truck-load of well-decayed manure per 1,000 sq. feet of garden space. If you do not have the manure, then use well-decayed compost. If you do not have compost you have been making yourself, then you may have to purchase it. Mushroom compost will suffice when other compost is not available. Till the manure or compost into the soil to a depth of eight inches or more.

Rows should be four to five feet apart. After measuring off the rows, add bone meal in the rows at the rate of approximately one pound to ten feet of row. Broadcast the bone meal in a twelve to fifteen-inch wide area down the rows you have laid off. This should also be tilled into the soil, and then set the plants at a depth of four inches and fifteen to eighteen inches apart in the rows.

If you do not obtain plants (crowns) locally, then when the plants arrive, they should be soaked in a solution of two table-spoons of liquid seaweed to a gallon of water, and let soak for twelve to twenty-four hours. Sometimes in shipping, the roots become dry, and if planted without trying to restore the lost

James A. Eagle

moisture, they may never put out growth in the spring. They will stay in your soil until the following spring. The liquid seaweed has natural hormones that help the plant overcome the stress of dehydration, and will stimulate root growth.

After the crowns are in the soil, mulch to a depth of four to six inches. Cover the area with mulch from one row to the other. This mulch is necessary to insure a moist soil and to keep the roots cool in our hot summers. It also helps to control weeds. Mulch should be added each year. As the old mulch decays, it adds nutrients to the soil and insures you of continuous supply of large spears year after year.

After the first year, add approximately two pounds of fishmeal or three pounds of alfalfa meal to ten feet of row in the fall or early winter. Composted animal manure is one of the best additions that can be added for continuous large spears each spring.

Asparagus has separate male and female plants. Tests conducted have shown that the male plants are heavier producers of large spears than the female plant. You will be able to distinguish the male from the female, because the female will be the one that sets the red berries with seed. Some nurseries sell just male plants, so it is possible to purchase just male plants.

If your soil is prepared as outlined above, then you may be able to start harvesting young spears as soon as they are one-half inch in diameter or larger. This could be as soon as the second year that some can be harvested. The third year, you may harvest for about three weeks, and after the third year you can harvest five to seven weeks. After that, let any spears that come up grow to replenish the root system. You can harvest asparagus for fifteen or sixteen years before you need to replenish the plants.

Asparagus can be grown further south than it was once believed. I grew it in Florida, Zone Nine, and had success. Mulching makes this possible.

Garlic: Garlic has been grown and extolled for many thousands of years, and we are still discovering many of its benefits. The Greeks used it in ancient times to cure snakebite and pneumonia.

During World War I, garlic was used to treat typhus and dysentery. It was also used to successfully treat battle wounds in order to prevent infection and gangrene. Many people, even today, will take a clove each day to prevent colds and other infections.

Why is this herb heralded so highly? Although it is known as the "Stinking Rose," we still have adoration for its qualities as an aromatic herb. Each year there is a Garlic Festival held in Gilroy, California, to extol its qualities as a culinary herb. Hundreds of thousands flock to this town to partake of the many culinary delights served, everything from appetizers and hors d' oeuvres to desserts

We now know that it truly acts as an antibiotic. When the garlic clove is minced or crushed, an antibiotic known as allicin is formed that has the antibacterial action equal to one percent of penicillin. We know that it has been used as an antibacterial agent for hundreds of years.

During WWII, while I was in Italy, I came across this old Italian in the field working like a young man. He could speak some broken English. I asked him how old he was, and he told me he was ninety-three. I asked him what the secret of his longevity was. He reached into his pocket and pulled out garlic cloves. He said he ate several every day.

This magical herb can also be used as a fungicide for preventing diseases of your plants. It will also repel many insects and pests such as rabbits, deer, and others. Here is my formula: Mince or crush approximately four ounces of garlic, put into a glass or plastic container and cover with two tablespoons of mineral oil or vegetable oil. Let set for several days and then add one pint of water and shake well. Strain this mixture through a cotton piece of cloth to remove all fiber in order to prevent clogging of your sprayer. This mixture can be saved until you are ready to spray. At this time, use one-half cup of the mixture to one gallon of water and one teaspoon of dishwashing liquid for each gallon of liquid.

Now you wonder if you can grow your own. You certainly can. I grow from eight to ten varieties each year and the fall of the year is the time to get your cloves for planting. Most of the varieties sold in the grocery store will not do well in our area, Zone Eight. There are many places you can order cloves from.

December is the best month to plant the bulbs in our area, but very early spring would be best in the North. If the ground is frozen, then plant in the spring as soon as the ground thaws. They should be planted approximately four inches deep in a good loamy soil approximately four inches apart. If the cloves are planted too early, they will come up immediately and may be hurt by a heavy frost

The bulbs are ready to harvest in late spring or early summer when the tops start falling over. Dig at this time and air-dry in a shaded area for a couple of weeks. At this point, you are ready to prepare them for storage. A lady's hose is one of the best storage containers you can use. You can also use the netting, which can be purchased in a fabric shop, and cut this approximately six to eight inches wide. Fold over and sew the side and bottom. You now have a tube to store them in. Store them in a cool room until ready for use. Mine is stored in the room I use as an office. If you come to my office, you will see a lot of garlic hanging in the closet. It repels the evil spirits (a joke).

Here are the names and addresses of places you can purchase the cloves for seed: Johnny's Selected Seed, Foss Hill Road, Albion, Maine 04910-9731. The catalog is free and they also give culture data. They also sell Elephant garlic, which is not a true garlic, but is related to the Leek. Nichols Garden Nursery, 1190 North Pacific Highway, Albany, Oregon 97321-4580. Catalog free. The best source of all is Filaree Farm, Route 2, Box 162, Okanogan, Washington 98840-9774. They offer many varieties, more than any other source I have found. The catalog is free.

Jerusalem Artichoke: Jerusalem artichoke is not an artichoke, but a member of the sunflower family. It grows from four to eight feet high and has a flower, like sunflowers, up to three to four inches in diameter. Underneath the soil is the prize you want to grace your table. It has a delicate, sweet, nutty flavor that can be the envy of the most discriminating cook. The tubers can be fried, stewed, boiled, steamed, stir-fried, or used fresh in salads. The cooked tubers can be mashed like Irish potatoes, or steamed and served with a sauce or butter.

The calorie count of the tubers of the Jerusalem artichoke is only about one-tenth of those of potatoes. It is lacking in heavy starch content, and is one of the easiest to grow plant that I know. In fact, if you do not dig all the tubers, they will put up more plants the next year. In my opinion, you can grow them in most areas of the United States. There is no storage problem, simply leave the tubers in the ground during the winter and harvest as you need them. If the tubers are dug and stored, they have a tendency to shrink as potatoes sometimes do. But these tubers will shrink much faster than potatoes. Dehydration is the problem.

They can be started from seed or by planting the tubers. I prefer planting the tubers, because there have been strains developed that are much improved over some of the older varieties. Most seed catalogs sell the tubers only. Many do not even give a variety name. My favorite source is Johnny's Selected Seeds, Foss Hill Road, Albion, Maine 04910-9731. The catalog is free. They offer a variety called Stampede, which is maturing earlier than the common varieties.

Another source is Pinetree Garden Seeds, Box 300, New Gloucester, ME 04260. Their catalog is also free. They offer the Nova Scotia Redskin. It has an attractive purple skin with creamy white interior.

Prepare the soil by adding approximately two inches of compost and working into the soil. This will provide all the nutrients needed unless your soil is extremely poor. Plant the tubers in early spring. The tubers can be planted whole or cut, leaving at least two eyes on each piece. Plant four to five inches deep, spacing about fifteen inches apart in the row. After planting, mulch with approximately five to six inches of leaves, straw, or hay. This will control the weeds and hold moisture in the soil. After this, forget them until harvest time.

You can start harvesting the tubers when the leaves start turning yellow in the late summer or early fall. Only harvest what you need at the moment, leaving the rest in the soil, and pulling the mulch back over the opening you dug. In the spring, you will get your new crop from the pieces of roots and tubers you leave in the ground.

In the spring, mulch the bed again for the new growing season. No nutrients need to be added. The rotting mulch you used the year before will provide all the nutrients you will need.

The real treat comes when they are brought to the table. Some people prepare them by washing and leaving the skins on. Others scrap the tubers to remove the skins. That is your choice. Any recipes you have for Irish potatoes can be used in preparing the Jerusalem artichoke, and they can be prepared many other ways. Take the raw tuber and slice thin over a salad, or cut in larger pieces for stir-frying. They have a crisp, sweet flavor you will not forget.

Stevia rebandiana (Sweet Leaf): The common name for this plant is *Sweet Leaf Plant,* because it is ten times sweeter than sugar. When the leaves have been refined, it is 100 times sweeter than sugar. One teaspoon of refined stevia is equal to three cups of sugar and contains only eight calories. Compare this to three cups of sugar which contains from 2,100 to 2,200 calories.

Stevia is much safer than the artificial sweeteners, and much safer than refined sugar, so you wonder why it has never been used before as a sugar substitute? Well, it has been used for 400 years in its native country and other countries around the world as a sugar substitute. Then why not in the USA?

Here we have the Government looking after the interest of big corporations and the special-interest groups to protect them. This is the sugar industry and the manufactures of the sugar substitutes. They are not concerned with your interest. Their only desire is to control the common man. Since it is an herb, they are not able to get a patent on the plant and control its use, so they use their influence of big bucks to keep it controlled.

Ten years ago there were several US companies that started marketing food products sweetened with stevia. Then there was an anonymous complaint filed against Celestial Seasonings, which was one of the companies using it. The FDA then banned its import as an unsafe additive. Why? It has been proven safe for over 400 years. The FDA remained mum on why this was done. Pressure was then applied by the Lipton Tea and the American Herbal Products Association to relent their ban. The FDA has never given the reason it is unsafe as a sugar substitute.

In 1994, after the passage by Congress of the Dietary Supplements Health and Education Act, the FDA eased their ban by allowing it to be sold as a dietary supplement only, and not as a sugar substitute. This allows you to purchase the plant products, and you can use it as you wish. Stevia is stable at high temperatures, so it can be used in baking and cooking. Other sugar substitutes are not stable at high temperatures. Some years ago, the FDA had a company that had published a recipe book using stevia destroy all the books and would not let them release it. This is a good example of how your government works for you.

Stevia rebaudiana is a subtropical plant. It is a native of Brazil and Paraguay. It can be grown here year-round in a heated green house, or when protected in the winter from temperatures below forty degrees. It can be grown in the open during spring, sum-mer, and early fall, then brought inside for the winter. If you have a greenhouse, then it would be an ideal place to keep the plants over winter. You can also grow it in the home as a houseplant. It seems to thrive in shade or full sun. I have tested it by growing it both ways, but the leaves are sweeter when grown in the sun. I have kept stevia alive all winter here in Zone Eight, by using a 'Wall-O-Water', around the plants.

If you have only one plant, then multiply the number of plants by rooting cuttings (see Chapter Eight). They are very easy to root without any hormones, and they root in a short time.

The natural sweet element in stevia, which is steviocide, will greatly enhance the flavor of any foods that need sweetening. The leaves and stems are harvested and dried. They should be dried at a temperature of around ninety degrees. Higher tem-peratures will cause it to lose some of the element steviocide.

The ideal place to dry them is in a food dehydrator that has temperature controls that can be set at different temperatures. If a dehydrator is not available, then tie bunches of stems together, placing them upside down in a paper bag, and dry them in this manner The bag should be placed in an area where there is good air circulation and low humidity. Drying your own stevia is not the same as refined stevia. It will take much more for sweetening than the refined stevia.

The dried leaves can then be shredded in a blender and used in foods that you wish to sweeten. If you use the powder, it will turn the cakes or muffins darker from its own color. You can make a liquid by using one cup of dried stevia to one cup boiling water. Let it set for twenty-four hours, strain, and use it to sweeten coffee or other beverages, or use in baking. You will have to experiment as to the amounts to use to suit your taste.

If you have health problems, such as diabetes, then this is a perfect substitute for sugar. One important question I have been asked many times is whether it is safe for diabetics to use? Here is a quotation from the Internet.

> "A number of studies have been conducted using stevia in a variety of therapeutic applications. Several preliminary studies in Paraguay and Brazil have examined the herb's hypoglycemic action. Researches found that hypoglycemic diabetics showed approximately 35 percent drop in normal blood sugar levels six to eight hours after consuming stevia extract. Other studies have concluded with similar results. These studies, coupled with a substantial amount of empirical evidence, have led physicians in Paraguay and Brazil to prescribe stevia in the treatment of diabetes."

My advice would be to consult your own physician on this. Please note that stevia extracts were used to lower blood sugar.

Recently stevia extract has appeared on the market in packets as other sugar substitutes. Some have trade names of their own.

The Rose: The rose is the favored choice of flowers for many gardeners, but many gardeners have been discouraged by failure after spending large amounts just to have many of the plants die. The reason I have decided to write about roses is because of the many questions I have received from readers of the newspaper columns I wrote. Most of us have been disappointed by trying a prized rose, then having it to die shortly after blooming only once or maybe not blooming at all.

I do not consider myself to be a rosarian. I am strictly an amateur when it comes to understanding the world of roses. The ones that I grow have proven themselves to have stamina and hardiness even with neglect. This eliminates many of the hybrid teas, but not all.

Most of us will choose a rose because of its beauty and aroma, but more important is to select one that has stamina and a long blooming-season. Many of the hybrids have one blooming period in the spring, and then they are finished blooming for the season. There are groups and varieties of roses that can provide us beauty and a wonderful aroma all summer long. These should be the choices of the amateur. Leave the ones that require lots of attention to the experts.

I have some roses that date back to the 16th century. When I first obtained them, about twenty years ago, I planted them in an open space next to my daylilies, which I had hybridized shortly after I was diagnosed with cancer, and had several surgeries. I was unable to do much for some years. Weeds, bushes, trees, and shrubs came up in that space. Those roses and daylilies are still living and blooming without any attention whatsoever, and are surrounded by trees. These are roses with stamina.

Roses are divided into several main classes. There are the Hybrid Tea, Grandiflora, Floribunda, Polyanthas, Hybrid Perpetuals, Shrub, Ramblers and Climbers, and Miniature China Roses. Of course, there are crosses between these groups. There are nearly 100 species of roses and many crosses between these species, and thousands of cultivars. In fact, most of the roses sold in the United States are the modern hybrids that have

James A. Eagle

been derived from the following species: Rosa chinensis, R. damascena, R. foetida, R. moschata, R. multiflora, R. odorata, R. rugosa and R. wichuraiana.

At this point I probably have the amateur completely confused. I even get myself confused when trying to trace the ancestry of a rose. Pick your rose because you like it, regardless of parentage or species. Choose your roses for beauty, fragrance, vigor, stamina, and hardiness (ability to take cold). At this point, you will have a rose that will please and give you much joy for a long time.

Many of the hybrids today do not produce a vigorous root stock that will thrive and produce a healthy plant. Therefore, they are grafted onto one of the root stock of a hardy species rose. Even then, many of the hybrids have a short life-span. Many of the roses today are sold on their own root stock. There is one nursery that sells only roses on their own stock. These are usually vigorous and will have a longer life-span. Many times, the drafted varieties will die, but a new shoot will put up below the draftee. The root stock that it was drafted on may be hardy, but you may not be pleased with the flower it produces. At this point, it is better to replace the rose. When purchasing a rose on its own root stock, be sure it meets your requirements of hardiness, stamina, vigor, fragrance, and beauty.

The old heirloom varieties are very popular today. You will find that many meet the requirements you desire in a rose. Some rose nurseries specialize in these varieties only. If ordering your plants, start by ordering a few at one time, and see what kind of service the nursery gives. Never choose a nursery that will not ship in the fall of the year. The fall of the year is the ideal time to transplant roses to insure they get a quick start in the spring. During the cold winter months, the roots are healing and establishing new roots to overcome the shock of transplanting.

There are plenty of places you can buy roses locally, but you have to buy whatever they have to offer. When buying by mail, you have a much wider choice of the kind of rose plant you desire.

To be successful growing roses, they should be located in an open sunny location. Be sure that they are fifteen feet or more from the drip-line of any large trees. The feed roots of the trees will certainly find their way to draw on the nutrients and moisture from the roses.

To display the roses to their best, it is better to set them in beds, rather than mix them with other plants. Beds can be circular, square, or rectangular. Beds should be six feet or more wide or circular beds eight feet in diameter. Bush roses can be planted as close as eighteen inches to two feet apart, depending on their height. Larger-growing roses must be spaced according to their size. We will cover climbing and trailing roses later.

Remove the top soil, then dig down into the subsoil and loosen it up as deep as twenty to twenty-four inches. Add completely composted manure or other compost to the subsoil, or peat-moss or leaf mold. Mix this with the subsoil. If you have clay or silt soil, then adding perlite will assure good drainage. The roots of the roses will be seeking this depth for moisture and nutrients. This is why it is important to have a well-prepared area to transplant the roses. The top soil you removed should also be mixed with well-composted manure and other compost, such as leaf mold. Also add five ounces of alfalfa, two ounces of bone meal, and five ounces of greensand for each plant. Mix this with the top soil.

Most roses perform best in a soil with a pH of 6.0 to 7.0. If you think your soil may be more acidic than this, then some limestone may be required. A soil test can be made by your County Extension Service to be sure it is not too acidic. Call them for instructions before taking soil samples down to their office.

Now you are ready for the arrival of your plants. If they arrive bare-root, then unpack them and soak the roots in water with two teaspoons of liquid seaweed to each gallon of water for six to eighteen hours before setting out. If any branches look withered, then bury the whole bush in loose soil and soak it with water for a day or more. This will restore the plant in many cases. Any

James A. Eagle

broken roots or limbs should be pruned off at this point, and cut all limbs back as much as eight to ten inches from the root stock.

You have your subsoil removed and mixed with the above listed amendments. Make a cone-shaped mound with the subsoil at each place you wish to set a plant. Spread the roots out over this mound and start covering with the top soil. Plant the roses the same depth they were in the nursery. Pack the soil firmly around the roots. Any extra topsoil left can be used to make a mound around the plant so it will hold water. Water well, filling the area around the plant. Several applications of water may be applied after each has soaked into the ground. Now level the soil and mulch the plants with four to six inches of mulch such as leaves, straw, hay, decomposed wood chips, or sawdust, some wish to have a beautiful display by mulching with stones or pine bark. Roses should be mulched each year, unless you mulch with stones. When mulching with hay, straw, or leaves, you are providing additional nutrients when the mulch decays. Add new mulch over the old each spring, adding the additional nutrients as needed before adding the new mulch. The only time you need to remove the old mulch is if there is a severe black spot disease problem, then all mulch should be removed in the fall after the plants lose their leaves and the old mulch is destroyed. An application of good composted cow manure is the ideal amendment to add at this time. In addition to the cow manure, also add approximately one-fourth cup of bone meal for each plant. Work this into the top couple of inches of soil, being careful not to get too deep so that you do not damage the root system. If you do not have cow manure to add, then add a mixture of four parts alfalfa meal, two parts fish meal, two parts bone meal, and four parts of greensand. This is by weight instead of measurement. Mix all these ingredients together and broadcast approximately one-half cup around each plant.

Mulching is more important for roses than most plants, but still beneficial for all plants. It is the natural way of preserving moisture and cooling the root system during hot summers. Mulching also prevents erosion during the summer thunder storms, and holds the water so that it will soak into the soil instead of running off. It also prevents water from splashing from the soil to the leaves spreading diseases.

If you discover that your roses are not growing as they should during the summer, it may be necessary to apply a liquid fertilizer, such as fish emulsion, liquid seaweed, or a combination of the two. Some of the best liquid fertilizers you can apply are teas made out of compost or manure. In making compost tea, use one quart of compost, or for each gallon of water, and soak for twenty-four hours or more. Strain and apply with a sprinkling can. If using manure for tea, use one quart of manure to a gallon of water and steep for three days, strain, and dilute until it is a light tea color. These manure and compost teas are one of the best natural fungicides you can apply to help prevent diseases.

The pruning of your roses should start in the spring just as new growth is beginning to bud. Good, sharp pruning tools are a necessity to insure smooth, clean cuts so the healing process will begin without danger of disease infections in the wound. Cuts should be made about one-fourth of an inch above the bud. On the larger limbs cuts should be at a forty-five-degree angle to shed water. On smaller limbs it isn't that important. Take a good look at each bush and thin out limbs that are rubbing others and prune the plant to a good balanced shape. Prune out any dead or diseased limbs and destroy. Pruning can continue throughout the summer. On roses that continue to bloom more than one time, cut back the limbs that have all spent flowers. This cutting back will stimulate new growth that produces the new buds.

During hot summer days, be sure your roses have adequate moisture. They should have approximately one inch of rainfall each week. If it fails to rain, then it will be necessary to water your rose plants. If you use a sprinkling system, be sure to water in the morning and no later than 2:00 p.m. in the afternoon. This will allow the foliage to dry before nightfall.

One of the most troublesome insect pests of roses is the aphid. These are little light-green to white soft-body insects that love the young, tender leaves on the tips of the branches and buds.

They can be controlled with insecticidal soap, neem, or diatomaceous earth. Spray the insecticidal soap following the directions on the container. The diatomaceous earth can be dusted in the morning while the dew is on the plants. One spraying will not get rid of them. Leave one and it multiplies to many in a short time. Spray at least once each week, or more often, until you get rid of them.

Spider mites are another small insect that you may be bothered with. The symptoms are light-yellow speckles on the leaves. Look under the leaves for these pests. You may even need a magnifying glass to see these small, reddish insects. They also form a small, fine webbing around the leaves. The same controls as for the aphids works very well for these insects also.

Scale insects are another problem for many. This insect is identified by tiny bumps on the stems and bark of the plant. They are grayish or brown in color. The scale is a soft-bodied insect that forms a hard covering over its body for protection. It stays at this one spot and sucks the juices from the plant. Winter time control should be done in the late fall or early spring, before new growth emerges. Spray with one of the oil sprays, following directions on the container. This will seal the hard shell over their body and they will die. In the summer, use insecticidal soap or neem. There is a summer oil-spray that can be used, but before spraying the whole plant, try a small limb first and see if any damage is done to the foliage. It will show up within twenty-four hours if it does burn the leaves. This summer oil-spray can be used for aphids and spider mites as well.

Japanese beetles are easily seen. They can eat large holes in the leaves in a short time. In fact, they can skeletonize the leaves if left unchecked. The Japanese beetle is about one-half inch long and blue-green in color, with bronze wing covers. The grubs over-winter in lawns, eating the roots of your lawn grass. A long-term treatment is using the milky spore disease (see Lawn Care in this chapter). This will kill the grubs and will keep multiplying to keep them controlled for years. This attacks the larva of Japanese beetles and the June bugs.

If you have the beetles on the plant destroying your plant, then you need immediate control. One way to control them is by knocking them off into a can of kerosene or fuel oil. Spraying with neem or pyrethrum will also control them.

The slug-like larva of the rose sawfly can also skeletonize the leaves of the plant in a very short time. This usually occurs in the late spring or early summer. These can be controlled with insecticidal soap, neem, or pyrethrum spray.

The rose-chafer may give you some trouble in the South, but usually they are more common in the northeastern states. I saw a few several years ago, but none since. They are a tannish, long-legged beetle about one-fourth inch in length. The grub of this small beetle also over-winters in the lawns and feeds on the roots of grass and weeds. These grubs can also be controlled with the milky spore disease. The adults that you encounter can easily be controlled by hand picking.

The milky spore disease mentioned above comes as a white powder, and can be sprayed or sprinkled on your lawn after mixing with water. Always follow the directions on the container for proper use. You should avoid inhalation of the powder, or avoid any contact with the eyes. Use a mask and protective glasses while using it. It should be applied in the early spring and up to early summer to your lawn and flower beds. Always follow directions on the container.

Mints: The mints are the best known of all herbs, and one of the easiest herbs to grow. It could be considered a must in the organic garden. One small plot will provide all the mint you will have need of in, most cases. It not only has medical properties, but is one of the best plants to repel unwanted insects from the garden. It also has antiseptic properties that could prevent some types of disease. One important use of peppermint and spearmint is using it for tea, or even to flavor other teas that may not be as tasty. It also makes a cool drink for summer as well. It is also used to flavor foods.

There are many herb nurseries and seed companies that sell peppermint seed, but you should get plants from a reputable dealer. The plants started from seed, in most cases, will be inferior from the true peppermint. Peppermint (*Mentha x piperita*) is a hybrid that was produced by crossing *Mentha spicate,* which is the spearmint, and *M. aquatica.*

The mints will reproduce by underground stems or *stolons.* If the proper growing conditions are provided, you will have a speedy reproduction. To control and confine peppermint, I recommend using a planter or burying a border into the ground to a depth of at least ten inches to prevent it from taking over a garden spot. One of the easiest ways to do this is getting one of the fifty-five gallon plastic drums and cut rings twelve to fifteen inches wide. You will be able to plant at least two or three plants in this space. All of the mints should be grown in a contained area.

The culture of all mints is the same, so if you have spearmint or any of the other mints, then the culture should be the same.

After a couple of years, it will be necessary to lift the old clumps and reset the well-rooted pieces. This is necessary because mint multiplies so fast. The old, woody parts should be discarded and destroyed. If you dispose of them by throwing them in an unused area, you may find that you will have mint all in the garden and lawn. The extra plants can be given to a friend.

Mint does best in a moist, ordinary soil, and in our area, it will do best in an area that is shaded for about half the day. It will grow in full sun if it gets enough moisture. During hot dry seasons, it will be necessary to give it plenty of additional moisture by watering it every several days

Mint should be harvested in summer before it comes into bloom. Cut the stems and tie into bunches and hang upside down in a paper bag in a shady, dry area with low moisture. If you have a dehydrator, then put stems in the dehydrator. As soon as the leaves are dry and crumbly, strip the leaves from the stems and place in jars that will seal in order to keep out dust or insects.

You can have a fresh supply of mint during the winter by making flats about eight inches deep and using a good sandy loam soil and filling it about four inches deep. Place the roots on the soil, then finish adding soil until the flat is full and place in a greenhouse or sunny window inside. Large pots can also be used for this purpose. The roots will start fresh, new growth in a short time.

Mint plants can be obtained from Nichols Garden Nursery, 1190 North Pacific Highway, Albany, Oregon 97321-4580. Get the one called Black Mitcham Peppermint. It is one of the best. The catalog is free.

Aloe Vera: The home that does not have an aloe vera plant growing on the window sill or on a table or planter near the window is losing a wonderful benefit of a first-aid treatment for burns, cuts, stings, sunburn, and scratches. Of course, using it as a first-aid treatment is not the only thing they are good for. The gel in the leaf of an aloe plant has antibiotic qualities that kill microorganisms that cause infection, so it can be used for many things to improve our health.

The clear gel in the leaf of the aloe vera plant was first documented to the effect of its healing powers in 1935, when an American medical journal documented a case where a woman healed the x-ray burns she had received by treating the wound with gel straight from the plant leaf.

I had an experience recently when using the stronger Capzasin HP for my arthritis aching joints. I had been using Capzasin P, but thought I would try the stronger HP brand. I woke up in the night with my knees on fire. I put cold towels on them and it relieved the pain long enough for me to get back to sleep. The next morning, I went to the garden. When the heat and perspiration hit those knees, it set them on fire. I went in the house and tried every ointment I could find, to no avail. Finally, I saw an aloe plant there in the house. I cut off a piece of a leaf and opened it and rubbed it on my knees. Almost immediately, it stopped burning and the red was gone shortly after. It works!

James A. Eagle

Aloe is one of the few nonnarcotic plants to cause a war. In 332 B.C., when Alexander the Great conquered Egypt, he heard of a plant with amazing healing powers on an island off Somalia. Determined on trying to heal his soldiers' wounds, he sent an army to seize the island and prevent it getting into the hands of his enemies.

Each thick leaf of the aloe is filled with the healing gel. It can be applied to a wound by cutting off a piece of a leaf and cutting down the middle of the leaf. Rub it on the wound and let it dry. It will form a protected coat over the wound.

There are more than 600 species of aloe, but aloe vera is the one that has the greatest healing powers. It contains more of the chemicals that act as an antibiotic.

Most people think of the aloe as a shade plant, but its natural habitat is in the sun. It can be adapted to many different climate conditions. It will grow and multiply in the shade, but it does equally well in the sun, or better. The only thing is that a radical change can damage the plant. If you take one that has been growing in the shade and place it in the sun, it will shortly change color to a yellowish-bronze, and you may be inclined to think it is dead. But in most cases, it will recover and turn green again. Changes should be done slowly so it can adapt to its new surroundings.

The aloe is a tender plant, but it has survived light frosts. It will die if left outside in cold weather. Aloes are natives of hot, tropical climates, so it can survive in heat and dry weather.

Over-watering can be more damaging to the plant than letting it become too dry. The leaves store the moisture it needs during times of drought.

The aloe vera plant is easily propagated by the offshoots that put out from the mother plant. The offshoots can be potted separately even before they are rooted. They will soon take roots and grow. The potting soil mix I use is equal parts of peat, leaf mold or compost, and sand. Add a pinch of bone meal to the mix. Do not fertilize the plant with a high nitrogen fertilizer. An application of fish emulsion and liquid seaweed in the spring and again in the summer is all they need. It can go from September to March without any feeding at all. You only water when the soil is dry, or the leaves show signs of wilting. The aloe can go years without repotting, as long as the side-shoots are removed and repotted. If the side-shoots are not removed, they can eventually crowd the pot.

Some aloes do not multiply as fast as the aloe vera, but all aloes will, in time, put up a shoot that has a flower and even bear seeds if pollinated. It will need to be grown in the sun to produce a flower. They even make a good rock garden plant.

There are some cactus specialists that have the seed to start them. You may find it interesting to try propagating one by seed.

Daylily (Hemerocallis): The Daylily is not a true lily of Lilium Genus, but it is a member of the Lily family, Liliaceae. The botanical name of the Daylily is Hemerocallis, pronounced hem-er-o-KAL-is. The word is derived from two Greek words, *hemera*, a day, and *kallos*, meaning beauty. In other words, we have beauty for a day, since their bloom only lasts for a day. Some plants send up several scapes with as many as ten to thirty-five buds on each scape. Therefore, you have beauty for weeks and months with many of the new hybrids re-blooming even up to frost. It is amazing the progress that has been made the last thirty years in the improvement in the beauty, colors, and patterns of this exquisite plant. You are cheating yourself if you deny yourself of the joy in growing this beautiful plant. *Warning*: Once you start growing the Daylily, it is easy to become obsessed with them. It is very addicting.

The Daylily does not have a bulb, but has large roots with a crown. The plant multiplies from this one plant, or fan, as it is referred to by Daylily enthusiasts. Some cultivars are more prolific in multiplying than others. Some are very slow in increasing their off-spring. Recently I dug some clumps that had not been separated in ten years that had more than forty fans. If they had been separated more often, they would have produced even more.

James A. Eagle

To say that the Daylily is a hardy plant with exceptional stamina is an understatement. Today it is grown in all fifty states and most foreign countries. For the novice, it is the ideal plant to start growing if you have no experience whatsoever in gardening. It can take neglect, drought, poor soil, cold weather, shade, and many more hardships and still survive. Although it will survive abuse and neglect, it performs much better when you give it Tender Loving Care. With TLC you will be rewarded with beauty, pleasure, and joy. Your spouse and children may survive with neglect and abuse, but it brings more pleasure when you bestow them with love, and the necessary care they deserve for complete happiness. The daylily is the same.

The plant and flower size varies greatly among the different cultivars. Flowers vary in size from two inches to more than eleven inches in diameter, and from nine inches tall to more than four feet. Today, with more than thirty thousand Daylily cultivars registered, there are cultivars to meet your every taste and desire. They come in most colors and combinations of colors. Also, there are many different shapes and patterns. With the many dedicated hybridizers today, what was once the lowly Daylily is being transformed into a splendor of beauty.

An exciting new phase of Daylily breeding has been ushered in with the introduction of the tetraploid daylilies. In nature the Daylily is a diploid plant, its cells containing twenty-two chromosomes. Through the use of a drug known as colchicine, breeders have now produced cells with twice the amount of chromosomes, forty-four instead of twenty-two. This, in turn, has produced variations in the cultivars that have been so treated. Tetraploid being crossed with tetraploid has created a new area in the culture of the Daylily. The tetraploid passes these double-chromosome cells to their offspring. Today, we have daylilies that are tetraploid and diploids. They are referred to in the trade as tets and dips.

To assist you and provide information and knowledge, there is a great organization known as the American Hemerocallis Society, Inc. It has fifteen regions with many local clubs in each region. Shows are put on each year during the prime bloom season by these local clubs, by the regions and the National Association. Anyone wanting more information about joining this organization should go on the internet and type in "American Hemerocallis Society."

Azalea: A two-page letter was received from a reader who had moved down from New York to our wonderful state of South Carolina. He had been having trouble growing azaleas here, although he grew them without trouble in New York. This letter has prompted me to write this section on the azalea, since it is one of our favorite flowering shrubs.

The azalea belongs to the Rhododendron genus. There are more than 4,000 species, varieties, and hybrids that have been cataloged of this genus that are being grown in the United States, and new ones are added yearly. For our purpose, we are going to discuss the small-leaf azalea. There are the deciduous and evergreen azaleas, but the most popular one in the south is the evergreen.

Azaleas do best in a cool, moist climate with plenty of moisture, so the most ideal way is to plant them in an area that can provide some shade and adequate moisture. To provide the cool, moist climate they need, plant them around shade trees, such as pine and oak. The pine and oak leaves will keep the soil in an acidic condition, which the azalea loves. They can also be planted as a foundation shrub, especially if planted on the north, northwest, or northeast side of your home, where they will get some shade during the hottest part of the day during the summer.

The soil should be an acidic soil with a pH of 4.5 to 6.5. If you do not know the acidity of your soil, you should have it tested by the County Extension Service. There is a small charge for this test. You may also test your own soil with the many devices they now have for testing. Some are as simple as the instamatic pH meter to a simple soil testing kit. If you have already been growing azaleas successfully, then this test can be dispensed with. You probably have the proper pH.

James A. Eagle

The soil should have an abundance of humus or decaying organic matter. This can be provided by adding composted oak leaves or pine straw. Also, use the oak leaves and pine straw to mulch your plants with. Never use maple or elm leaves for mulch on azaleas, because they do not produce an acidic reaction. Also, maple leaves are too prone to compact, which can inhibit good growth. By mulching with oak leaves or pine straw, they will help maintain the needed moisture in the soil and also produce an acidic reaction in the soil. Sometimes it may be necessary to add some other form of fertilizer. This can be provided by well-rotted manure, or cotton-seed meal. A foliar spray of fish emulsion or compost tea can also be used for a quick foliar feeding. Mix the fish emulsion according to the directions on the container. As I noted in Chapter 4, compost tea can be made by inserting compost in a bag and putting it into water to soak up to one to two days. Add enough water to it so it will appear as weak tea.

Azaleas love and need plenty of moisture. During periods of dry weather, you should water the mulched plants with about one inch of water each week. If it is extremely hot, then watering more often may be necessary provided the soil has good drainage.

It is necessary that the soil is acidic soil for azaleas. Even if the nutrients needed are present in the soil, the plant cannot utilize them without an acid soil. If you are planting azaleas as a foundation plant next to your home, you may have problems with an alkaline soil if your home has brick and mortar or stucco. Watering with a sprinkler, or rainwater splashing on the surface of the mortar or stucco, will wash down lime from these surfaces and make the soil extremely too alkaline for azaleas. I encountered this condition where I worked in Florida before retiring. The facility had a stucco finish and azaleas were planted as foundation plantings. Many had already died, and others were yellow with the lack of iron and magnesium. There were plenty of iron and magnesium in the soil, but the plants could not utilize these minerals because it was too alkaline. We purchased several bags of cotton-seed meal and applied to the plants, then mulched with oak leaves which we had plenty of. In one year, it was hard to realize the difference in the plants. They had lush, dark-green foliage and heavy with bloom.

Azaleas require little pruning, but if you do prune, it should be immediately after they get through blooming. The plants will be forming the buds for next year's bloom during the summer growth. Never prune in the fall or winter, because you are cutting off the buds that would provide the beauty you want in the early spring. Actually, the only pruning needed is removing dead limbs or shaping the plant. Some use azaleas as a hedge. If you are using them for this purpose, then prune right after the bloom season for maximum bloom in the spring.

There is a new hybrid azalea on the market today called *"Encore."* It is a species that has been patented, so you cannot reproduce them unless you get permission of the patent holder. They are supposed to bloom all summer and until frost. We have six plants of six varieties. I do not have a high opinion of them. They never have the amount of bloom as the regular ones in the spring, nor at any other time of the year. Blooms are scarce in the summer. Since they are patented, the price is high.

Flax: Can flax prevent colon and breast cancer? I will not answer that question, but I will tell you what some of the latest findings have been. According to the winter edition of *The Herb Quarterly* in 1998, flax seed or flaxseed oil, looks good as a possible herb for the prevention of breast cancer. Researchers with the Center for Food Safety and Applied Nutrition at the Food and Drug Administration in Washington, have examined flaxseed and found that it contains high levels of plant estrogens. Plant estrogen is different from pharmaceutical estrogen. Where pharmaceutical estrogen increases the risk of breast cancer, plant estrogen does not have the side-effects as pharmaceutical estrogen.

According to *The Herb Quarterly,* tests conducted on rats have proven that flaxseed and flaxseed oil (linseed oil) prevented colon cancer in rats.

The crushed seeds of flax have long been used as a poultice for sores. The oil (linseed oil) has good qualities as a laxative. A

James A. Eagle

poultice made of crushed seed, or linseed oil, has been used in treating burns.

When I was just a small boy, and that was a long time ago, I can remember my mother using flax seed to get a foreign object out of our eye when it could not be found by sight. She would put us to bed and place a flax seed in the eye, by morning the object would be outside the eye along with the flax seed. I still can't understand how it worked, but it did. Flax seeds are very smooth and slick. It will not irritate the eye.

There is only one species of flax that is grown for the seed and oil for medical purposes. The botanical name is *Linum usitatissimum*. There are many more species of flax, and many of them are perennial, some are even evergreen, but the one mentioned above is the medical flax, and it is an annual, so you will have to plant it each year to provide a source of seed.

The stem fiber of this plant is the source of linen thread and cloth. The ancient Chinese used the flax plant to make paper. They soaked the material in water, then beat it with stones into a paste. It was then dried in the sun to form a sheet that was used to write on. The seed is the part used for medical purposes.

Seed of the annual flax can be started indoors in early spring, or outside, after all danger of frost is past. It should have a nice, sunny place in your garden. It is especially good as a rock-garden plant, or in the border with other flowering plants. It prefers a light well drained soil.

This species of flax has blue one-half inch flowers that bloom most of the summer. It has a lovely lace-like foliage that is attractive, and it is a pleasure to grow for its beauty alone. This species grows to a height of four feet.

The soil should be prepared with a liberal application of good organic compost worked into the soil. If it is good compost, no other nutrients are needed. An application of mulch will also be beneficial in holding the moisture during hot dry periods.

Seeds should be harvested as soon as they start drying, or you will lose many of the seeds. After harvesting, place the seed in a warm, dry, and shady area for a couple of weeks to be sure the moisture content is reduced. They can then be stored in an air-tight container in a dark cabinet or colored jar. Best of all, store them in your refrigerator. Exposure to light can reduce their medical benefits.

A tea can be made of the seed by crushing them, and then steeping them in boiling water for ten minutes. Use one teaspoon of seed for each cup of tea. Adding honey, or some mint leaves will improve the taste and benefits. If you are using it for medical purposes, then three cups of tea each day should be taken. You can eat the seed raw, or they may be roasted. They make a tasty snack. They are also used in baking pastries and bread.

Echinacea: There are hundreds of herbs that are classed as benefiting mankind in preventing or healing the ailments we encounter. Science is now investigating, more than ever, the effects certain herbs can have on the body in restoring health. I believe that God has a plant to cure any disease we have due to sin, if we can only find it. One of my fourth great grandmothers was the daughter of a Cherokee Indian Chief. It has been told that she had a recipe of herbs that would cure cancer. It was passed to a daughter, then lost.

There was an article in *The Wall Street Journal*, sometime back, about the effect of using the herb Echinacea to destroy the effects of an on-coming cold or the flu. This was also repeated in more detail on the 700 Club on television.

We will not get into prescribing herbs, or dosages, but I will cover the methods in growing them and give details as to what they are, and what part of the plant is used. You can have your own drug store in your garden. If you are interested in the healing herbs, then you should get one of the many books available on them.

Let us explore the plant Echinacea, pounced el-in-Asia, its common name is Cone Flower. The flowers are very similar to the Rudbeckia, which is also known as the Cone Flower. Many of you may already be growing both in your flower garden. It has large daisy shaped flowers up to four or five inches in diameter with colors ranging from purple to white. It grows approximately four to five feet tall, and it is a native of the central plain states, growing along road banks, fields, prairies, and dry open woods. The flowers will bloom from midsummer until fall. They make an excellent cut flower, and an excellent addition to any flower arrangement.

The Echinacea is an easy plant to grow and start from seed. Good germination can be achieved if you wait until the air temperature is seventy degrees or more before sowing. By starting seed in the spring, it will be the second year before you can have bloom. Older plants can be divided in the fall for bloom the following summer, but I do not advise for this when you are harvesting the roots for a supplement.

It may be necessary to have a soil test before sowing. The Echinacea likes a neutral or alkaline soil. The pH reading should be seven or higher. Add lime at the rate of five to ten pounds per 100 square feet if your soil is acid.

Add a liberal amount of compost, a layer of two to three inches, and work into the soil. Add kelp meal at the rate of one pound per 100 square feet. Rock phosphate at the rate of two and a half pounds per 100 square feet. This will give a good seed-bed for starting your plants. Some lime may be needed. It depends on your soil pH.

The root is the part used for healing purposes. It should be harvested in the late fall after top-growth has been killed by frost. It should be killed back after several hard frosts. Harvest the roots the third or fourth year of the plants' growth. At this stage, the roots will be the most potent. The roots will lose potency after the fourth year. Also, if the crown is divided, the plants will not have the potency as plants started from seed.

The root should be cut up into small pieces and dried. Drying can be done in the sun or a dehydrator. The Native Americans used the plant to treat snake and insect bites. Many American herbalists consider the Echinacea to be an excellent blood purifier. Medical researchers in Germany, Russia, and China have shown much interest in Echinacea and are investigating its health properties.

Most major seed companies carry the seed of this garden flower and herb. You may find the seed locally.

The Ginkgo Tree: There is no doubt that many of you have heard of *Ginkgo biloba* for its claim in aiding the memory. Actually, it is being used today in treating some Alzheimer patients. By its ability to inhibit the PAF (platelet activation factor), it has shown that it has enormous healing potential, and especially conditions associated with aging. Before using this herb, be sure you consult your doctor. It could cause problems if you have blood clotting disorders.

The Ginkgo tree is the oldest surviving tree known, and it can also help us old people to survive. The common name of this tree is the Maidenhair tree. As amazing as this tree seems to be, you can grow it in your own yard. There is only one species grown, and that is the Ginkgo biloba species. The sexes of this tree are separate. The female tree bears fleshy drupes that are vile smelling when they fall to the ground and start decaying, so if you do not want the fruit, then grow the male tree only. The kernels of the seed are edible, and form a desirable food for the people of China, from which it is a native. Male trees are available from many mail-order nurseries. Also, seedlings are available at a much cheaper price, but you will not know whether they are male or female until they start bearing fruit, which takes about twenty years.

The tree is an attractive tree with peculiar fan-shaped leaves. The leaves are dark green in summer, turning to a bright yellow in the fall. It is a very hardy and beautiful tree, growing to heights of 90 to 100 feet after many years. This tree is pest-free, so this is especially a desirable trait. Maybe the leaves could be used to repel insects from your garden?

The tree will give good results in a good, well-drained, loamy soil. Mulching with leaves, straw, or hay will insure a fertile and moist soil for it.

James A. Eagle

Several variety names have been given to selective varieties grown from seed. One is fastigiata, which is a male tree with a stiff, erect habit. Others are laciniata, pendula, and variegata, which have variegated leaves. To me, there is none as beautiful as the unnamed varieties with the dark green leaves. Prices on these named varieties are much higher than seedlings.

Fall and early-winter is the ideal time to set the trees out, giving the roots time to establish themselves before new growth starts in the spring. Dig a hole twice the spread of the roots and at least six inches deeper than the tree was in the nursery. Add a liberal amount of good compost and mix with the top soil. Put some of this in the bottom of the hole, and then insert the tree, filling the hole with the topsoil mixed with compost. Water the tree liberally with a solution of two tablespoons of liquid sea weed (kelp) to each gallon of water. This will stimulate root growth, allowing the tree to recover from the shock of transplanting. In fact, soaking the roots in this solution before setting out will help stimulate root growth quicker. Mulch with leaves, straw, or hay to help maintain the moisture. If set out in this manner, you should see new growth in the spring.

Propagation of this tree can be made in several ways. Seed can be planted as soon as they fall from the tree. They should not be allowed to dry out before planting. When planting the seed, remember, you will not know whether you will get male or female. Young stem cuttings can be rooted the last of May and during the month of June with fair success. Some varieties will not root as well as others. Grafting can be done on seedling root stock of a preferred variety

The leaves of the tree are the part used to cure our afflictions. If you wish to harvest the leaves for your own use, then I would recommend the advice of one knowledgeable in their preparation. The young leaves can be harvested and dried by placing in a well-ventilated room with very little moisture, or better yet in a dehydrator. If using a dehydrator, set it on eighty-five to ninety degrees. They will retain more of the oils and nutrients at this temperature. Higher temperatures will deplete them of much of the beneficial ingredients.

Pineapple: A few years ago, I received a call from a reader that propagated a pineapple plant from a pineapple fruit purchased in the grocery store. She wanted to know if I had ever heard of that before. Hers had started forming a fruit in the apex after five years.

This is one of the best ways for the inexperienced person to get a plant started. The fruit that you purchase in the store is some of the choice varieties, so you would be assured of getting a fruit of excellent flavor. Some varieties of pineapple are very acidic and sharp and the tastes are not very pleasing.

The Pineapple (Ananas comosus) is a member of the Bromiliaceae family. It is a native of South America, and after the discovery of the Americas, it rapidly spread to all tropical areas of the world. Some believed it to be a native of Hawaii, since so many of our pineapples are grown there, but it only was introduced there in the 18th century. The pineapple was cultivated by the South American natives long before the continent was discovered by the Europeans.

The pineapple can be seriously damaged with temperatures below thirty-two degrees. The fruit can be damaged at temperatures below forty-two degrees. This is important to remember, so you can bring your plant inside the home or green house before temperatures drop this low.

To propagate a plant from a fruit, cut off the crown of leaves from the top about three-fourths of an inch down from the crown, getting a small amount of the fruit. Let it air dry for twenty-four to forty-eight hours, then place it in a five or six-inch pot of sand and peat moss, covering the fruit section up to the leaves on the crown. You can propagate other plants from the side-shoots, or slips that your plant will grow as it matures. It should be rooted enough after several months to transplant to a two or three-gallon pot. The pineapple is a heavy feeder, so you should make a potting soil of equal parts of well-rotted compost, peat moss and perlite (one gallon of each). To this, add one cup of fish meal, one cup of bone meal, one-fourth cup greensand, and two tablespoons of kelp meal. The plant will be able to remain in this size container for one to two years. It will depend on the amount of nutrients and the amount of sunlight the plant receives that will determine repotting time.

The pineapple also requires a large amount of water, but does not like wet soil. Just keep it moist.

A pineapple plant grown partially as an indoor plant will not be as large, in most cases, as one grown outdoors. Because of our cold winters, we will have to take them indoors for the late fall and winter months. To keep the plant in a healthy state, place it next to a sunny window. On warm days during the winter, when outside temperatures are above sixty degrees, place it outside in the sun for an hour or two at a time. If it has been inside too long, then be careful not to overexpose it to the sun at any single time. It can cause the leaf spikes to turn yellow when it is not conditioned to sun exposure. It must be conditioned slowly. When it gets warmer in the spring, then slowly extend the time you leave it outside until it is getting six hours or more sun each time. It still may be necessary to bring it inside if temperatures drop in the fifties or lower during late spring and early fall months.

Pineapples planted outside will grow three feet high and four to five feet wide, but growing one as an indoor plant in a container will restrict the size of the plant. After a couple of years, it may be necessary to transplant it to a four or a five-gallon container. This can be placed on a platform with three swivel casters. This will allow you to easily move it from inside to outside.

Pineapple plants suffer much from the lack of micro-nutrients, so I recommend that a feeding of liquid seaweed be used every few months, and a feeding of fish meal twice yearly. Make a small trench in the potting soil around the plant and place one-fourth of a cup of fish meal in the trench. Pull the soil back over the fishmeal. This will eliminate any smell you may get from fishmeal.

The plant should have seventy to eighty leaves before flowering to insure large fruits. They will flower with less, but this is an excellent way to determine if your plant is getting all the nutrients, water, and light it requires.

Easter Lilies: Have you been discarding your Easter lilies after the blooms fade? If you have, then you have wasted a lovely plant that can be increased and have beautiful flowers for many years.

The general requirements of the Easter Lily (Lilium longiflorum) are about the same as for all major species of lilies. The Easter lily has been developed with many different varieties from the L. longiflorum species. They have been promoted as the Easter lily, but it does not bloom at Easter in a natural environment. This lily is forced into bloom to reach the stores at Easter time. The white beauty and fragrance of this lily are ideal flowers to symbolize the resurrection of Jesus Christ.

If the soil is prepared properly, this lily will thrive in most areas, and even improve in its beauty as the years roll on. Lilies like a well-drained soil with plenty of humus (decayed organic material) in the soil. If the soil stays wet for too long, the bulbs will rot. The humus provides the proper drainage you need. This can be applied as compost. It can be mixed with manure for quicker composting. After working several inches of this into the soil, add a little fish meal or alfalfa meal and bone meal, or other good organic fertilizers. After this has been accomplished, then you have an excellent place to plant your Easter lily bulbs.

Prepare a solution of water and liquid seaweed in a bucket large enough to submerge the pot. Mix two tablespoons of liquid seaweed to each gallon of water (optional). Submerge the pot until there are no more bubbles coming to the top. Remove plant from pot and transplant into your garden to the depth it was in the pot, or an inch deeper.

Mice and voles love the bulbs of lilies, so to insure your that lily is not ravaged by voles, plant it with your daffodils. This is one flower they will stay away from. Daffodils can be planted within a foot of the lily plant.

James A. Eagle

In the southeast, the Easter lily bulbs will live in the soil through the winter when kept mulched. Although the stem will die, it should not be pulled out. Leave it alone until spring, when you see new stems starting to emerge in the spring, then you can cut off the dead stems from the prior year, within a few inches of the soil level. The stems of the Easter lily grow from two to four feet tall, with each stem being crowned with three to five large trumpet shaped flowers. They become more beautiful each year, multiplying and making more bulbs.

The Easter lily is one of the lilies that have the scale type bulb. The mature bulb looks like it has a large amount of scales. These scales can actually be used to propagate new plants. If a few of the outer scales are removed in the fall and put into a rooting medium, they will, in time, produce minute bulblets. These will usually take several years to produce bloom.

The Easter lily will also produce new bulbs in the soil as off-shoots. When these bulbs are ready to separate and plant, then they should be planted approximately six to eight inches deep. The Easter lily is a stem rooting lily, and will form roots along the stem in the soil.

This lily also produces small bublets along the stem near the soil, or even under the soil. These bublets can also be used to increase your stock.

At the State Institution, where I worked in Florida, we had lilies growing all over the place in the landscape. They would start blooming sometimes as early as June. It will bloom later as you go further north. These plants became a main target of the people that worked at night to increase their plant selection.

If you think your potted Easter lily is beautiful now, wait until you have a clump of multi-stems: three, four, five or more blooms on each stem.

Confederate Rose: When this lovely flower is in bloom, there are not many flowering shrubs that can match its beauty. Most of these beautiful flowers are white or pink in the morning, and turn to dark pink or red as they are exposed to the sun during the day. The Confederate Rose is a member of the Hibiscus family. Its botanical name is *Hibiscus mutabilis*. The Confederate Rose comes to us from China. It is also called the Cotton Rose.

This shrub is a tropical species of the Hibiscus, but we are fortunate here in that we can grow it with the proper care and maintenance in Zone 7 and 8. Naturally, it does better in Zone 9 and 10. I am sorry, but you folks farther north cannot have the joy of growing them. Your weather is too cold.

In the winter the cold will kill the upper-growth. That is why we grow it in our area with multiple trunks or canes. In the spring, it puts up May canes from the crown that is left in the ground or it will put out new canes from the large roots. In tropical climates it can be grown with one trunk and becomes a small tree.

The Confederate Rose usually starts blooming in August, but I have seen it wait until the first of October, and then had many of the buds get killed by an early frost.

Care and maintenance is about the same for all of the hibiscus family. They prefer a loamy soil with plenty of organic matter. Mulching will aid in protecting the roots in the winter, if there should be a severe cold period. In the spring, remove the mulch and put a layer of clear plastic down around the plant to hasten the growth of new canes. This should be done about the middle of March or first of April. Keep the plastic on until new growth has occurred and the canes are about six inches high. At this point, remove the plastic and mulch with leaves, straw, hay, or other organic mulches. By doing this, you will hasten the budding and blooming process by getting them blooming earlier than normal.

It is fairly easy to propagate new plants from the confederate rose. In June, you can take tip-cuttings of about six to eight inches long and place them in a rooting medium of equal parts of peat moss, sand, and perlite. Dip stems in some rooting hormone, such as Rootone, and place in the medium you have prepared. Place containers in a shady area and mist with water daily until rooted. They should be well-rooted within four to six weeks. They can also be reproduced in the winter if you

James A. Eagle

have a green house or other area that the temperature does not get below fifty-five degrees. Cut the canes down to the ground right before the first frost. Then you can cut them into lengths of about one or one and one-half foot long. Put them in pots with the above rooting medium of peat, sand, and perlite. They will root and have plants to set out in the spring that have a start on the others. I have also rooted them by placing these stems in a five-gallon bucket of water. Roots will form, and then you can pot them and have them ready for spring. Be sure you place the butt down into the medium, or the water, whichever you use. Be sure you cut the canes in the fall, before the first frost for rooting. A heavy frost can damage them and prevent the rooting process.

About the only pruning you need to do is cutting the old canes off in the fall after the first frost. Cut them within an inch or two of the ground and mulch heavy with leaves.

The older your confederate rose is, the larger the root mass it will have in the ground. The roots will be so established that you can get growth as much as eight to twelve feet, or more, in one season of growth. In a tropical climate the tree will keep growing without freezing, requiring severe pruning if you do not wish it to grow into a tree. Where it gets frozen to the ground, growth will be restricted for only one growing season because of it getting killed to the ground each year.

Blueberries: The Blueberry is a native American plant. Many of you elderly people, like myself, can remember harvesting them wild when we were young. It was about 1910 that a breeding program was begun by the United States Department of Agriculture to improve and domesticate the Blueberry. There has been miraculous progress since then to give us a greatly improved Blueberry. Today there are many varieties that far exceed the wild Blueberry we harvested as kids. They are larger, sweeter, and much better flavored.

Most of the domesticated blueberries grow to six to twelve feet tall if not controlled by pruning. Most of the Blueberries for the Southeast were developed from the Rabbit-eye Blueberry.

Some were crossed with the High-bush. New varieties are coming out almost every year. It is hard to keep up with all the varieties. Just make sure that any you purchase are adapted to your area. The blueberries for the Southeast has been bred for our region. The ones for the northern states are bred for that area.

The ideal soil for Blueberries is a sandy loam soil with plenty of organic matter. The ideal pH is 4.5 to 5.6, but they will grow with a pH as low as 4.0 and as high as 6.0. The best way to provide the correct pH is by adding plenty of organic matter composted out of oak leaves or pine straw, or by mulching with oak leaves or pine straw. A mulch of six to eight inches each year will provide all the nutrients and proper pH needed in most cases. If additional nutrients are needed, they can be in the form of cottonseed meal. This will insure an acidic soil and provide nutrients as well. For young plants one to two feet tall, apply one-half pound per plant. Three to four feet plants apply up to one pound per plant. Older plants should have up to two pounds.

After the first two or three years, mulching the blueberries as outlined above will be provide all the nutrients they will need.

If you live in the south, then set your plants in late fall to early winter. It will insure that the roots get established for the plant to get a good start in early spring without stress. If you live in Zone Six or further north, then it is better to set them out in early spring. At the time of planting, add a liberal amount of peat moss to the soil, or better yet a compost of pine straw and oak leaves. Mix this into the soil and plant the Blueberry plant at the depth it was in the nursery or container it came in. Apply your first mulch at this time and water the plants to settle the soil around the roots. Always mulch blueberries with oak leaves or pine straw. They lower the pH reading of the soil.

Little or no pruning is needed until the end of the third growing season. Blueberries set fruit on the previous season's growth. To insure large berries, the weaker canes can be pruned out in late winter or early spring before flowering or new growth starts. If Blueberries are left unpruned, they have a tendency to bear too heavy, and the fruit will be reduced in size.

James A. Eagle

There are few diseases for the Blueberry in our area. With the care outlined above you should have healthy plants that will give you many years of good fruit. Sometimes when the plant is stressed by lack of moisture or proper fertilizer, lichens may grow on the stems. Lichens are a combination of a fungus and an alga growing together forming on the older stems of the plant. It will not hurt the Blueberry, but it doesn't look good. Prune out canes that are badly infested and keep plants watered and apply cottonseed meal as a nutrient.

Most Blueberries are self-sterile, but you will get better fruiting by planting two or more varieties.

Tilling is never necessary around Blueberries. Just keep them mulched and watered during dry periods. The roots are shallow growing and can easily be damaged by tilling. The mulching will also help to retain moisture.

Birds love the Blueberry, so if you have been trying to attract birds to your yard, then this is one way. Of course, if you only have a few plants, you probably don't care to share them with the birds. The bushes can be covered with netting during the ripening season.

Any excess Blueberries you have can be frozen. We wash ours and put them on a cookie sheet and pop them into the freezer. After they are frozen, they can be stored in a Zip-Lock bag. When you get ready to use them, you can take them out and only use what you need, because they will separate easily this way.

There is nothing like a hot Blueberry muffin for breakfast. Here is my favorite recipe: Two cups all purpose flour, one-half cup sugar, three teaspoons of baking powder, one-half teaspoon salt, three-fourths cup milk, one-third cup olive oil, one teaspoon of vanilla flavoring, and one beaten egg. Combine flour, sugar, salt and baking powder in a bowl, add milk, oil, and egg and blend with dry ingredients. Add one cup of fresh or frozen Blueberries and blend into batter. Bake at 400 degrees for 18 to 22 minutes. When the heat hits those Blueberries, they will burst and send that flavor throughout the muffin.

Blackberries: The erect, or bush-type blackberry is ideal for the home garden. But the outstanding feature about the new bush blackberry is that they are thornless. That is correct. We have blackberries that you can pick without catching blood-poisoning from the thorns on the bush. When speaking of blackberries, you think of an unmanageable thicket of canes and thorns, then forget it. With the new thornless bush varieties that stick is something in the past.

Cultivation of the thornless varieties is the same as for thorned blackberries. They will grow in most types of soil, but they do not like a soggy or swampy area. Before setting out plants, make sure a good supply of organic matter has been added to the soil. Then mulch the plants with straw, hay, or leaves to hold moisture, which will add organic matter when it decays. Mulching should be done each year. This will provide all the nutrients you will need in most cases. Set plants about three or four feet apart in the row and place the rows approximately eight feet apart. If you completely mulch the rows, then there will be no need to till the soil to control weeds.

The blackberry canes are biennial; they grow one season, bear fruit the next and then die. While you are harvesting your blackberries in the summer, you will see new canes coming up to replace the old canes for the next season. After the blackberries are through fruiting, you can cut the old canes off and discard them, leaving the new canes to grow for the next year. Some people top the new canes after they reach about three feet. This will produce stronger branches.

If you desire more plants, then you can propagate them by placing the tip of a cane into the soil a few inches while it is attached to the mother plant, then in the spring cut the tip from the mother plant and set out the new rooted plant. They can also be propagated by taking tip cuttings. I take a new cane and get eight to ten cuttings from it. Place the cutting in a sterile medium of peat, sand and perlite. Place in a shady area and keep the rooting medium moist until rooted.

James A. Eagle

Root cuttings are another method of propagation, but the horticulturists tell you that root cuttings of the thornless varieties will have thorns. I have used root cuttings with excellent success, and none had thorns. That is why I always tell gardeners to experiment. Don't take the word of anyone as the complete truth. You may be surprised at the discoveries you may make.

Some of the thornless varieties available are Navaho, Arapaho, Lochness, Black Satin, Hull, and Chester. These are varieties I have tried, and my favorite is the Navaho. The taste and growth habit is ideal for me. It has a nice bush shape and delicious berries with a large harvest.

The best features of the bush and self supporting blackberries are that they are easier to control and do not need support. Many of the thorned blackberries have a trailing nature and must be supported.

The blackberries should not be picked until fully ripe. At that stage they are sweeter and can be eaten fresh from the plant. The berries will not ripen any more after they have been picked. That is why it is important to be sure they are fully ripe.

Use the berries for making jellies, jams, pies, and many other delicious things. They can also be canned and frozen. There isn't a genuine Southerner that hasn't had *Blackberry Cobbler*. If you have not enjoyed this delicious treat, then be sure you have one this summer. You just do not know what you are missing until you have a dish of blackberry cobble with whipped cream.

Figs: Figs that are grown to supply fruit to the home gardener are grown in all the Gulf states and up the eastern seaboard to Virginia. They are delicious eaten fresh off the tree, dried, or made into jams and preserves. They can also be used in many types of pastry. Substitute them for raisins, dates, or prunes in your favorite recipe.

Figs have many health benefits. I know from experience that they are an excellent laxative. When bothered by constipation, I just go by the fig tree and eat a dozen of fresh figs, and the problem is solved. There have been claims that they are good for the heart. In some cultures the leaves are used to stabilize blood sugar.

The most popular varieties for our area, Zone Eight, are Brown Turkey, Celeste, and Texas Ever-bearing. There are others varieties, but many of them are not as cold-hardy as the three mentioned. About twelve years ago we bought one called *Chicago*. It was supposed to be hardy as far north as Chicago. It has frozen to the ground every year, and we still have not gotten any figs from it.

When we first moved to South Carolina, I tried to purchase some figs locally. All that I found was what they called the Sugar Fig. I have come to the conclusion that it is the Brown Turkey Fig. It is similar in size and color as the Brown Turkey Fig.

You have probably heard that the best place to plant a fig tree is on the south side of a building to protect it from the harsh winter cold wind. This does not always hold true. On a cold, frosty morning look around and see where the spots are that has less frost. It indicates that the area has better air circulation, which is better to prevent cold damage than some South sides of buildings. Most of the figs mentioned above will take temperatures down to eighteen degrees before there is negligible cold damage. If your fig gets killed to the ground with extremely cold temperatures, it will survive if you have a good mulch around it. Mulch out to the drip-line of the tree or beyond.

A good mulch around your fig will provide about all the nutrients that you will ever need for the fig. If you get too much nitrogen, then you will sacrifice fruit production. Also, the mulch will protect the roots from severe cold, and help hold the moisture during dry periods. Mulching is preferred to cultivation, because cultivation can damage the shallow roots, inviting cold damage in the winter. The mulch will provide about all the nutrients you will ever need. If you still think additional nutrients are needed, then a light application of alfalfa meal around the drip-line of the tree will probably be sufficient. That is where the small feed roots are located.

James A. Eagle

During extremely dry conditions, the figs should be watered long enough for a deep soaking. If the roots can get moisture by shallow watering, then they will keep their roots shallow instead of going deep. You should water deep about once every week to ten days during periods of drought, at least one inch of water or more. If you use a sprinkler, then put a can about four feet from the sprinkler. When you have one inch or more of the water in the can, then you know you are getting the proper amount. The lack of moisture can cause the figs to drop.

Figs can be trained with a single trunk, or with multiple trunks. That is up to the grower. Just be sure you leave good strong stems and cut out the slender ones. You will want strong trunks and limbs to support your fig crop.

Your first crop of figs will form on the prior year's growth. If there is a late cold after they start forming, you will get a heavy drop of figs, sometimes all will fall if there is a killing frost. Don't despair, as the fig starts putting out new growth, then you will get a second setting of this luscious fruit. It will be later than the one you lost from the cold, but just as good.

Figs can be propagated by hardwood cuttings taken in the late fall or early winter. The method of doing this is covered in Chapter Eight.

Strawberries: The Alpine and Musk strawberry are ones that you never see in the grocery store, but yet they are sought after by the finest restaurants of Europe in preparing the most delicious and most sought-after desserts. These strawberries are truly a gourmet treat. Each variety has its own flavor and aroma, and I mean flavor and aroma like nothing you get in the cultivated varieties that we think of as a real treat in the spring. Here in the states it is grown as a specialty or hobby.

The Alpine (Fragaria vesca) and Musk (Fragaria moschata) strawberries came to us from the Alpine Mountains of Europe. The reason they have not made the popularity polls here is because they are much smaller in size, but the flavor and aroma make up for this.

If any of you have ever grown any of the modern hybrids that are grown here for maxim production, you are familiar with the many runners they have, and in order to get the best production and prevent diseases the runners must be kept cut off. This does not occur with the Alpine and Musk strawberries. They do not send runners out, like our hybrids. They can be increased by division or you may start them from seed. Because of the lack of runners, they make an excellent border plant, and especially where they get partial shade. In fact, in our hot climate, here in the south, they do much better if they only get sun for a few hours in the morning and a few hours in the late afternoon. I have propagated many different varieties, and all of them do better in mostly shade in our area. The hot summers in the south can really put a strain on them.

Another wonderful feature of the Alpine strawberry is that they bear fruit in our area from April to frost. They are truly an ever bearing strawberry. Even if you lose the first blooms from a late frost, you can be assured that you will still get a crop as they will soon be putting out new bloom scapes. This is one that you can harvest fresh all summer long for your breakfast cereal or for delicious desserts. Fruiting will taper off during the hot days of summer, but it immediately picks up during the cooler days of fall.

The normal leaf cycle on the Alpine strawberries is from forty-five to sixty days, so don't worry when the bottom leaves start turning brown. Pick the browning leaves off and discard. At this stage during the summer you can cut all the leaves off, but *do not* cut out the heart of the plant. Within a few weeks new leaves will be growing back. You may even see bloom scapes shooting up and blooming before the new leaves occur.

These strawberries are extremely hardy. They will grow in all parts of the United States with possibly the only exception being the extreme northern part of Minnesota and North Dakota. You can even grow them in Miami.

James A. Eagle

One of the most outstanding features of these wonderful jewels is that they laugh at diseases and insects. It is a rare occasion to see one die of disease, or have insect infestation.

Another good trait of these jewels is that they put the bloom scape up above the leaves, thus preventing the berries from contacting the ground where many soil bore diseases are transmitted to our regular cultivated varieties.

The Alpine strawberries produce either red or white fruit with an intense wild strawberry flavor. The White Alpine tastes more like pineapple. Musk varieties can have a mixture of flavors of raspberry, strawberry and pineapple into a single fruit.

Prepare the soil by adding two or three inches of compost, and the following amendments to each ten square feet of space: one cup alfalfa meal and one-fourth cup each of bone meal and greensand. Work this into the soil about a week before planting.

When transplanting these plants, do not set them lower in the ground than they were in the pot. If you are setting out bare root plants, then leave the heart of the plant above the soil line. They should be placed about fifteen to eighteen inches apart in the border or rows. For maximum production, be sure they are shaded during the heat of the day. Mulch the plants so as to hold moisture, and then wait for a delicious harvest of the most unusual berries you have ever eaten.

Now we will cover the commercial types of strawberries, those that are grown for heavy production, and have a ripening period in the early spring. We have conditioned ourselves to the large red juicy berries we see in the grocery stores, so we want a similar berry for our table.

For the home gardener there is varieties that can be grown which have much better flavor, but may not be as large as the ones we see in the stores. Many of these varieties are not suitable for shipping, but make ideal fruit for the home gardener. Many of the commercial varieties are also suitable for the home gardener as well, but most are lacking in flavor and sweetness.

For the gardeners in the southeast, November and December is the time to transplant the plants for a spring harvest. If you wait until spring you will get a very small harvest. Although the foliage will die down during the winter months, the roots will be developing to produce a heavy harvest in the spring.

Selection of the site is very important. You should not plant them in an area that has grown tomatoes, eggplant, peppers, or potatoes the last three years. These crops infect the soil with verticillium wilt, a very troublesome root disease of strawberries. Also select a site with plenty of full sun and with good air circulation. A slight slope would be ideal, especially a southern slope. This will help protect against a late frost that could damage the early crop. Strawberries on a southern slope will also ripen earlier than those on a northern slope.

A large supply of organic matter is ideal, and can be supplied by the addition of compost, rotted manures, etc. Compost should be applied at the rate of approximately 100 pounds per 100 sq. feet An additional amount of organic amendments can also be added to insure all needed nutrients are available such as four to five pounds of alfalfa meal, two pounds of rock phosphate, and three pounds of greensand per 100 sq. feet I also add some cornmeal to the soil where I plant mine. It helps to prevent many diseases.

Planting the plants fifteen inches apart is adequate if you keep all runners cut off. This is necessary to provide necessary air circulation. If you let the new runners remain on, then they should be set twenty to twenty-four inches apart.

When setting out your plants, be sure not to set them too deep. The crown of the plant should be exposed above the ground level. If planted too deep, the plant will die.

Strawberry plants are shallow rooted, so they should receive at least one inch of water each week, even during the winter months. If you water with a sprinkler, set a can about middle way from the edge of where the water reaches to the sprinkler. When the can has an inch of water in it, then that should be sufficient.

Many instructions from the northern growers will tell you that all blooms should be cut off the first year. This does not apply to the southern areas where you set them out in the fall. You can

James A. Eagle

harvest a good crop the first year. Most northern growers set their plants out in the spring. In Florida, strawberries are grown as an annual. Plants are set out in the fall or winter and the crop is plowed under after harvest in the early spring. Strawberries are grown from Alaska to Florida. The only difference is in the culture and management requirements of them in the different areas. I have seen them set out near Fairbanks, Alaska in June and they harvested huge strawberries before the first freeze, usually the first of September.

Mulching the plants in the fall will protect them from severe cold, provide a covering to hold moisture, and keep the strawberries off the soil in the spring. Letting the berries touch the soil can cause rot. The mulch will also keep the berries clean.

Most of the large nurseries, which specialize in producing plants for commercial purposes, do not sell small amounts of plants for the home gardener. It is best to buy plants locally or from a retail seed house such as Park Seeds and Burpee. They sell plants in small amounts.

Lawn Care: While writing gardening columns for our local newspaper, I was flooded with questions on lawn care, pest control, and diseases. Actually, this could take a book to cover it in-depth, but we will cover the highlights of chemical free lawn care here.

Most of our lawns have become a sponge for the pesticides, herbicides, and fungicides that are on the market today. Many have their lawns treated by some commercial firm that tell them that the chemicals they are using are safe, because it was approved by the EPA. That is not just misrepresentation, it most cases it is down-right fraud.

If we want a disease and weed-free lawn, then we should get our soil in balance. Charles Walters, Jr. in his book, *Weeds: Controls Without Poisons* writes:

> "A proper calcium level with magnesium, potassium and phosphates in equilibrium will do more to roll back weed pro-

liferation than all the herbicides in the Dow and Monsanto armamentarium."

This item on lawns will be devoted to those who already have established lawns, but want to improve them or correct those that have been damaged by insects, disease, and herbicides and other conditions created by excessive use of chemicals.

Some of the main causes of weeds and bare spots are inadequate fertility, excessive nutrients, compaction, poor drainage, an inadequate amount of organic matter, or incorrect pH. Most of these causes can be exposed by a soil test.

Test your lawn for compaction by taking a probe, such as a six-inch screwdriver, and push it into the lawn. If the lawn is firm and the screwdriver will not penetrate down into the lawn for six inches, then you have a compacted lawn. This can be corrected several ways. First if you do not own one of the spike disk cultivators, you may be able to rent one from a tool rental shop. One of these will aerate your turf and get it ready for other methods we will cover.

Poor drainage may be caused by an excess amount of thatch. Thatch is the buildup of matted grass clippings, roots, and stolons on top of the soil surface. Thatch can be beneficial if it is not more than one-half inch thick. If over that amount, it should be removed. Thatch is not caused by returning your grass clippings to the lawn, as most lawn services will tell you. It is caused by the use of chemicals that prevent grass clippings from decomposing, thereby adding compost to your lawn. So, if you have a buildup of thatch over one-half inch thick, then most likely you have been using chemicals to control weeds, or chemical fertilizer that causes a spurt of lush growth. This lush growth will create an excess of clippings that will not decompose as fast, especially when hampered by other chemicals.

Most of us are afflicted with a frenzy to get that lawn growing in early spring, so we head to the garden centers and load ourselves with bags of chemical lawn fertilizer with a high nitrogen content to get that lawn growing. Sure, it will make a flush of new growth that is so green that it is almost blue in color. Out comes the lawn mower and cutting must be done each week or more. This application of chemical fertilizers will also make the weeds grow as well, and invite the insects and diseases that afflict our lawns.

If you want a beautiful, healthy lawn, then stop using herbicides, poison pesticides, fungicides, and chemical fertilizers. Convert it to an almost care-free healthy lawn, using organic methods- a lawn that you will not be afraid for your children or pets to play on.

One of the first things you should do before trying to restore your lawn is to have a complete soil test made by the Extension Service. You will want to know not only the nitrogen, phosphorous, and potash needs, but if your soil is lacking in calcium, magnesium, and other nutrients.

If you have been using chemicals in any form, then the clippings should be caught, or raked, for the next two cuttings, and destroyed. These clippings will have chemicals that will inhibit the proper decomposition of them into organic matter in your lawn.

It is urgent that you start adding organic matter by returning the healthy clippings back onto the lawn. Chemical-free clippings will decompose into organic matter in a few weeks, you will be ready to start the restoration process, provided you performed the compaction test, and corrected it if you had compaction. It is an absolute necessity that the soil be able to breathe. The roots need oxygen for proper root growth, and proper utilization of the nutrients in the soil.

If good rotted-compost is available, then apply an inch all over your lawn. This gets the lawn started immediately with some of the nutrients it needs, and it starts restoring the microorganisms needed to convert the nutrients and minerals already in the soil in the form needed by the grass. Instead of catching your grass clippings, return them to the lawn now. This adds organic matter that will also help aerate the soil and it will have the ability to retain moisture longer. After restoring your lawn to an organic care lawn, the grass clippings will provide most of the nutrients your lawn will need in most cases.

If you have centipede grass, as many of the lawns in the Southeast are, then you have a low maintenance lawn. Centipede grass dislikes heavy fertility. Excessive fertilizing can cause disease and insect problems in this type of lawn. A centipede lawn requires very limited mowing- usually every two weeks or even longer on a properly-maintained centipede lawn.

If your lawn is in bad shape with bare spots, check for insects around the edges where it is still green. One method is by using a two-pound or larger coffee can, or any kind of can, with both ends cut out. Insert it into the turf about two inches deep and in an area that is not damaged, but close to the damaged area. Fill the can with water. Insects, especially the chinch bugs, will start coming to the top within five minutes. The chinch bugs are very small, with the adults measuring only about one-sixteenth of an inch. The immature bugs are even smaller. If there are less than fifteen bugs appearing in the can, then there isn't that much of a problem. You can soak your lawn with a neem spray. This is made from an extract of the neem tree. The most important thing is to restore your lawn to its health. Therefore, it is necessary to provide the nutrients to get this process going. Apply the formulations listed below according to what the pH of your soil tested, and provided you have centipede lawn or other grass that loves an acid soil. If your soil tested above a pH of 6.0, then apply a combination of cotton seed meal, rock phosphate, and kelp meal (seaweed). It depends on how your soil tested for nitrogen, phosphorus, and potash as to the amounts for each. If your soil is very low in all of these, then a standard formulation of eighty pounds of alfalfa meal, twenty pounds of rock phosphate, and thirty pounds of greensand to every 1000 sq. feet of lawn should prove adequate.

If your soil tested above a pH of 6.0, then the following formulation should be adequate for each 1000 sq. feet of lawn: Eighty pounds of cottonseed meal, twenty pounds of rock phosphate, thirty pounds of greensand. Your lawn will not be affected

James A. Eagle

too much if this is adjusted slightly for pH and the content of nitrogen, phosphorus, and potash.

If an application of compost was applied as outlined above, then half of the above formulations should be sufficient.

An application of one of the above formulations should restore your lawn to a more healthy lawn where it can resist disease and insects. It may also be the last time you will need to apply nutrients, if you maintain your lawn in an organic healthy manner.

Lawn clippings are a great source of free fertilizer for your lawn. Rake them up or catch them, and you are robbing your lawn of over half of the nitrogen it will need, also you are robbing it of the moisture retaining organic matter it will provide. The speed the grass clippings break down depends on how chemical free your lawn is. The chemicals destroy the earthworms, bacteria, fungi, and other microorganisms needed for a quick decomposition of the clippings in order to prevent thatch build up.

Most of us like that nice evenly-mowed lawn, and we pull out the mower each week and mow the same day, usually Saturday, regardless of the lawn's growth or condition. Mowing is one of the most important things you will ever do to your lawn. It can be beneficial, or it can be the most harmful. The rigid mowing schedule most of us follows may not suit the grass. Grass grows at different rates throughout the year. The rate of growth depends on many factors, such as water, heat, fertilizer, disease, and the season of the year.

How you mow will have an important impact on the health and appearance of your lawn. Grass, like all other plants, carries on a process known as *photosynthesis* in its leaves. Using the energy of sunlight it manufactures the energy it needs for growth. The more of the grass leaf we cut off, the more we reduce the ability of the grass to manufacture the food it needs. Food production is not the only thing to suffer when you mow. Cutting grass creates points of entry for disease organisms, especially if the lawn mower blade is dull. It tears the grass leaves, leaving more openings than a sharp blade will leave. One of the benefits of mowing properly is that it will produce a thicker lawn. If you left the grass to its own choice, it would grow until it produced seed. But mowing prevents the development of seed, so the plant then responds by producing stolons and rhizomes and spreading horizontally, therefore producing a thicker lawn. If the lawn gets too thick, then there is greater danger of disease, so you have to judge your lawn as to the need to mow and how often. It has proven to be more beneficial to mow at higher heights with less frequency for the healthiest lawn. The lawn will spread, but not as fast, and is able to produce the food it needs as well.

During extremely hot weather and especially hot dry weather, the less you mow, the better it is for your lawn. If two weeks pass without having any rain, or manually watering the lawn, then it is time to raise the mower to a higher length.

Insects can be a problem. There are several ways to keep insect damage to a minimum. One of the best methods that has worked very well for us is a bird habitat. These feathered friends will provide you with many hours of pleasure in watching them and trying to identify them. The next best control is having a healthy lawn. It will deter more insects than one lacking in nutrition, water, poor drainage, etc. We will assume you have already established a healthy lawn, so what do you do when you have attacks of insects? Usually, the pest that will cause you the most trouble is *Yourself*. We get the idea that our lawn must be maintained like a golf-course. We use herbicides if we see one little weed, or spray with pesticides when we see a single bug, and sometimes we spray just to prevent a bug infestation. These methods can eventually destroy the lawn ecological system whereby there will surely be an infestation of weeds, bugs and disease.

There is evidence that all living things emit radiation in certain wavelengths that can be recognized by other organisms. Insects rely on these signals for their survival; whether its food they are seeking or a mate for breeding. Infrared frequencies given off by plants will tell an insect when that plant is stressed, thereby attracting the insect to the plant that is stressed. Major things that cause stress is lack of moisture, too much moisture, improper nutrients, or stressed by excessive use of poisons.

James A. Eagle

When an insect invasion occurs, it is necessary to identify the insect. You may have an invasion of beneficial insects that are after some insect that has made your lawn its dinner table. If this is the case, leave things alone for a few days and observe to see if your lawn is being damaged. If it is not, then refrain from applying anything.

One of our most common lawn insect pests is the chinch bug, but there is another insect that can control the chinch bug, and that is the big-eyed bug. If you spray with a poisonous pesticide, then you will destroy the big-eyed bug. If you later have an infestation of the chinch bug, then you will not have the big-eyed bug to control it, and the chinch bug may have developed immunity to the pesticide by this time.

The chinch bug nymphs can do more damage to the lawn than the adult chinch bug. The nymphs are about half the size of a pin head when first hatched and are bright red with a white band across the back. The adults are approximately one-eighth of an inch long and are orange-brown to black in color.

The big-eyed bugs are the good ones. They are about one-eighth of an inch long, oval, and somewhat flattened, with yellowish or brownish in color with tiny black specks. One of the most distinctive identifying features of the big-eyed bug is the bulging eyes. You may need a magnifying glass to identify these and the chinch bugs. Although the big-eyed bug is small, both the adults and nymphs have a big appetite. They eat a variety of insects' eggs, mites, aphids, and leafhoppers. If there is a source to purchase these beneficial insects, I do not know of one. It is best to have a habitat that will attract them. The adults feed on nectar of flowers and fallen seed when there is not enough insect prey available. Try sowing clover as a ground cover and scatter shelled sunflower seeds beneath your flowers and other plants to provide food for them.

There are two other insects that love to make your lawn their breeding ground, and that is the Japanese beetle and the June bug. The grubs of these beetles eat the roots of the grass, and the roots of other plants, as well. We will cover the life cycles of these two, so you will have a better understanding of them.

The Japanese beetle is one-half inch long, with a blocky, metallic blue-green in color. The adult beetles seem to prefer your flower plants, but feed on many vegetables as well, such as beans, corn, okra, asparagus, and tomatoes. They chew on the leaves during hot weather, sometimes completely defoliating the plant. They feed on plants until late summer, then burrow under the grass to lay their eggs. The eggs hatch and the larvae feed on the roots of your grass until cold weather arrives. In the spring they will continue eating on the grass roots until they pupate and emerge as beetles in early summer. The beetle larvae are fat and dirty white in color, and C-shaped with brown heads. They obtain a length of about three-fourths inches before they pupate. The best time to treat for them is in early spring or late summer. Treatment will be the same as for the June bug grubs. During heavy infestations you will find patches of wilted or dead grass, which you can easily lift because the roots have been destroyed. You may also find raccoons or crows digging in your lawn for the fat plump grubs.

There are several different species of the June bugs. The adult averages from three-fourths to more than one and three-eights inches long. Most of these beetles are shiny brown or black. Some species have lengthwise stripes on the back. The adults feed on the leaves of trees and are rarely damaging. It is the grub that we need to worry about. The adult beetles lay their eggs in batches of fifty to one-hundred eggs in balls of earth in the soil. The eggs hatch after about two to three weeks, and feed on decaying veg-etation the first year. Then they hibernate below the surface of the soil until spring. The second summer, they feed on the roots of your grass as the Japanese beetle grubs do. That winter, they hibernate again in the soil, and feed until June on grass roots. They then pupate and emerge as adult beetles after two to three weeks. The beetles remain in the soil until the next spring before emerging and feeding on tree leaves and laying their eggs to start a new generation. One most effective control is applying one of the beneficial nematodes, which are available from many sources by mail. There are two kinds that are available. The one most-preferred for the grubs of the Japanese beetle and June bugs are *Heterorhabditis bacteriophora* Another one that is also effective is *Steinernema carpocapsae* Both of these nematodes will enter the body of the grub and feed on it from within. They will also feed on many other grubs and worms that live in the soil. These are nearly microscopic in size, so don't expect to be able to see them with your naked eyes. Go to the internet for sources.

Another treatment is the milky spore disease, *Bacillus papilliae*. The milky spore disease turns the clear blood of the grubs to a milky white, thereby killing the grubs. This was one of the first biological controls used for these grubs, and it is still doing a good job today. The grubs have never built a resistance to it. It is best to apply after the temperatures in the spring have reached seventy degrees or more, so the disease can build up in the soil. This is a long-time treatment, and will last for years. The milky spore disease is harmless to humans and all other warm-blooded animals. It is also harmless to your plants as well.

If you are bothered with moles in your lawn, then by getting rid of the grubs, you will destroy the food source the moles are seeking, and therefore it will be necessary for them to move somewhere else for a meal.

A plant is much like the human body when it comes to protecting itself from disease. Our body can protect itself from disease when it is in best of health. When we expose ourselves to pollutants and improper eating habits, then we weaken our immune system and we then come down with diseases when exposed to bacteria, viruses, and other disease causing microorganisms.

Most of the protection of a plant comes from a component of the growing system, the soil. When the soil is at its peak in health, then you will have a healthy plant. The one promotes the other. A soil that contains all the plant nutrients necessary to produce an excellent lawn may be lacking in other resources necessary for prime health. One of these resources is organic matter. Although it may be a fraction of the total soil content, it is crucial for the plant to have an immune system, or better yet, be able to resist diseases. The organic matter contains billions of soil organisms that destroy disease causing organisms, or gives the plant the ability to resist diseases. The occurrence of diseases is diminished significantly when your soil is enriched with organic matter. This is one suggestion you will notice me mentioning time and time again. Your soil health depends on organic matter.

Cornell University has done a significant amount of research on adding aged organic matter to your lawn to suppress diseases. They found a significant reduction in the amount of diseases where it was added. They tried to identify the species of microorganisms that was responsible for this. They found that many species of microorganisms are responsible. This is not only true for your lawn, but for all plants you grow.

Experts in lawn care have found that diseases are rare in lawns that have been restored to their prime health with the use of organic matter. This again emphasizes the saying, *"Better to prevent than try to cure."* Is it any wonder that the compost teas, I have recommended so many times, help to prevent the diseases that afflict our plants? Too many times we have altered our lawns' ability to resist diseases by altering its ability to defend itself. Our maintenance methods are at fault. What are some of these mismanagement techniques we use which cause so much trouble? One of the most outstanding procedures we practice is excessive use of pesticides, herbicides, and fungicides. We destroy our lawns' ability to fight diseases. We open it to a weakened condition where it is impossible to defend itself against the onslaught of microorganisms that cause disease. The beneficial microorganisms are destroyed, leaving your lawn open to attack. The vast majority of soil microorganisms in an organic soil are the beneficial kinds that suppress disease.

Inappropriate applications of lime to correct a pH deficiency, adding too little or too much can be harmful in that it inhibits the plants' ability to resist disease. Be sure you know what your pH is before adding lime.

James A. Eagle

Excessive vehicle or foot traffic on the lawn will compact the soil, restricting the movement of moisture in the soil, which reduces the amount of oxygen available to the plant roots. This causes stress on your lawn turf and decreases the ability of the grass to resist diseases. Compaction can be relieved by tine aeration and a program for increasing the organic content of your soil. One sure way to increase your organic content is by leaving your lawn-clippings on the lawn.

Excessive utilization of fertilizers, especially nitrogen, is one of the greatest causes of diseases. This is one that has been stressed before. Excessive nitrogen pushes growth in exchange for poor health and the invasion of diseases.

There are several commercials on TV that are nauseating to me, the ones that advertise lawn food that has a herbicide in it to kill the weeds. This is very stressful to your turf. They have to add excessively high amounts of nitrogen to try and overcome the extreme stress the lawn grasses must deal with when it is used. This, in turn, puts more stress on the lawn. Believe me that is no real fix.

Not all the fungal organisms in your soil are harmful. In fact, most of them are beneficial in helping to prevent diseases. Use the many fungicides to try and cure a disease, and it will kill the beneficial fungus as well. So how do we solve a disease problem? There are no easy cures for most of the diseases that can attack our lawns. They attack when the lawn's health is not ideal. To be sure you know the disease, take a sample and have it analyzed to determine the disease. Plant pathologists spend years studying the differences among diseases, so I am not going to try and tell you the type of disease anyone is afflicted with. Some cannot be identified any way except under a microscope. When you are afflicted with disease of any kind, there is one basic step you must take to control and get rid of the disease. Remove the diseased area and destroy the diseased turf. Build the soil with a two-inch layer of compost and work it into the soil. Apply lime to raise the pH if a test proves it needs it. This will vary according to the variety of grass you have. The bare area can be reseeded, or sprigged with sprigs from a healthy section of your lawn. Now soak this area in a compost tea. This will provide food for the bacteria and fungi that control the bad bacteria and fungi. If there is disease in one portion of the lawn, then that is an indicator that the rest of the lawn is under stress and needs to be improved with organic matter as well. Many will head to the garden shop when you see these disease areas, and load themselves down with fungicides to try and get rid of the disease. If they succeed, it will be for a short period only. You must restore the health of the soil to be successful in the long term. If you just use poison fungicides, then you will be fighting the problem constantly.

There is a biofungicide available known as *Mycostop*. The active ingredient is natural occurring soil borne bacteria. It is mass produced and then formulated as a wet-able powder. It is packaged in hermetically sealed packets. The packets should not be opened until ready to use. Mycostop works in three ways. The first method is by out-competing several undesirable pathogenic fungi for their living space and nutrients by colonizing the plant roots more efficiently then other microorganisms. The second method is by excreting various enzymes and metabolites that inhibit the growth of undesirable pathogenic fungi. The third method is that it impels growth in the host plant, making them more vigorous, healthy and strong. This makes the plant more capable of warding off unwanted pathogens.

There is also a soil inoculant known as *Actinovate*. Under warm moist conditions, the spores in *Actinovate* germinate and form mycelia which attaches themselves to the roots of the plants. Reproduction runs rampant. Before long, the complete root system is covered with protective mycelia. The mycelia converts minerals and nutrients into food for the plant. It also protects the plant from harmful disease causing pathogens.

Actinovate comes in a glandular form which can be used as a top dressing. One pound would treat 1000-2500 sq. feet of lawn. To find a source for any of the products mentioned, just type in the name in your favorite search engine on the internet.

James A. Eagle

Chapter Eight

Propagation of Plants

Miracles of Plant Life. *In Psalm 19:1, David declares that the Heavens declare the glory of God, and the firmament sheweth His handiwork.* To me, the plants of the earth do the same thing.

We think of a plant as starting from a seed, which is true, but there is so much more in this miracle of plant growth and production. The seed must have the proper conditions before it will germinate and bring forth a new plant. Regardless how small the seed, it will contain the food and energy to give it a start when life bursts forth from it.

If my memory serves me right, I think it was in the 1940's that some seed of wheat was discovered in one of the pyramids of Egypt. It was believed to have been there for thousands of years, but when it was planted and given the proper moisture, it germinated and brought forth wheat plants.

Some seeds can maintain their viability for many years when low humidity and cool temperatures are provided, but when proper moisture and warmth are provided for growth, then new life comes forth. Some weed seeds, and other seeds, will lay dormant for years before germinating because they are buried too deep. The seed waits for the right moment or proper depth to occur before it starts breaking the outer shell and germinating. Have you ever noticed that just pulling weeds up from the soil will finally reduce the number of weeds that will germinate, but as soon as you plow or till the soil, a whole new crop of weeds occur? The seed was raised to the proper depth and germination took place. Even at the right depth and correct amount of moisture and temperature, some seeds may take several years before germinating.

An example is the Southern Magnolia. The seed must go through what is referred to as a *stratification process*. This is when the seed is planted and goes through the winter with the temperature lowering, then warming, lowering, and warming over and over again in order to break the hard seed covering. Sometimes they will germinate in one year, other times it may take several years before they germinate. Many of the woody plants require this stratification process before they will germinate. Many seed that require stratification can be stratified by birds or animals eating the fruit, with the seed in. Then when they deposit the seed it will germinate. The radish seed is one that can break its covering and germinate in a few days without stratification.

When the seed germinates, the first thing that takes place is that it sends down the roots, regardless of the position the seed is planted. The root then must be able to take up moisture and food so the plant can be nourished in order for it to grow and mature and bring forth more after its kind.

Have you ever even considered what must take place for this to happen? The decaying vegetable waste in the soil is providing microorganisms to break this materiel down whereby it can make the nutrients available to the plant. Healthy soil is occupied by millions of microorganisms that are necessary for healthy plant life. The plant is then able to take the moisture and nutrients from the soil which is necessary for its growth to bring forth more after its kind.

For the plant to be able to mature, bloom, and bring forth more seed, it must be pollinated. Some plants have been created to be self-pollinating. Others must have some method of getting pollen from another plant before it will produce seed. Here, God has provided many methods to accomplish this. Many are pollinated by many different kinds of insects. There are birds that

James A. Eagle

also help pollinate some flowers, such as hummingbirds. Other plants are pollinated by the wind carrying pollen, sometimes for miles until it reaches a receptive female flower.

Even the distribution of new seed varies from one type of plant to another. The dandelion has light, cottony material that provides the necessary buoyancy to move through the air until it finds a home to start another plant. The seed of the pine tree has winged seed hulls that allow it to float through the air for hundreds of feet before resting to start a new pine tree. Some seed use methods of attaching themselves to animals which can be transported for long distances before the seed is removed and then it establishes a new home for it to grow in.

The corn plant is one that amazes me. When the tassels on the corn just start to burst out at the top of the stalk is when you will find a slightly raised protrusion on the stalk. This is an ear. There may be two or more of these. The silk will not protrude out until the tassel at the top starts blooming and producing pollen. Each silk on that ear must be pollinated or that grain of corn will not mature. Have you seen a cob of corn where some grains didn't mature?

Man does not have the knowledge to put together everything necessary to carry on the species of plants we are blessed with. Only God, the Creator, can do this.

Propagation From Seed: Propagation of plants from seed can be easy when you know the basic needs for success. We can get into a rut sometimes in planting seed and assume they will germinate naturally, but different seeds require different techniques for success sometimes.

Most of our vegetables such as corn, beans, peas, etc. can be successfully planted by most, but there are several things needed for success. Some are: time of planting, depth to plant seed, and proper soil preparation. The smaller the seed, the finer the soil must be to insure maximum germination. A good method of determining the depth is to plant three to four times the diameter of the seed. Large seeds are planted deeper than small seeds. For example, a bean that is one-fourth of an inch in diameter is planted approximately one inch deep. Fine seed such as petunias are barely covered with very fine soil. Some seeds need light to germinate and must be planted on top of the soil, and just pressed down. The soil must be kept moist until they germinate. If planted early and there is another cold spell, the seed can lie in the ground and rot before germination. It depends on the type of seed. We are prone to blame the seed, when, in fact, it was the weather or our failure to abide by proper practices that were needed for that plant.

Most of us buy our bedding plants instead of starting the seed ourselves. This can be because we do not have the facilities to start them inside while it is still cold. We want them out as soon as it gets warm. Take a look at the garden shops as soon as we have a warm day of seventy to eighty degrees. People get the gardening fever and can't wait to get them set out. Beware! We may have another frost and it could destroy tender plants. If we have the patience to wait until it gets warmer, many of the plants can be started outdoors and outperform plants you purchased. I have started seed outside, where I wanted them to grow and they outperformed purchased plants that were set out the same time. You will also have the joy and pleasure of selecting the variety you wish to plant when you start your own plants from seed.

If you are planting the seed in the location where you want them to grow, prepare the soil with plenty of organic matter and well-rotted manure. If this is not available, use sifted peatmoss to enhance the soil to hold moisture. If you are not adding manure or organic matter, then apply an application of organic amendments, such as fish meal, cottonseed meal, or alfalfa meal. Rock phosphate or bone meal should be added for the phosphate, which promotes fruiting or flowering. Add green sand for the potassium. Wood ashes can be used in place of the greensand if it is available, but do not overuse the ashes.

If the seeds are very small, you should level the surface of the soil and slightly pack it with a board, or by hand. Cover fine seed with very fine soil, and only barely cover them. Water lightly daily until they germinate, and let God do the rest.

James A. Eagle

Seed can also be started in pots or trays. Make sure there are drain holes in the bottom for proper drainage. If you want a sterile soiless mixture, then milled peat-moss mixed with fine perlite and vermiculite is good. If using garden soil or some of the so-called potting soils sold in garden shops, then make sure it has been sterilized before planting. Soil-borne bacteria can cause dampening off of the young, tender plants. When a young, tender plant weakens at the soil line and falls over, then you have experienced this disease. Many garden shops today carry small bags of peat moss with perlite and other substances just for starting seed,

You can sterilize your soil in your oven or microwave. This will kill bacteria and weed seed. Let the soil cool before planting. *Warning:* This will smell-up your oven for a while. You can leave the oven open to air out. I mix cornmeal with the soil to kill fungal diseases, or soak the soil with hydrogen peroxide and water. This will not kill weed seed, but kills most diseases.

Do you ever find yourself looking at a seed catalog and wishing you could have some of the beautiful and outstanding varieties they picture? Well! You can have all of these outstanding varieties when you start your own seed. Some flowers that you may try are Achillea, Aster, Astilbe, Begonia, Coreopsis, Daylily, Dahlia, Geranium, and many more, and by starting them from seed. I wanted to whet your appetite for the more unusual types. Most seed packets have instructions for each specific variety. *Parks Seed* lists the germination time, culture requirements, and bloom season on the index page of the catalog. The catalog is free.

You can really whet your appetite for fresh vegetables by scanning thorough the catalog of *Johnny's Selected Seed. Johnny's* is a family-owned company. When they first started out the catalog was in black and white. Today it is a masterpiece of color. For example observe the many varieties of lettuce. They have lettuce tinged with red, purple and other colors. The same holds true for string beans. You can observe the actual colors of the bean from purple, yellow and different shades of green. This applies for other seed they offer.

Very small seed started in pots or trays should be watered from the bottom. To accomplish this, use a larger tray and put water in the tray until it comes up about half way of the pots you are watering. Let it sit in the container of water until the top of the mixture is moist, then remove. It may take a number of hours, or a day or more to completely soak the soil to the top..

We start most of our seed directly in the garden. This way there is no transplant shock to the plant.

You may want to save seed from your own vegetables and flowers. I'll try to give you the very basic of the different flower structures. This basic knowledge can aid you in producing seed that are true to variety.

(Deleted paragraph because it was a repeat.)

Some plants carry both male and female organs, and many of them are within the same flower. The male part of the flower is called the *stamen*. It consists of two parts: the filaments and the anther. The filament is the small stem which supports the pollen bearing anther. Some flowers have two or more anthers.

The female portion of the flower is called the pistil, and consists of three parts; the stigma is the portion which is receptive to pollen. It can vary in size and shape, according to the plant you are working with. The stigma of the tomato flower is nothing more than the tip of the style. Compare this with the flower of the daylily. The daylily has a long style with the large stigma sitting on top. Another magnificent difference is the style and stigma of the corn plant, which is the corn silk. A single strand of corn silk can receive pollen along its entire length. The other portion of the female pistol is the ovary. When a single grain of pollen touches a receptive stigma, the pollen grain begins to form a pollen tube which grows down through the style to the ovary, where it fertilizes ovules within the ovary. The ovary then develops into the fruit or pod which bears the seed.

Some plants have separate female and male flowers. An example would be the squash. Insects are required to pollinate the flowers, carrying pollen from the male flower to the female flower.

There are other plants that produce male flowers or female flowers only. Spinach has plants with only male flowers and producing pollen only, and female plants which produce seed only. Again insects are needed to pollinate the flowers.

Some of the flowers that produce both male and female parts, still need insects to pollinate. I am going to use the daylily here because the flower is large and you can observe the male and female parts more easily. The stigma in the daylily is elevated high above the pollen producing anthers. The pollen will fall down into the flower, but never reaching up to the stigma. Unless an insect gets pollen on itself while inside the flower, then brushes the stigma on leaving the flower, it will not get pollinated, unless it is hand pollinated.

I am giving these references as if everything is pollinated in accordance with the Divine plan of creation. Man enters the picture and pollinates the flowers by hand in many cases today to overcome the difficulty of getting variety pure seed or to produce a hybrid.

At this point, let us describe what is considered a hybrid seed. If the flower of a standard variety is crossed with the flower of another standard variety, the seed of that cross would be what is called an F1 hybrid. This cross would have to be accomplished between these two standard varieties each time this hybrid is produced. Breeders may take two varieties that is not considered quality fruit, but they can have certain qualities which they wish to produce to make a better fruit or flower, so these are crossed. Suppose you had a delicious tasting tomato, but it had poor saving qualities when picked. You have another tomato that has excellent saving qualities, but poor taste; by crossing you may be able to obtain the good qualities of both.

If seed from a hybrid variety is planted, you may get many different-looking flowers or different-tasting fruit. Some may be excellent, but most would be inferior to the first year hybrid. Different varieties can be stabilized by selecting seed from the plant you desire most, and replanting. It could take eight to fifteen years to stabilize a variety. Once it is stabilized, which means producing the same type of fruit each year, it is referred to as a standard variety. It requires much work and effort to standardize the qualities of a variety. This type of work is beyond my scope and time span today.

Asexual Reproduction of Plants: Most plants will reproduce themselves in nature by seed, but propagation by seed will give you many differences from the mother plant. In most cases, these differences will be inferior to the mother plant.

Evolutionists will tell you that this is due to evolution. Evolution is evolving from a simple form to a higher form. Every time a seed comes up, it has lost some of its DNA, which makes the difference. To evolve it would have to gain DNA. This just doesn't happen.

To insure your ability to obtain the same qualities of the mother plant, you must produce this plant by asexual reproduction. There are many forms of asexual reproduction. The most common is by rooting cuttings, but it can be done by grafting, budding, layering, and division.

When you asexually reproduce a plant, it will have the characteristics of the mother plant. No DNA is lost. The most common methods of asexually reproducing plants by the layman are stem cuttings. Of course, the grafting and budding methods are desirable in many cases. Asexual reproduction is a very extensive subject to cover, so the very basic methods will be covered only. This book is not for the professional nurseryman, but the methods discussed here will be for the average homeowner that wishes to increase a tree or shrub that they have, or maybe obtain a cutting from a friend or neighbor. You may wish, during the summer, you had some plants of a tomato to set out for late tomatoes. You have a variety growing in your garden which you like. What do you do? The answer is below.

The easiest method for the layman is by using cuttings. The types of cuttings and the time of year you take the cuttings depend on the type of plant you wish to reproduce. Some of the

James A. Eagle

different kinds of cuttings are stem cuttings, leaf cuttings, and root cuttings.

There are four different kinds of stem cuttings. They are hardwood, semi-hardwood, softwood, and herbaceous.

Hardwood Cuttings: The average homeowner does not have the facilities for the propagation of many plants, especially hardwood evergreen cuttings, so we will cover deciduous hardwood cuttings only.

Some of the shrubs, trees, or vines that can be rooted by hardwood cuttings are: blackberry, blueberry, figs, dogwood, grapes, trumpet vines, Ben Franklin tree, and the list goes on. There are many others, so if you wish to try any deciduous shrub or tree you have, you only have your time and labor to lose. Experimentation is the way to discover answers when you cannot find them anywhere else.

To clarify some things from the beginning, there may be words or terms used you may not understand. Go to Addendum I for explanations.

Take stem cuttings from deciduous plants when they are completely dormant, that is when all their leaves have fallen. It depends on where you live when this happens. It could be September, October, November, and even December in Zone Nine and Ten. Cut the last six to eight inches of the stem, making sure you have two or more nodes. Make your cut right below a node with a sharp knife, leaving a smooth cut. You can also take a whole limb and cut it in six to eight inches long pieces, as long as the butt does not exceed three-fourths of an inch in diameter. Dip the butt in a rooting hormone, Tie all cuttings in a bundle and label with a marker that will not fade or smear when it gets wet, with the name on the label. Bury these in a container that has holes where excess water can drain, and cover the cuttings with sand, or a mixture of sand and peat moss. Lay the cuttings on their side. Leave them in storage this way for a period of three to four months. The storage area should be in an area that is cool but not freezing. The ideal temperature is between forty-five and sixty degrees. This can be an area under your home if it is enclosed, a basement, or a cool room or greenhouse. The sand or mixture of sand and peat moss should be kept moist for the next three months.

Another method of storage for your cuttings is a plastic garbage can with a lid. Drill one or two holes in the bottom to allow drainage. Put a layer of sand or soil and a layer of cuttings, then repeat as often as necessary. Leave at least one foot empty from the top of the can. Bury this can in the ground up to about four inches of the top. Pack leaves, straw, or other dry mulch in the top of the can, and put on the lid. Mulch over the top of the can to keep the inside warm during extreme cold periods. You can remove the cutting in the spring and line them out in a shady area, or put in pots. By this time they will have roots, or will be calloused and ready to sprout roots. If you got them mixed and don't know which was the butt, when you take them out you will be able to tell. The calloused or rooted end will be the butt. If any cuttings have not calloused or rooted, then discard them. Keep the soil moist until new growth has started and roots can be seen around the edge of the pot when removing from the pot. At this stage, you may plant your successes in their permanent location or you may line them out instead. Lining out is digging a trench and placing the cuttings in the trench at an angle, and covering them with several inches of soil. You can plant them in their permanent location the following fall. *(Lining out is an old term used by old farmers and nurserymen.)*

Semi-Hardwood Cuttings & Tender Cuttings: The procedures for rooting softwood and semi-hardwood cutting are the same, except when you take the cuttings. Some species of plants root better from tender cuttings than from semi-hardwood or hardwood cuttings. Sometimes it may be even among the different varieties. Roses are one. Some roses root very easy, and other do not. Most of the roses that can be purchased on their own rootstock root easy. Here is where you experiment.

James A. Eagle

Take softwood cuttings in the late spring or early summer. When the plant you wish to root from has new growth about four inches long or longer, then take the tip cuttings and remove where the new growth started.

Semi-hardwood cuttings are taken in the summer after the new growth has started hardening. Some plants root better when taken in summer and late summer.

The system explained here is for the homeowners that want a few plants of their own. It may be cuttings you received from a friend, or from a plant you have, but wish to have more of. The commercial growers use elaborate systems that are too expensive for the average homeowner.

Here is a mixture that works well. It can be increased according to the amount of plants you are rooting.:

- 1 gallon of peat moss
- 1 gallon of sand
- 1 quart of perlite
- 1 cup of cornmeal
- ½ cup of kelp meal

The cornmeal is to prevent fungal diseases and provide nutrients, and the kelp meal will stimulate root growth and provide nutrients. Using small containers with holes, fill with the rooting mix. Wet the mix thoroughly. Dip butts of cuttings into a rooting hormone about one inch. Insert into the pots about one and a half inches deep. Place the containers in a gallon Zip-Lock bag, or if you have a large amount, you can insert them in a clear garbage bag. They must be able to get light. Place a few holes in the bag to provide some air circulation. If you have your potting mix wet enough, you should see condensation inside the bag within twenty four hours. If not, then wet the mix more. When you fail to see any condensation inside the bag, open the bag and wet the mix some more.

It depends on what you are rooting, but many plants will have started rooting within weeks, some take several months.

I promised to explain how to reproduce that annual, the tomato. Take a tip-cutting and treat it as you would the above cuttings. They root within seven to ten days. You might try other annuals as well.

The above procedures are given whereby the novice can have some success of reproducing plants. There are other ways more complex and expensive. If you wish more information I would advise you contact your local Extension Service, or purchase books to expand your knowledge.

Layering: This is one of the easies methods to root. Grapes are especially easy using this method. If the plant is low growing plant where you can bend a limb to reach the ground, then try layering, using this method: About six inches from the tip of the limb, remove the bark, leaving a small strip where some sap can flow to the tip end. Bury the limb at the place you removed the bark in about two or three inches of soil. Leave the rest to God. Do this in the spring or early winter. Within six months you should have a new plant. Cut it loose from the mother plant and plant it where you wish it to grow, or it can be potted in a pot for another year or two before setting out in its new location.

There is one other type of layering. It is what is referred to as *air layering.* You can take the tip end of a limb and prepare it as you did the layering above. But here, you wrap it with wet peat moss and wrap it with clear plastic, so as to see when roots are formed. Tie both ends of the wrap. If the peat moss shows signs of drying out, open it at the top and wet it again. You will be able to see the roots when it has rooted. When it is rooted, cut below the rooted area and either pot it or set out in its permanent location.

This is where I want to tell about an experience I had while attending a special course for the local nurserymen on propagation, given by the Extension Service and the University of Florida. One nurseryman wanted to know if the Southern Magnolia could be successfully rooted from cuttings. One of our local Extension Agents stood to answer. He said the Southern

Magnolia was very hard to root, and it would be better to propagate by seed, which takes one to two years. I guess he saw the look on my face, and he kept looking at me. Finally he said, "Mr. Eagle, you have been rooting them, haven't you?" Of course my answer was yes. At that point, about everyone one wanted to know how I did it. The main method I used was air layering as described above. I have also rooted them as a semi-hardwood cutting given above. This is why I say don't take for granted everything you hear or read by the university educated for the absolute truth. Experiment.

Division: There are many plants that can be increased by division. Some can be separated by pulling them apart. For others, it will be necessary to cut them with a sharp knife. By separating by pulling them apart, they may break off without any roots, so I like to use a knife, in most cases

Some of the plants you can divide are: Daylilies, hostas, peace lilies, ferns, irises, and many more. If the plant keeps increasing with new stolons, then it probably can be divided. Any plant that puts up a new growth on its side, for example the daylily, or a plant from a stolen, such as a bearded Iris, can be divided after the plant forms some roots.

Chapter Nine

Questions and Answers

While writing gardening columns for the local newspaper, many questions were received in writing and over the telephone. And yet today, almost ten years later, I receive calls or visits by individuals. I also received a complaint from a schoolteacher, who went directly to the editor, when I referred to the tomato as a vegetable. She stated that she had been teaching her pupils that the tomato was a fruit. The editor wanted me to give a written apology to the teacher. I told him I would write an article on the subject. Here is the article:

What is a Fruit: Do you know the true definition of what a fruit is? The botanist definition of a fruit is the fertilized ovary of the flower that has matured to form a seed-bearing container. In other words, it is the ripened ovary of the flower.

My dictionary has three botanical definitions. The first one describes it as any plant product, as grain, flax, vegetable, etc. The second definition describes it as a sweet and edible plant structure, consisting of a fruit (see Addendum I) or false fruit of a flowering plant, usually eaten raw or as a dessert. Many true fruits that are not sweet, such as tomatoes, beans, peppers, etc. are popularly called *vegetables*. The third definition is the mature ovary of a flowering plant, together with its contents, and any closely connected parts, such as the whole peach, pea pods, cucumber, etc.

Why am I getting scientific in what a true fruit is? I was chastised on my reference to the tomato as a vegetable by a schoolteacher for calling the tomato a vegetable. Truthfully, there is a lot of fruit that we refer to as vegetables, such as corn, beans, cucumbers, squash, pumpkins, etc. Now she can teach her students that the ripened ovary of a plant, along with all its parts, is the fruit of the plant.

Usually we refer to vegetables as any herbaceous plant that is eaten raw or cooked, but not as a dessert. It can be any part of the plant, such as the fruit, leaves, roots, or even the flowers. Yes, the tomato is a vegetative fruit.

Some may say that they do not eat the flowers of plants. Do you mean that there is no flower or flower bud that you eat? If you have ever eaten cauliflower or broccoli, then you have eaten flower buds. There are many flowers that the flowering part of the plant is delicious. Two that I have had the pleasure of partaking of are the daylily and the nasturtium. They are delicious in salads, soups, and stir-fry dishes.

The leaves and roots of plants are some of the most delicious and nutritious of all the vegetables. We eat the leaves of many vegetables, such as collards, turnips, mustard, kale, beets, etc. Some we eat both the leaves and the roots, such as the beet and turnip. There are others that only the roots are eaten, such as carrots and radishes. Take the kohlrabi: we can eat the leaves and the bulb that grow above the ground. It resembles a turnip in taste, only it is more delicious. The leaves taste more like the collard or kale.

Let us reevaluate as to what a fruit really is to the botanist. If the seed or seeds of a plant with all the parts that enclose the seeds, then it is a fruit. An ear of corn with the husk still on is the fruit, as is the bean pod that we eat and the milkweed pod that we all have seen. The pod of seed of the daylily plant, the pecan nut, and, yes, the red tomato, is a fruit. Whether we eat it as a vegetable, or as a fruit, it is a fruit in the eyes of the botanist.

James A. Eagle

We laymen think of fruit as those that have a sweet fleshly covering over their seed, such as peaches, plums, cherries, oranges, grapes. etc. The tomato is not sweet, and is eaten as a vegetable, so we laymen refer to it as a vegetable.

Through questions and complaints we all can learn. That is why I enjoy receiving mail with questions. You make me go back to reference books many times to confirm my theory of a situation, and in doing this, I learn even more. Instead of complaining to the editor of the newspaper, complain to me. We will learn the answer together.

Another incident was when two senior citizens came to my home. The gentleman came to the door and introduced himself and then informed me that he had a lady in the car that had a question for me. I looked out toward the car and told her to come on in. She came to the door and opened her hand which contained the seed pod of an amaryllis plant, and she asked, "What can I do with this?"

Answer: "Plant them," I replied, with a grin. I invited the couple in. After they were settled in our home, I told her that it contained the seed of the amaryllis plant. I opened it enough to remove one seed and showed her the black, flat thing that was shaped like a small wing, with a small bump in it, which was the seed. I told her to plant all the seed, the wing and all. There is no need to try to remove the seed from the wing covering. Use a sterile peat mixture and barely cover the seed. I then took them out to my propagating place and showed her amaryllis seed I had planted and had just come up. I wanted them to see what the new emerging seedlings looked like.

If any of you have bought these large amaryllis bulbs and forced them in your home, take the pollen from one and implant on the stigma of another flower. This way you will get a cross and wait to see what colors or combination of colors you will get. This can be done with many other flowers as well, especially your daylilies. Some of the new hybrid amaryllis are sterile and will not produce seed.

Here are many other questions received. I have answered only those that I considered worthy or may be of interest to others. It is impossible to cover everything that may be of interest in one book. The answers to questions will cover many items not covered in other Chapters which are of interest to someone. It may be specific culture methods on some particular plant, or pruning of a specific plant, or specific methods of insect control. Whatever it is, someone can profit by the answers here in this chapter.

Question: I purchased cabbage seed and on the packet it stated that it took eighty-five days to maturity, but mine took about one-hundred and thirty days before the heads were large enough to eat. Why would mine take so much longer?

Answer: Seed companies give the time from when you set out the plant to the time of maturity. Some companies will give this information, others do not. You will find the same is true for some other vegetable plants. They were not giving the time from planting the seed to production of the fruit.

Question: I have noticed that you seem to always recommend such things as baking soda, cornmeal, and hydrogen peroxide for disease control. Are there others that are safe?

Answer: Yes! I use to use sulfur and copper sprays on many plants for diseases, especially apples, peaches, and pear trees. You can obtain these products at most garden centers. There is a warning. If you spray during moist, warm weather, it can damage the leaves on the plant. It will take the form of reddish or brownish spots, and sometimes the tree may shed the damaged leaves. There are many commercial sprays today put out by different companies that contain safe products, such as sodium bicarbonate and potassium bicarbonate. Why not just use the baking soda out of your cupboard? It is much cheaper. There are other commercial and safe pesticides and fungicides that are safe containing neem and pyrethrum.

Question: I grow African violets in my home, but this past year they have quit blooming. I had a friend tell me it might be propane gas causing this. We did have a propane gas heater installed in our fireplace over a year ago. Could this be the cause?

Answer: Yes, it certainly can! The burning of manufactured gas will *not* harm the plant, but unburned gas will. Have your heater tested for leaks. Insufficient light can also be at fault. You should have them at a well lighted window or provide artificial light for them.

Question: It seems that all the eggplants I grow are bitter. What causes this?

Answer: There are several things that can cause bitterness in eggplants. If the plant undergoes stress, such as dry weather, it can cause bitterness. There are varieties that are less prone to be bitter than others. See what the seed catalogs have to say about the eggplant seed you purchase. Always pick the eggplant while it is still bright and glossy. Do not leave them on the plant until they lose their gloss. Do not try to grow it the size of the ones you see in grocery stores. These are grown to full maturity and are prone to be bitter. If you buy your eggplants, then select the ones that have firm flesh and have the bright glossy look. If it is soft and has lost its gloss, then it will most likely be bitter.

Question: Last spring something ate just about all my potatoes before they came up, or shortly after. What do you think did this, and what can I do to prevent it?

Answer: If you had holes in the soil, then it was most likely voles or mice. Voles are similar to mice, except most are larger. They have a blocky body and short tail compared to the house mouse. They are more similar to the field mouse.

Recently there was an article in a newsletter I take, where tests were conducted using oyster shells to repel the voles and mice. If you are planting potatoes or bulbs of any kind, then line the hole with oyster shells and plant your potato or bulb in it. Be sure it is surrounded by a thin layer of the oyster shells. The oyster shells will also provide calcium for the plants as they break down over the years. Some tests were conducted where oyster shells were tilled into the soil. Both of these tests kept mice and voles from the potatoes and bulbs. It appears that they do not like to travel in soils that have anything with sharp edges in it. Egg shells crushed should do the same. You must add enough oyster or egg shells to prevent their travel through the soil.

You were not the only one to have this problem. I encountered it in my potatoes. I finally resorted to using a rat poison, which I object to, but I was desperate. I placed one or two round balls of poison in every hole I found. I used a poison, which was made in round balls about one-half inch in diameter. They seem to have reduced the population in the area where they were used.

Question: I have been told that citrus fruit would kill insects. Is this true?

Answer: The rinds and seed of citrus contain a substance called limonids. Tests conducted in the early 1980's showed that it would repel several types of insects. There were some tests conducted where insects were confined in a container where the rinds had been placed. Within twenty-four hours the insects were dead, so I guess there is truth in what you have been told. To prepare a spray, grind or process the rinds and seed in a processor or blender and pour warm water over the mixture and let set for twenty-four hours; strain and spray. You should dilute the mixture according to the amount of rinds you use. You should experiment to find the right mixture.

James A. Eagle

Question: Is there an easy method of cracking black walnuts?

Answer: According to the Northern Nut Growers Association, they recommend the following method to make it easier to crack black walnuts: Lay the walnuts out on canvas or heavy plastic and run over them with your car until the outer husks are removed. Put the walnuts in a container and pour boiling water over them and let soak for two hours. Drain and let set overnight before cracking. After performing this process they should crack much easier.

Question: I have a peach tree that the bloom or fruit of gets killed just about every year. Is there anything that can be done to prevent this?

Answer: You must have a variety of peach that does not require very many hours of cold below forty-five degrees to set bloom. I find that it is best to have peach trees that require 650 or more hours to set bloom in our area. (Zone Eight). If this is your trouble, then there is one method you can use to delay blooming. As soon as the buds start to swell or whenever we have several days of night temperatures above forty-five degrees, then start laying blocks of ice around the base of the tree. Freezing water in a milk cartoon will provide you with enough ice for several times. One half-gallon milk carton of ice will be sufficient for four days. This should be done every four days as long as it remains warm. If you have the trees mulched, pull the mulch back and place ice under the mulch. The mulch will help to hold the cold in around the root.

Before buying any fruit tree of any kind be sure the tree is suitable for the Temperature Zone you live in.

Question: I have heard that sprouting seed for eating is healthier than the vegetable. Is this true?

Answer: Yes! If you wish to have fresh vegetables that will grow the year round, rival meat in nutritional value, mature in three to five days or longer, requires neither soil or sunshine, and rivals citrus in vitamin C, then sprouting is the answer. Seed is loaded with nutrients to feed the plant until it is able to obtain nourishment from the roots, so when you sprout the seed you are feeding on the highest form of nutrients. You can have fresh, vitamin-rich vegetables in three to five days by sprouting some seed. Most of us are familiar with the alfalfa and mung bean sprouts you will find in many of the salad bars today, but there are many more that can be sprouted. Besides the alfalfa and mung beans, you can sprout radish, onion, buckwheat, wheat, rye, blackeye peas, lima beans, lentils, chickpeas, soybeans, sunflower, and all the beans. There are others, but be sure that by sprouting, it doesn't turn them into a poisonous dinner. An example would be sprouting potato or tomato seed. They belong to the nightshade family, and sprouting them will produce sprouts that are toxic. Make sure the seed you use has not been treated with fungicides or dyes. It is best to purchase seed that is sold especially for sprouting. Seed sold in the grocery stores, such as beans and peas, are also good provided they are still viable and will sprout. Many seed catalogs have seed especially for sprouting. *Be sure the seeds haven't been treated.*

It does not take any special equipment. You can probably start with items you already have in your home. If you have a quart canning jar or a used mayo jar, it will suffice. With small seed, such as alfalfa and radish, use about two level tablespoons of seed for the quart jar. Use about one-fourth cup of the medium seed such as grains and lentils, and one-half a cup of the larger seed such as beans. Put seed in the jar and cover with room temperature water and let soak overnight. In the morning, drain the water off and rinse the seed. To accomplish this, cover the mouth of the jar with cheese-cloth or nylon netting, and screw the open jar lid on the jar. You will be able to drain the water off the seed without losing any seed. The jar should be placed in a dark area for several days, with the room temperature about

James A. Eagle

seventy to seventy-five degrees. Lower temperatures will delay sprouting, and higher temperatures will promote mold. Tip the jar with the mouth down, where the seed can continue to drain. The mouth of the jar can be placed into a bowl and the bottom end propped up. Run room-temperature water over the seed at lease twice every day. It is even better to do this procedure three times each day. Drain the water off each time and place the jar in the drain position. Within a couple of days, you will begin to see the seed starting to sprout.

The rinsing process is necessary to prevent fungus from growing on the sprouts. Never eat any sprouts that show signs of mold. It could be toxic.

You will find that the jar will be filled with sprouted seed in four to five days in most cases. Some will require a longer time to sprout, depending on the type of seed. At this point, rinse the sprouts again and drain. Place them near a window for plenty of light for another day or two. This will give the seed a chance to form leaves and turn green, providing you with healthful chlorophyll. At this stage they can be placed in a plastic Zip-Lock bag and placed in the refrigerator.

Sprouts can be used in many ways. I like the alfalfa and radish sprouts for an addition to a sandwich, instead of lettuce. Use them in fresh salads, and all sprouts can be used in many recipes in preparing other dishes. The grains are especially excellent in adding them to the dough mix of delicious yeast breads.

Sprouts can also be dried to make a sprout powder for thickening soups and gravies, or added to the top of casseroles. They can be dried in an oven set at the lowest temperature, or using a dehydrator. After they are dry, blend them in a blender until you have a fine powder.

There is no other food that you can eat that adds more nutrients to your diet than sprouts. When the seed sprouts a magnification of energy takes place bursting forth with several times more vitamins and minerals than the food we harvest later. Sprouts can be your food supplement for the day.

Here is a recipe for breakfast or a quick lunch or supper. Beat six eggs together with two chopped green onions, two table-spoons of chopped fresh dill or one teaspoon dry dill, with salt and pepper to taste. With a wire whip, stir in one-fourth of cup milk. Put this into a no-stick pan, and when it begins to set, add one-half of a cup sprouts and one chopped tomato. Fold the omelet over the sprouts and tomato. Cover with a lid until top is set. This will serve four hungry people, especially when served with grits.

Question: Just about the time my squash plants start bearing, they start dying. I have seen a deposit at the base of the plant that looked like some insect dung. What can I do to control this?

Answer: You probably have the squash vine borers. They will attack squash, pumpkins, and cucumbers. The sawdust-like excrements you saw at the base of the plant was just what you believed it to be. If they have already entered the plant, about the only control at this point is to slit the vine open, cut lengthwise of the steam, and remove the borer and kill it. Another treatment I have used with success was to inject a solution of Bacillus Thuringiensis, better know as Bt. This bacteria will attack only the larvae of insects such as cabbage worms, corn earworms, tomato worms, and many more. It is safe to use around wild-life or other animals, including yourself. After applying it, you can eat the fruit without washing and without harm. I used a syringe to inject the solution into the base of the stem. Where it was used, I never had any trouble. Bt comes under several trade names. Two of the most popular are *Dipel* and *Thuricide*.

The squash vine borer is the larva of a moth that lays her eggs at the base of the plant. After the eggs hatch, the larvae will bore into the vine of the plant. One method to keep the moth away is by placing a layer of aluminum foil around the base of the plant. The reflection will cause the moth to pass over your plants to seek others.

James A. Eagle

The easiest way to prevent squash vine borers is to smear a small amount of mentholated petroleum jelly at the base of the vine. It will keep the moth from laying her eggs there. This will also deter many other types of moths from plants.

Question: My irises have not bloomed the last two years, what have I been doing wrong?

Answer: When irises become crowded, they will stop blooming. It could be overcrowding or lack of nutrients. The best time to dig and separate the irises is in the fall. If you move them to another location, or even put them back in the same area, be sure and prepare a good, fertile bed for them. Apply several inches of compost and approximately five pounds of bone meal to each one-hundred square feet of garden space. When you reset them, space them approximately two feet apart and leave the top of the rhizome exposed to the air. If you plant them too deep, it will inhibit bloom. Be sure to water regularly during dry spells.

Question: This year I started my own tomato plants, but they are skinny and they lean toward the window. How can I prevent this?

Answer: Your plants are not getting enough light. The cells in the stem on the side away from the window will elongate turning the plant toward the window. Other plants will do the same thing, but it can be prevented by rotating the container each day. When the temperature reaches fifty-five or more outside during the day, take the plants outside in the sun for a period of two hours or more each day. After a week, or more, you should be able to extend the time outside to four or more hours. Keep extending the time until the plants are hardened off and ready to plant in your garden. Plant the tomato plant into the ground three inches or more, stripping the bottom leaves allowing more of the stem to be covered by soil. It will grow new roots all along the stem giving it more roots to absorb the nutrients and water.

Question: Is it safe to use mushroom compost on my garden?

Answer: I have answered this question in the past with a positive answer, because I used it all the time while I was in Florida. Since then, I had the opportunity to see the test results conducted by an independent laboratory. The results of the test were amazing! The compost contained numerous pesticides and fungicides. Since horse manure is used in the compost the mushrooms are grown in, and also straw, then, no doubt, many of these pesticides and fungicides come from the use of them around the horse stables and in the fields where the wheat is grown. The mushroom growers are also heavy users of the fungicides. Since I am trying to grow everything organically, I cannot recommend it as the best source of compost any longer. The contents will vary from different mushroom farms.

While working for the state of Florida as a Grounds Superintendent, we had a mushroom farm nearby operated by Purina Mills. I began wondering what they did with all that spent mushroom compost. I knew that it was used once and then disposed of. One day, I went out to the farm in my pickup and stopped at the reception office. I asked the attendant what they did with the compost. He laughed and said, "We give it to anyone who wants it, and we load it." He gave me directions to where it was. I went to where it was located and there was an individual on a tractor with front loader carrying compost out to an area where they had rows of compost stored. Some appeared as though they had been there for years. He wanted to know if I wanted a load, and I followed him to an old pile while he loaded my pickup with one big scoop. That was just the beginning. I started telling others and the first thing I knew they started charging $10.00 for a pickup load. Within a couple of years they were bagging it and selling it by the bag.

I believe that first compost I hauled was free of chemicals, because it had probably been leaching them out for years. When you purchase it today, it is fresh from growing of the mushrooms.

James A. Eagle

Question: How can I get rid of the snakes and lizards in my garden?

Answer: I hope you are kidding me. They are your friends. If there was not a lot of food for them, they would not stay. Snakes will eat rats, mice, voles, and many other critters in you garden, They also eat large insects such as grass hoppers and crickets. Let them live; you will have a better garden for it.

Spiders are critters that most of us just can't stand. There are only two spiders in our area that are poisonous, and they are the black widow and the brown recluse. Spiders destroy more insects than most people realize. Some build webs to snare their prey, others hide and prance on their prey. After they capture it, they suck its life juices from its body, but they are doing this to some of your enemies. They eat beneficial insects as well. It is reported that many kinds of spiders hide in the mulch we put around our plants. They hide and attack many of the insects that are eating our garden. Some studies claim that some spiders could destroy hundreds of insects each day.

Many of us recoil from a lizard. Why? Is it because of the way it looks? When you see one scooting along in your garden, be thankful. It is searching out your enemies. The little chameleon that moves around on your hedges changing color to suit its environment is looking for those white flies, aphids, and even larger insects. It can destroy hundreds each day. We are constantly finding the eggs of the chameleon in our garden tubs when we stir up the soil getting ready to plant in the tub. We just bury the egg again and let it hatch.

We just can't stand the wasps that build their nests under the eaves of the house, in our tool shed, even on and under the tiller or mower we use regularly. We go around destroying their nests every chance we get. They are one of your best friends. When they sting you, it is because you interfered with their home, or they thought you were a threat to it. Wouldn't you do the same thing if you had a stinger? The U.S. Department of Agriculture lists more than 700 different species of wasps that benefit us.

Aren't we lucky? When I encounter a wasp nest now, I try to avoid an encounter with them. They are eating our enemies, or feeding them to their young. Let them live whenever possible.

If anyone has a reason to hate the wasps, then I guess it should be me. About twenty-six years ago, I ran over a nest in the ground of wasps with a tractor. The nest was more than three feet in diameter. The ground gave way and the tractor got stuck. About that time they were all over me. This was the wasp that we call yellow jackets, which build their nests in the ground. The doctor thought I would never come out of the emergency room alive, but I did. While in intensive care, the nurses tried to count the number of stings. They gave up after more than 200 were counted on my upper body. They didn't try counting any below the belt line. Why do I tell this? Today I try to pass around these little friends if I see them in time. I do not destroy them just for the sake of killing them. Let them live.

Toads are not considered as fearful as the other critters that have been mentioned, but it is amazing how many will recoil at the sight of one. They are one of the best friends you can have in your garden. They like a nice, cool, moist place to hide in the day time, but at night they become dangerous hunters to our enemies, the insects. You can increase the populations of the toads by putting down a small pool about one foot deep and a foot or two in diameter. It can even be a half of a barrel, especially the dark plastic barrels that are available. Fill with water and they will come. They lay their eggs and in a few days there will be hundreds of small tadpoles. They will consume the mosquito lava so the babies are helping also.

I recently had a niece to tell me that she and her daughter were sitting on the porch one night watching a toad eat the insects. Suddenly there was a snake that came up and swallowed the toad. She got a butcher knife and killed the snake, then cut it opened and removed the toad which was still alive.

Provide hiding places for the toads during the day. Old tile-pipe or an old clay pot buried in the ground with one end left

James A. Eagle

open will soon become home to them. Fill half of the pot with soil and keep moist. Be good to your critter friends.

Question: My tomatoes are rotting on the blossom end. What is wrong?

Answer: Two things can be the cause. It can be caused by inadequate or irregular watering during dry spells, or by the lack of enough calcium in the soil, or both. I prefer bonemeal as my source of calcium. Apply at the rate of approximately six to eight ounces per plant and work it into the soil in an area approximately three to four feet in diameter around the plant. This should have been done before setting the plant out.

Here is a quicker way to replenish calcium in your soil. Pour a quart of milk around each plant. The milk will provide the calcium.

Question: I live in an area where I have my own well. This summer, with the extreme dry weather, my well is almost dried up and I can't water my garden anymore. Is there any way I can protect my garden from drying up?

Answer: This seems to be a puzzle to many gardeners as to what they can do to solve their moisture problem. Sometimes the good Lord does not bless us with an adequate supply of rain for our plants to flourish and grow as they should, so we have to substitute by watering our plants, if we have a water supply.

This past summer, I received many calls and letters about conditions readers were experiencing with plants, lawns, and shrubs due to the excessive dry period we experienced.

If you are truly an organic gardener, then you will not experience as much trouble as one who is not using organic methods. During dry periods, you will experience damage to plants when using chemical fertilizers. Chemical fertilizer is not the answer.

An organic gardener knows that the best means of retaining an adequate supply of moisture to his plants is by applying organic matter regularly to their garden. The organic matter acts as a sponge to absorb and hold moisture and retain it until it is needed by the plant.

Of course, this is not the only function of organic matter. It also provides food for the plants, and aerates the soil where oxygen can get to the plants' roots. Oxygen is needed for the plant to be able to take up nutrients into its roots to stimulate proper growth. Organic matter will make heavy silt and clay soil soft and pliable, making them easy to till. It is the best health benefit you can provide for your soil.

Another thing organic gardeners should do is to provide a mulch of straw, leaves, or hay to help retain moisture and keep the roots' cool during the hot summer months. Plants with cool roots are much healthier than when the hot sun raises the soil temperature into the nineties or hundreds, where there is no mulch. This requires the plant to take up more moisture and give this moisture off through its leaves in order for it to stay cool. Mulching reduces the amount of moisture the plant will need and helps prevent evaporation of the moisture in the soil.

One of the worst things you can do is apply a little water each day to the plants. This will encourage the roots to grow shallow and near the top of the soil in search of moisture. Encourage them to grow deep by not watering more often than every seven to ten days. Then apply one inch of water if there has been no rain.

Every gardener should have a rain gauge and an empty coffee can. If it has been five or more days since I watered my garden, and we have one-half inch of rain, then I will apply another half-inch of water with a sprinkler, making a total of one inch of water. The rain gauge will tell you how much water you received from the shower, and the coffee can acts as your rain gauge to indicate when you have applied the necessary water with a sprinkler. The coffee can, or any kind of can, should be placed one-half of the

James A. Eagle

distance from the sprinkler to the outer limits where the water from the sprinkler reaches.

Vegetables and annuals and many perennial flower plants will wilt when there is a short supply of moisture. Most shrubs and trees, including fruit trees, show their moisture deficiency by the leaves turning yellow, especially the older leaves, and then dropping off. Now excessive watering can cause the same effect. When the soil is water logged, the roots cannot get an adequate supply of oxygen, causing the roots to rot. This will make the plant unable to absorb the moisture even though there is a great deal of moisture in the soil. If you have been constantly watering plants and they show these signs, then most likely your trouble is from excessive water and not a shortage.

I am constantly trying to instruct my wife in the proper methods of watering plants. This past summer, she was constantly watering different parts of the garden when it did not need the water. I would take a hoe and dig down a few inches and show her that there was adequate moisture in the soil. My wife had a fixation on watering like an employee I had before retiring had on adding chemical fertilizers. Before I took over the grounds' maintenance at this Florida State Institution, the former supervisor used chemicals. When this employee saw a plant wilted or leaves turning yellow, he wanted to add chemical fertilizers. He had to be reeducated in his desire to do this. No wonder there was so many dead plants when I assumed this position.

Words of Wisdom:

"For as the rain comes down, and the snow from heaven, and do not return there, but water the earth, and make it bring forth and bud, that it may give seed to the sower, and bread to the eater, so shall my word be that goes forth from My mouth; It shall not return to me void, but it shall accomplish what I please, and it shall prosper in the thing for which I sent it."

Isaiah 55:10 (NKJV)

Question: How do I prune my trees and shrubs and when should I do it?

Answer: This is a very broad question. Learning the growth habit of a plant is the best way to be successful in pruning any shrub or tree. Selecting the proper plant for the purpose you want it to accomplish will also greatly reduce your pruning time and labor. If you want a large tree for shade, then do not purchase a small growing tree to provide the shade you desire. If you wish some small evergreen shrub to adorn the entrance to your home, then do not select a large growing species that will reach your rooftop in five years or more. Good sound reasoning can reduce the need for much of the pruning we perform.

If you are selecting plants for your landscape, then make an endeavor to get the type you wish to accomplish the outcome you desire. Talk with nurserymen and order catalogs of nurseries that specialize in the kind or variety of plant you wish. New species are being created constantly. If you are not sure of the type and kind of plant you wish, order the catalogs to study so as to be able to make the proper choices and decisions. If you do not know where to get addresses of the nurseries, then go on the internet. This information is available.

Many times a large growing species has been planted and the individual thinks they can keep it small by constantly pruning the plant. Remember, ever time a cut is made off the tip of a limb, it will put out many side-branches, making the plant dense and compact. If you wish the plant to be dense and thick with growth, then you are sacrificing the plant's health. Dense pruning will make formal hedges look neat and full but can create problems. It reduces air circulation and light to the inside branches, creating an atmosphere that can cause disease and insect problems. Take a look at a very dense shrub and notice how the foliage of the inside branches has died. Eventually the limbs may also start dying.

If you purchase a plant according to the size you wish it to be within five to ten years, then this condition can be avoided.

James A. Eagle

The only pruning the plant will need is to remove dead branches, and to thin the plant by cutting the branches off back to the next limb. The above types of pruning can control the excessive branching and thickening of the plant. If it becomes necessary to prune tops to control the height of the plant, then when the side branches put out where it was cut, remove all side branches accept one. This will control the thickening and density of the plant.

Indiscriminate pruning can be much more trouble than proper selection of your cuts. When pruning a tip of a branch, select a bud that is in the direction you want the new growth to grow, then make your cut approximately one-fourth inch above the bud making a slanted cut, with the high side pointing up. The high side should be above the bud, so it will shed water without rotting the limb back further than the point it was cut. This will force the new growth out from the bud where you made the cut.

Not all plants respond to a cut the same way. Learning the habit of a plant can soon be discovered if you will observe what happens after you prune a plant. Pruning, as outlined in the above paragraph, may not apply to some plants. Good examples are the azaleas, rhododendrons, and camellias. You can cut off the tip of a branch, and it will, in return, sprout many other branches at the point the cut was made, regardless of where you made the cut. Pruning of this type of plant should be done immediately after blooming, because the flowering buds, for the next bloom- ing season, will form on the new growth.

There are many shrubs that form their buds on the new growth. Some types of these plants can be forced into more excessive blooming by cutting back the plant to force new growth. One of these plants is our crape myrtle. The buds are always formed on the new growth, so in late winter or early spring, cut back all growth from the prior year to approximately one-third. This will stimulate more growth, forming flowering buds. If excessive cut- ting is performed on the plant, it may only put out growth the first year without flowering buds. Learning the proper amount can be quickly learned by experience. Always take notice of what happens when you prune, and remember that not all plants are the same. Treating one plant the same as we do another of a different type or genre, is like feeding a pet snake like you would feed a rabbit. Of course, you could feed the rabbit to the snake

Question: My crape myrtles have not bloomed very much the last several years. What am I doing wrong?

Answer: You probably need to prune them back about one-third of their height to stimulate new growth. The buds are formed on new growth. If you haven't fertilized them lately, then apply a good organic fertilizer or compost around the drip line of the plant. The larger the plant, the more fertilizer you should apply. Crape myrtles like an acidic soil, so I recommend cottonseed meal. It will lower the soil pH. Also, water during dry spells. If you prune your crape myrtles back after they bloom the first time, then, in many cases, you can get another blooming before frost the same year in our area.

Question: Should I prune my perennials back to the ground now? (This was asked in the fall.)

Answer: That depends on what you desire most. If you want a neatly kept yard, then now is the time to prune them back to about one inch from the ground. If you want to provide shelter and feed for wild life, then let them stay until early spring. Many perennials have seeds that are readily consumed by birds. This will attract birds to your yard.

Question: I have ligustrums next to my home. They are getting leggy and too tall. When should I prune them, and how much?

Answer: Many evergreen shrubs can be pruned very heavy during the dormant period, usually from the middle of November to the first of March in our area. If you prune heavy now, then you will have a lot of bare stems without any foliage on them until they put out new growth in the spring. I would wait until late February or early March before pruning. You will find that new growth will put forth as soon as it gets warm in the spring, covering the bare limbs with beautiful foliage.

Question: When should I prune my roses?

Answer: Some pruning on roses can be done the year round. During the dormant season, I prune mine in the late winter, or early spring back about one-third of their height, and before they start putting out new growth. This pruning stimulates new growth and budding. Pruning too early can cause damage to the plant should there be a very severe cold spell. Cold can enter that cut and kill the rose back even further.

During the spring and summer, prune as soon as all the roses have bloomed on a stem. Cut the stem back about one-half of its length from where it attaches to another stem. This stimulates new growth and budding on roses that bloom all summer when pruned properly. Many of the new hybrid teas and some others do not have but one blooming period. This is why I like the old fashion roses which will bloom all summer and have a very fragrant smell.

Question: When pruning larger limbs, should the wound be painted with some of these solutions I see for sale for this purpose?

Answer: At one time, most information in books and articles from extension stations recommended painting the wound of a cut with some of these solutions. The reason was to prevent disease bacteria from entering the wound.

Tests conducted since have proven that this can inhibit proper healing of the wound. If the cut is made without damaging the collar around the limb, then the recovery is much faster, and without decay going back into the cut. The new tissue will cover the wound much quicker.

When I first read of this controversial procedure of painting the wound, about forty-five years ago, I conducted my own tests. I cut two large limbs of about the same size off the same oak tree,. I painted one wound with an asphalt base commercial formula. The other I left unpainted. In five years, the painted wound had rotted back into the trunk. The other wound had formed new bark covering the entire wound.

I have always recommended to my readers to not be afraid of testing different methods of anything they think will work, or may not perform as many writers recommend. The knowledge obtained can be very valuable.

Question: I have a white or grayish scale on my azaleas and dogwoods. What can I do to treat it?

Answer: I am inclined to think it is one of the lichens instead of scale, since it is on your azaleas and dogwoods. Scale on plants is a small insect that forms a protective covering on its body. There are three classifications of scale insects: armored scales, soft scales, and mealybugs. The armored scale has a very hard scale and once it is formed, it never moves. It will stay at that spot and suck the juices from the plant. The soft scales have a cottony or felt-like deposit on their bodies. Some will move around slightly, but mostly remain in one area. The mealybugs move around for most of their lives, but often live in colonies. Their bodies are covered by long, waxy threads that look like cottony threads. Where beneficial insects have not been destroyed, they usually will keep them in check. During the dormant season, they are easily controlled by one of the superior types of oil emulsion sprays that are available at garden shops. In the summer a good safe control is Safer Insecticidal Soap

Lichens are organisms that grow on tree trunks, branches, and rocks. It appears as a gray or greenish algae. Since lichens are not parasites, they will not usually harm the plants. It will form on plants that have not been getting proper nutrients. Try adding compost or another good organic fertilizer. Since they are dog-

James A. Eagle

woods and azaleas use cottonseed meal and oak leaves or pine straw for mulch.

Question: How do I save tomato seed for planting next spring?

Answer: Tomato seeds are easy to save when a few simple rules are followed. Remove the seed from the tomato. Don't worry about getting too much pulp. This method will remove the pulp and bad seed. Place seed in a bottle or jar. Fill the container with a couple inches of water. The seed will start fermenting by the next day. Shake the bottle each day and the pulp will come to the top and good seed will go to the bottom. After three days you can drain off the pulp and bad seed, leaving the good seed that went to the bottom. Rinse the seed and place on cloth or paper towels to dry.

Question: How can I grow my own vegetables?

Answer: I received this question from a telephone conversation with a woman who had always lived in an apartment, and now had her own home, but not much room. This question has been asked many times as to how one, with no experience, can learn to grow his own vegetables. This is a very important question, and I am afraid it will be asked many times in the near future. The way things are shaping up in our world, it may be necessary to be able to grow part of our food supply just to survive. I have lived through one of the greatest depressions this country ever experienced. If our family had not been able to grow much of our own food, I don't think we would have survived. We not only grew food for ourselves, but we shared it with friends and relatives that had no food.

If you have a small plot for a garden, it can amaze you as to how much food can be grown in a small area. The methods that I prescribe will give you a healthy, living, and thriving soil that will grow vegetables that is filled with nutrients.

We are all aware that a seed must be planted to start a plant, but there is more to it than just planting a seed. For that seed to grow into a healthy plant that produces food for us, you must provide some basic needs. The first requirement is a healthy soil. There are several methods one can garden with that have been used with great success. One that my wife and I use, since we are in our late eighties, is container gardening. Be sure your containers are located where they will get at least six hours of sun each day.

There are many types of containers you can use. The larger the container, the more you can grow in it. I wouldn't advise using anything smaller than a two gallon size. We purchase plastic twenty-gallon tubs with rope handles and drilled six one-half inch holes in the bottom for drainage. Drainage is very important to prevent water remaining in bottom and starting many fungus diseases.

Here is the method by which we do it today. It would have been different ten years ago. Age has had its toll. We fill the container three-fourths full with dry leaves, then we wet them down. They will settle right away to less than half full. Then we use about a one-half inch of shredded paper, and wet it down. I discovered that where I use the paper, it will repel ants. It may repel other insects as well. I think it may be due to the chlorine they use in the manufacture of the paper. To fill the rest of the tub, I mix equal amounts of peat moss, compost, and topsoil. I then fill the tub about two or three inches from the top. Now I use a layer of green grass clippings from mowing my lawn. The reason for this is that it will decay faster than the leaves, and produces methane gas, which will kill any nematodes, if there should be any in the topsoil you used.

Remember, green plants returned to the soil will break down in a couple of weeks to give organic matter, and the tub should be ready to plant in two weeks. It will have settled even more by now, so add extra of the mix you made above and fill it to the rim. If it is too much trouble making your potting mix, try some of the many commercial potting mixes on the market today.

James A. Eagle

If you don't get healthy growth from this tub, then add some alfalfa meal or small amount of blood meal and work it into the soil. Or you may add some '*Black Cow*' manure. There are many more things that can be used to add natural nutrients without using chemicals. If you can obtain it, you can use soybean meal, cottonseed meal, and corn meal, or even wheat flour. Remember that the seed of plants is loaded with nutrients. God has devised it that way so the plant can get off to a good start.

We do not throw anything away that is plant material or made from a plant, anything from sawdust to grass clippings and tea and coffee grounds. Even the coffee filters and paper towels and napkins. We have little buckets, with lids, that this is dumped in. When full, it is taken out to a tub that has nothing growing in it at the time. About five inches of the top soil is removed, and the organic waste is dumped into the tub and covered with the soil which was removed. It will be ready to plant again in two weeks.

Another system that can be used for those who have small areas, is what is called the *raised bed system*. This requires you to build beds of untreated timbers, such as cedar or cypress. Treated lumber has chemicals which can leach into your soil and be taken up by the plant. Or you can use bricks or concrete blocks. Heavy plastic can also be used. In fact, some companies are already selling this for raised beds, and it is expensive. The height of the beds should be at least six inches. It can be as high as you wish. You can make these beds about three to four feet wide and as long as you have room or desire. Some build squares of about three or four feet square, leaving space to walk between the beds.

After you have the beds built, you are then ready to prepare the beds for planting. Remove about four to six inches of the top soil inside the beds, and save. Now prepare the bed similar to the method used for containers. Dry material in the bottom and wet down, and continue as above as it was given for the tubs. Let set two weeks or more before planting.

Chapter Ten

Gardening Tips

Do you want to increase your spud yield? Add extra potash in the form of greensand or wood ashes. Add this in addition to your regular fertilizer. Add four pounds of greensand per 100 sq. feet This has increased yields up to 26 percent according to the New Delhi Agriculture Research Station.

Science now knows that nitrates may be bad for us. They also say that nitrates can break down into nitrites, which can then form cancer-causing agents in the body. Some vegetables, especially your leaf vegetables like lettuce and spinach, and also some root vegetables like carrots and beets, can contain an excessive amount of nitrates where chemical fertilizers are used. Tests have shown that using manure or compost to feed your crops can have the opposite effect. Tests showed that manure-fed crops had fewer nitrates than chemically fed crops, and yields were as good as or better than the chemically fed crops. (A Swiss and German study conducted in the Eighties).

There are several ways to control the squash borer. That is the worm that enters the base stem of the vine and bores up the stem. It will eventually cause the plant to wilt and die early; just about the time it is loaded with fruit. One way to prevent this is to place aluminum foil around the base of the plant. Cover an area about two feet in diameter. This will deter the moth that lays the eggs and she goes on somewhere else to perform her nasty chore.

Another method is to use the wetable powder Bt. Mix according to directions and use one of the vegetable hypodermic needles and inject this into the base of the stem about two to three inches from the ground. As soon as the worms consumes any vegetable tissue with the Bt on it, it will stop eating and die. And another method is to purchase a jar of medicated petroleum jelly from the drug store. Take your finger and put just a small amount at the base of the plant before the plant starts forming buds. The odor will repel the moth.

Do you remember the buttery yellow potatoes we had seventy years ago that made such wonderful potato salad? They are still available. You can get them from Wood Prairie Farm, RFD 1, Box 164, Bridgewater, Maine 04735. You can get organically-grown seed potatoes or potatoes to eat. Their catalog is free. Their spring catalog listed thirteen varieties of seed potatoes available.

Have you ever noticed a split in the trunk of your favorite fruit tree or shrub on the south or southwest side? This is usually caused in the winter when the temperature has been warm for several days, then drops rapidly on clear nights. The warm sun shining on the southwest side can raise the cambium temperature more than 60 degrees higher than the air temperature. When the temperature rapidly drops after sundown, it freezes the water in the trunk and causes it to split. The cambium tissue dries out and dies. You then have a large wound that can be an entry-point for bacteria to cause other problems. In some cases you may even lose the plant. This can be prevented several ways: one way is to lean boards against the trunk of the tree on the southwest side. You can get exterior insulation and place around the trunk of the tree. My favorite is to paint the trunk of the tree with white latex paint. The paint reflects the sunlight and keeps the cambium temperature from rising more than ten degrees above the air temperature. *Use paint that does not contain mildew-killing compounds,* and apply it in late autumn. Apply it from the base of the trunk up to the large limbs of the tree.

You can grow your own onion sets, and use the small white varieties for pickling. Prepare the bed in a weed free area. Go

James A. Eagle

easy on the fertilizer or manure. You do not want excessive, lush growth. Sow seed, in early spring, thick so that the plants will not be more than one-fourth of an inch to half and inch apart. You want them close so they will not grow large. Weeding the close onion plants can be tedious work, so remove any weed as soon as it emerges. When the tops start falling over, then they are ready to harvest. Dig and cure in open area for several days. Store in nylon-hose, in a cool place until time to plant, or pickle.

It is a disappointing experience to go out to your garden and find almost a whole row of corn or peas that didn't come up, when other rows did. You dig down into the row and find the burrow of the mole. You do not want pesky moles in your garden at all. Sure, they eat the worms and grubs of insects, but they also eat your seed as well. They will also eat earthworms, and you want them in your garden. How do you keep them out? Moles do not like any type of vibration. Have you seen the little whirligigs on a pole? When the wind blows, it may actuate an old man chopping wood, or it may be a duck flying, or some other object moving. Mount one of these in your garden to keep the moles out. If you want to kill the mole, there is a method that is safe to other animals and pets. Get a pack of *Juicy Fruit* chewing gum. It must be *Juicy Fruit*. They will not eat any other flavor. Use a pair of gloves and unwrap the gum, and roll it up into a ball. Take a small stick and punch a hole in the ground right over his burrow. Push the gum down into his burrow. *Do not* use your bare hand. They will never take it if they smell your scent. The mole will eat this. Then he cannot digest and pass it, so he dies. If you didn't kill your moles with the *Juicy Fruit* chewing gum, then repel them by punching a hole in their tunnel and placing a small onion or garlic clove in the tunnel.

When fall comes, many of us have garden plants we wish to bring inside for the winter. If the plant is already potted, you want to be sure you are not bringing in bugs and insects you do not want in the house. To prevent this, get a large bucket and make a mixture of sixteen parts water to one part household bleach. Mix enough to submerge the pot completely. Let soak for ten minutes, remove, and let drain. Your plant is now ready to go into your home free of insects. It will also get rid of a lot of disease bacteria.

If you grow potatoes, or other types of vegetables that you need a cool dry place for storage, but do not have one, then here is a substitute for a root cellar. Get a plastic garbage can. Dig a hole large enough and deep enough to bury it except for the last four inches. You want to be able to enter it when you need produce. Put a thin layer of straw in the bottom to allow good air circulation around the potatoes. Put a layer of potatoes, then a layer of straw. After it is full, put the lid on and cover the top with black plastic, then cover this with six inches of straw, leaves, or hay. A layer of soil may be put over the top of the straw if desired to insure the proper coolness or warmth desired.

Have you ever tried to save tomato seed, but after they were dry, they had all stuck together? Here is a method that works for removing the pulp from any kind of seed you may be saving. Put the seed in a small jar and fill with several inches of water over the seed. Let set for two to three days, but each day, shake the bottle. After several days, pour off the water and pulp or any bad seed which come to the top. The bad seed will float to the top. Add fresh water and shake and pour this off. Empty seed on a paper towel and let dry for two weeks or more, then store in a cool place. Better yet, store in your refrigerator.

Do you grow elephant garlic? For delicious and healthy greens cut the tops of the garlic when they reach eight or ten inches high and stir fry for a delicious treat. They are much milder than the garlic cloves. These tops can also be used to flavor other dishes as well. After cutting the tops, they will grow back out for more delicious greens.

Do not pull up your old vegetable crops. Cut them off and leave the roots in the soil. The roots are loaded with nutrients. If you mulched your garden, then cut the old crop off and pull the mulch back, dig a small hole, and plant your next crop. No tilling is required. When the plants come up, pull the mulch back around the small plants. This is also a good way to mulch small

James A. Eagle

plants. Mulch first, then pull the mulch back enough to plant the seed of the next crop.

It is safe to compost all leaves with the exception of the Australian eucalyptus. Even black walnut leaves are okay to compost, because the juglone they contain to restrict plant growth, will break down within a couple of weeks in the compost pile. Oak leaves will lower the soil pH, but maple leaves will usually raise the pH to near neutral. Leaves composted in the shade will break down much faster than in the sun.

There is a substance in the seed and rinds of citrus fruit called limonids. Tests conducted in the early 1980's showed that it helped repel several types of caterpillars. Tests conducted since have proved it not only will repel, but kill many insects. To prepare, grind up seed and rinds, then soak in water for twenty-four hours. Strain and spray the extract on your plants. There is a commercial extract on the market now.

You do not need beer to trap your slugs. Here is a cheaper and more effective solution: Mix one part molasses with three parts water and add a teaspoon of yeast to each quart. Use your large plastic milk or pop bottles and cut out holes on each side for entry. Dig a hole in the garden and bury up to one inch of the holes. Fill bottles to within one inch of the holes. You will not only catch slugs, but also many other kind of insects.

Obtain two crops of beans with just one planting. When the bean crop has just about expired, cut the tops off to within three or four inches of the ground, add some blood meal or fish emulsion or fish meal. Keep the plants watered during dry periods, and start harvesting again in about one month. This works for string or lima beans. Cutting the spent blooms of flowers will also stimulate additional blooming.

Have you read what the Bible says about sparing the rod and spoil the child? Some people believe the same about their plants. Fred Yoder, a gardener store owner of High Point, NC, advises customers to beat their plants if they want them to grow big, healthy, and strong. He said that he knew a guy with an apple tree that would not produce any apples. Yoder said, "He got so disgusted that he took the blunt end of an ax to the tree and beat it. The next year it bore fruit." His customers tell him similar stores. One man switched his okra, and a woman said her father took his belt to his apple tree. One man blasted his unyielding cherry tree with a shotgun. The next year it bore a large crop. Yoder believes that plants are like people. "Sometimes our friends respond better to a caustic remark than to too much kindness." You may ask, "What do you believe?" I do know that many times when a plant is put under stress, it will bear quicker and more abundantly. It is God's way of making sure the plant bears seed before it dies.

Did you know that a one inch layer of compost on your garden (not mixed into the soil) will do more to prevent diseases on your plants than chemical fungicides? You can also use a compost tea or manure tea, which will accomplish the same thing. To make the compost tea, take one quart to one gallon of water and let steep for twenty-four hours. Strain and spray or sprinkle with a sprinkling can. For manure tea use the same formula, but weaken it to a light tea color before applying.

If you keep hens for supplying your egg needs, then here is a tip to increase the winter production of the eggs, or any time of year, if they are kept confined: Give them a daily treat of greens. It can be most any kind such as cabbage, collards, kale, mustard, oat or wheat greens. An especially good green crop for spring and summer is alfalfa.

For a good root system, and to protect your early tomatoes from a late cold snap, dig a hole two feet deep or more in the soil. Add about a gallon of compost to the bottom and mix with some soil. Plant the tomato in the hole. As it grows, fill in the hole with good soil. If a cold snap should come, cover the hole with a board. You will not need the Wall-O-Water for this system.

For those early seedlings you plant, but have no way to sterilize the potting mixture of to prevent damping-off disease, sterilize the soil with boiling-hot water. Fill your planting tray or pot with the planting mixture, making sure you have drain holes.

Pour the boiling-hot water over the soil and let drain. After it cools, plant your seed.

If you have your peas, cabbage, turnips, etc. up and growing and a cold spell comes with temperatures below thirty-two degrees, there are several ways you can protect them, but one of the best is the fabric row-covers that are available. You can get several different weights for even more severe cold. Many garden centers sell the metal loops to hold them up off the plants, but you can make your own out of number-nine single-strand wire, or even coat hangers.

In the morning, after you have had your last cup of coffee and there is still coffee left, don't pour it out. Let the coffee cool to room temperature, then water your house plants with it. It not only provides the necessary moisture, but adds nitrogen and other nutrients to the soil, which the plant needs. Tea is also good.

If you use a sprinkling system to water your lawn or garden, then use it in the middle of the day. Watering should be completed by 2:00 or 3:00 p.m. This will give the plant foliage time to dry before sunset. If the plant still has moisture on the foliage by nightfall, it encourages fungus diseases.

You have probably heard of using human hair to repel deer and some other animals from your garden. Instead of human hair, try dog hair. It is especially effective in repelling squirrels, rats, and raccoons. If you don't have a dog, go to a pet grooming parlor and ask for their dog hair. Put the hair in a nylon hose or other netting and hang on the plants.

There is an item on the market that really works to repel birds from the garden. It is a line made of polypropylene that can be stretched from two stakes or posts. The slightest breeze will cause it to make a sound that scares the birds away. It is a patented device called "Birds Away." Many seed catalogs have it. You may be able to obtain it locally. If you cannot find one locally, then take an old video-tape apart and use it. It works just as good.

Do you have mulch, such as hay, that you believe to have weed seed in it? Here is a method that will rid it of the weed seed.

Spread the mulch out until it is six to ten inches thick. Water it thoroughly, then cover it with black plastic. In about a week, the mulch will have warmed up enough to sprout the seed. Since they cannot get any light, they will soon die. Leave the black plastic on for about three weeks. This can be done in the winter in our area, and in the spring, summer and fall in other areas.

There is a product that will rid your home of cockroaches. It is boric acid powder, not the granulated boric acid, but the fine powder. At one time, you could go to the drug store and, for less than one dollar, buy enough to treat your home. Today it is sold under several trade names, such as *"Roach Prufe"* *"Roach Away,"* and several other names, but it is still available under the generic name, "Boric Acid." Dust this powder in cabinets, behind appliances, or wherever the roaches hide. As they crawl over this powder, it will stick to their feet. The roach does not like dirty feet, so he cleans himself by eating the powder. Wherever the powder gets on the body of the roach, it will eat a hole into his shell which protects it. The roach will then lose its body fluids and die. The powder kills in about twelve hours after the roach comes in contact with it. It does not take much powder. A one-fourth pound box will treat the average home. When a roach dies, other roaches will eat the dead roaches and, presto! That is the end of your roach problem. Is it safe? Absolutely! When I was young, the doctors prescribed boric acid for making a solution of it by mixing with water to wash the baby's eyes. This was to prevent infection of the eyes. Also, I was a license pest control operator for the state of Florida and used it for roaches in a four-story building. The EPA had required it to be licensed with warnings to claim it as an insecticide. I wrote the EPA, "What was the dangerous zone?" Their response was, "If a child consumed two tablespoons, it would probably get an upset stomach."

James A. Eagle

Chapter Eleven

Was it Evolution or Creation?

Do you believe that there is a God? Do you believe in an All-Powerful, All-Knowing God, beyond all of our understanding and comprehension, the creator of the universe, including the earth and everything in it? There wasn't even time until God created it. When He created the universe, that is when He created time. You may think this is too fantastic to understand, but consider what most of you have been taught in school, that everything came by chance, and life developed from water running over rocks and it created a one-cell lifeform. *Life? Evolutionists still can't explain life.* We know for a fact that this is scientifically impossible. With all the false assumptions that have been developed to explain it, they still cannot prove anything. To learn the truth of our history read the book of Genesis, especially the first few chapters.

There are many answers you can obtain from the internet. One of the best is www.answersingenesis.org. Another site is www.icr.org . This is another scientific site that has answers as to the truth. Answers in Genesis have a book that has been published with many different authors titled, *Answers*. The latest edition is called, *The New Answers Book 3*. They also have

Answers 1 and *2.* I recommend getting No. 2, if getting only one. They have information not included in *3,* and *3* does not have some information as in *1* and *2.*

I am like a person I heard on the NRB network. I do not know his name, but he is very knowledgeable about science and the Bible. The title of the program is, *I don't have enough faith to be an atheist.* I am the same way. It takes more faith to believe evolution than believing a loving and *all powerful* God did it all from nothing. There is one thing that the evolutionists have never been able to explain scientifically, and that is the question of, "Where did all the elements and minerals come from to start this universe?" Others are, "Why did two sexes evolve? Why didn't things evolve without the need to have sexual communion with another? Did emotions evolve?" If it is survival of the fittest, then there is no need to love or have emotions. You are fighting for survival. God created emotion and the ability to love because He wished to have communion with us because He loves us and all of His creation so very much.

There is a dangerous deception being taught as truth in our schools that has been devised by Satan. Just as sure as God inspired the prophets of old to record the truth and the Gospel of Salvation for sinful man, Satan is inspiring his followers to fool people that will doom and separate them from a loving God for eternity. This deception is that all life came from a one cell animal in the slime of a pond, and over millions of years, all life evolved from that one cell, including plant life, and *you.*

Science has given us many wonderful things, and has greatly improved our existence and comfort. This type of science is accomplished by experiments and learning the laws and principals by which things operate, which God created. This type of science is called *process,* or *operational science,* and has given us great achievements, such as radio, television, computers, and space travel.

There is another type of science that deals with history. This is called *historical,* or *origins science.* Here is where science is limited: It is almost impossible to recreate conditions of things

James A. Eagle

that happened in the past. Here scientists speculate as to what happens in the past in most instances. Their beliefs will govern and control their thought processes to the extent that what is recorded as science is nothing more than their own opinions and speculations. If they are atheists, they will determine in their own mind things which they speculate happened without a creator. If one believes in a designer and God as the creator, then the Bible is your source of truth.

If you are an atheist, then there is no morality or purpose in life. Not even love. The Bible tells us that God is love. God has given the laws by which we are to live to have purpose, order, happiness, joy, and meaning in life.

Since an atheist has no morality, there is no reason not to commit actions against others, such as theft, abuse, murder, or not have any sexual immorality, either. There is no reason to reframe from adultery, fornication, polygamy, and homosexuality. There is no need for a family-life and proper rearing, nurturing, and educating children into moral beliefs. After all, everything is relative. There is no right or wrong. Whatever you wish to do, or feels good, then do it.

Man has always sought to have his own way. That is why Adam and Eve sinned against God, their creator. A curse was put upon the earth that brought death to everything. At this point, everything started declining to the point of death. Everything was eternal until Adam sinned.

The evolutionists claim that when one believes in creation and that there was a designer, then it is religion. I have news for them. Evolutionism is also a religion. It is an unproven belief system. It is taught in our schools as humanism. Humanism even has a manifesto of their beliefs, just as communism has.

Is it any wonder that crime has increased so? I can remember when we could go to bed at night and not even lock our doors. That certainly cannot be done in today's world.

To learn more on Creation go to www.AnswersinGensis.com. Better yet, visit their Creation Museum in Kentucky

God formed the earth to be inhabited. Today science is learning more and more about the harsh realities of other planets in our solar system that cannot support life in any form. God made the earth for the purpose of having it inhabited, and even with the disruptions of sin, we can still exist for a time on earth. One day, if we accept the Lord Jesus Christ as our redeemer, we can have everlasting life reestablished. Have you prepared yourself for this life? It is *free* gift of God.

God created us to have the freedom to choose. He did this for a specific purpose. He wanted for us to love Him through choice, not through forced love. He wanted us to respond to Him with love, as He has love for us. But man rebelled and sinned. That is why we need redemption to have communication with our Creator.

There is one outstanding feature God has established in all of His creations. That is a co-dependent relationship between man, animals, insects, plants, and all the other creations of God. You do not need to be a scientist to be able to observe them. I observe them in just about everything I do, especially in gardening. This would be impossible if everything evolved. One of the most common ones is the pollination of plants. As I asked above: *Why two sexes if everything evolved?"*

We depend on insects, birds, and even animals for pollinating plants. A few years ago, there appeared some kind of disease that was destroying the honey bee population. Honey bees are even used commercially for the pollination of plants. There are many that cultivate the raising of honey bees which they in turn rent out to farmers that need them to pollinate their crops. When we lived in Florida I knew one man that had over 600 hives that he rented to citrus growers in the early spring, when the citrus started blooming. He also hauled hives to the vegetable growers in South Florida to pollinate their vegetables.

Of course, there are many other insects that are native that pollinate our plants. When our blueberries are in bloom, there are all kind of insects over the flowers, going from one bloom to another. The humming birds are another source of pollination.

James A. Eagle

One of the most outstanding examples of the codependence God has created in nature is between the Yucca plant of the Southwest deserts of the United States and the Pronuba moth.

The Yucca plant starts its blooming cycle in the spring, which lasts several weeks. Beneath the plant lie the cocoons of the Pronuba moth. At the moment, the flowers of the yucca plant start opening the Pronuba moths emerge from their cocoons and flies up to the opening flowers, attracted by the emerging fragrance of the flowers. The moth goes from flower to flower, gathering pollen and rolling it into a ball with her jaws and tentacles, which God has made especially for this purpose. When the ball of pollen gets so large that she can hardly fly, she will enter the next flower. She backs down into the flower and pierces the ovary of the flower, and with a special tube she has for this purpose, she lays her eggs.

The moth then craws to the top of the flower and places the ball of pollen into the pistil. The pistil has a special built cavity, just the right size to hold the ball of pollen. She stuffs the pollen into this cavity. The pollen travels down the stem of the pistil and fertilizers the eggs in the ovary. The seeds of the Yucca start growing and developing. Now it is time for the Pronuba moths eggs to hatch. The larvae that hatch start feeding on the developing seed, but not all are consumed. Enough are left to carry on the species.

After the larvae have developed, they will crawl out of the flower and let themselves down to the ground by spinning a thin thread of silk. They enter the soil and develop into cocoons, where they lie until the following spring to start the whole cycle over again.

The female moth never eats. Her sole purpose is to gather the pollen to fertilize one flower and lay eggs. After this, she dies.

What tells the moth to emerge at just the right time to fertilize the flowers? If it is evolution, how did either plant or moth survive until everything was in place?

Another amazing thing is that there are other varieties of Yucca and they all have a different moth to perform this duty.

There is a difference in the flower of each variety, and each moth is designed to pollinate that particular flower.

You see many things similar throughout God's creations. I believe He did it purposely to demonstrate His wisdom and greatness, whereby we would have to realize that there is an all powerful God who has created all.

The evolutionists claim that since there are so many similarities in the creations, it proves they all evolved from one source. No! It proves that there was only one designer. .

There is a law of science that lies at the base of all modern science. Scientists refer to it as the first law of Thermodynamics, which is, *While you can convert matter to energy* (like burning wood to produce heat), *you cannot produce energy or matter out of nothing.* We know that our universe is made up of matter and energy, so we must face the reality that it had to come from somewhere. Evolutionists have no solution for this, but I do. God created it all from nothing. Science cannot perform this.

Even Albert Einstein, although he didn't like it, had to admit that all things have a beginning. If there was a beginning, then there must be a creator to start this beginning. In the very first book of the Bible, Genesis, and the very first verse we have the answer, *"In the beginning God created the heavens and the earth."* This says it all.

Would you say that everything on this earth and in the heavens had careful design? Would you say that the computer had a very good design? Which do you think evolved? Even one part of your wonderful body could not function without the heart. The eye is so wonderfully designed that it's impossible to function without the heart distributing blood to it for nourishment. Yet it is more complicated than any computer. Why would anyone think they evolved and their computer was designed?

Isn't it wonderful to know such a wonderful God that is all powerful and knowing? Don't you want to worship and serve such a God?

Although we have all sinned and separated ourselves from God, God has provided a way of escape from eternal hell, and whereby we can have communion with Him. *Salvation Consists of Three Things: Faith, Repentance, and Love* (All scripture quoted is taken from the New King James Version of the Bible.) Salvation is the deliverance of the soul from eternal hell. Sin cannot dwell in Heaven. Therefore, since we are of a sinful nature, we must have redemption. Where do we obtain this redemption? Through Jesus Christ who came to this earth as the Son of God. He was born of a virgin, lived a sinless life, and, although tempted as we are, he never yielded to the temptations of Satan. He took upon Himself all our sins, so we could receive redemption. He rose from the dead on the third day, then ascended into Heaven. Before ascending into Heaven, Jesus made this promise.

> "I go to prepare a place for you. And if I go to prepare for you, I will come again and receive you to Myself, that where I am you may be also."
>
> John 14:3 (NKJV)

> "In Him (Jesus Christ) we have redemption through His blood, the forgiveness of sins, according to the riches of His grace."
>
> Ephesians 3:7 (NKJV)

> "For God so loved the world that He gave His only begotten Son, that whoever believes in Him shall not perish but have everlasting life."
>
> John:3:16 (NKJV)

> "For by grace you have been saved through faith, and that not of yourselves, it is a gift of God."
>
> Ephesians 2:8 (NKJV)

Here we have the ultimate sacrifice for our sins. There is not anything we can do to receive this wonderful gift. It is a free gift of God, to be saved through faith. We only have to accept this wonderful gift.

Many seek salvation through other sources or by their good deeds, but this will not give us redemption. Only by faith in Jesus Christ can we have hope of eternal life. Jesus tells us:

> "I am the way, the truth, and the life. No one comes to the Father except through Me."
>
> John 14:6 (NKJV)

> "Nor is there salvation in any other, for there is no other name under heaven given among men by which we must be saved."
>
> Acts 4:12 (NKJV)

This gives us a firm message that there is no other way for eternal life with Jesus Christ in Heaven.

God, the Creator of all things, has provided us a way of escape. He will not turn us away.

> "All the Father gives Me will come to Me, and the one who comes to me I will by no means cast out."
>
> John 6: 37 (NKJV)

> In Revelations 3:20, Jesus says, *"Behold, I stand at the door and knock. If anyone hears my voice and opens the door, I will come in to him and dine with him, and he with Me."*
> "If we confess our sins, He (Jesus) is faithful and just to forgive us our sins and to cleanse us from all unrighteousness."
>
> 1 John 1:9 (NKJV)

So it is by faith we come to Jesus and repent of our sins, believing He is just and will forgive us of all sin. Here we have God who came to this earth for the exclusive purpose of providing a means of our salvation. He lived and died on the cross for all of

James A. Eagle

our sins. He took the punishment, which we deserve, for our sins, and then rose again to eternal life. We also can obtain this eternal life with Him in Heaven when we accept His gift to us.

Jesus laid down His life for us. There can be no greater love. If He was willing to die for us, then shouldn't we return His love and live for Him until we go to live with Him forever? Read John 14:21. How shall we escape if we refuse His great gift to us?

"How shall we escape if we neglect so great a salvation?"

Hebrews 2:3 (NKJV)

"…behold now is the day of salvation"

2 Corinthians 6:2 (NKJV)

You must choose this day whom you will serve. It is either God or Satan. We cannot serve both. Our eternal soul's salvation depends on it. Today is the day of salvation. Tomorrow could be too late.

Jesus Christ can come the next moment, or you could be hurled into eternity

Jesus Christ ascended back to Heaven. There, He is preparing for those who receive Him as their savior, a home that cannot be imagined. Read John 14:1-3. Here, He assures us of this wonderful place, and, most of all, that He will return. The scripture foretelling of His return is being fulfilled so fast today. Never in history was it possible for much of the book of Revelation to be fulfilled until now. The technology we have today makes it possible for the control of all human life on this planet. If you do not accept Jesus as your savior, then you will go through this tribulation period, which is foretold in Revelations. I do not want to be here. There may never be another day. Jesus Christ can come the next moment. There is no assurance that tomorrow will ever come for us. Make your decision today for Jesus Christ and His saving grace. We either accept Gods grace of salvation, or His wrath by refusing His gift of salvation.

A simple prayer such as, "Jesus Christ, I know that you died on the cross for my sins, and I accept this gift of Yours right now. Please forgive me of my sins. Come in to my heart and abide with me. I promise to live for you. I ask this in the name of Jesus Christ. Amen.

Addendum One

Horticulture & Gardening Terms, Words, Products, or Phrases Explained

Sometimes the terms, phrases, or words used by a horticulturist can be misleading or completely confusing, or misunderstood. I have had many to ask what I meant by pH, or when speaking of the hardiness of a plant they think I mean the vigor or the plant's ability to overcome cultural hardships. Here we will discuss some of these terms and their meanings. There are words and products that also need explaining. Hope this will help you to understand what they mean, and if it is a product, then how it is used.

Air Layering: This is one method of asexual reproduction of a plant. It is used mostly with very woody plants that are hard to root by cuttings. You do not remove the part you are rooting from the tree or bush to root. It is rooted while on the tree. You scarify, or remove the bark, about one inch wide and leave a thin strip of bark so tree sap can flow through to the tip to the tip you are rooting. Do this about six or eight inches from the tip of the limb. Put a rooting hormone around the scarified place and above it for about one inch. Pack the area with moist peat-moss and wrap with a plastic covering and tie it on each end. Use clear plastic, that way you can see through it and tell if the peat moss is drying out. If it is, untie the top end and pour water into it and re-tie. You will also be able to see the roots forming. When it has rooted, cut below the rooted area and transplant the rooted tip.

Ammonia: This is the household ammonia used for cleaning. Ammonia is a colorless, pungent gas compound of nitrogen and hydrogen. It is used as a fertilizer and in medicines. The household ammonia is mixed in a water solution making it a liquid. I recommend it as a spray for your plants for repelling insects and animals. Also, the nitrogen in it acts as a liquid fertilizer when sprayed on the foliage (see Addendum II for formulas).

Annual: This is a plant that has only one season life span. It is planted in the spring and dies after growing to maturity and bearing fruit. (See Fruit, biannual, and perennial.)

Asexual Reproduction: This is when you can reproduce a plant without the union of male and female cells. This is producing a plant that is identical to the mother plant. In other words, we are producing a clone. Personally, I do not believe in the cloning of animals or humans. But cloning plants is not the same. There are some plants that do it naturally. The willow tree is a good example. A small piece or limb can get broken off and it will root where it touches the soil and can stay moist. There are some plants that start growing little plants on the tip of their leaves that then fall off and take root. Another is the spider plant. It will grow a tentacle that will bear flowers, but the tip will form roots without it being in the soil. Transplant this and it will readily grow.

Baking Soda: This is the Sodium Bicarbonate that is used for baking. It is a long-time remedy for many fungal diseases. I get about the same results using it as I do using cornmeal and hydrogen peroxide. I especially like it for black spot diseases. Use two tablespoons per gallon of water and keep it shaken up as you spray.

Biennial: A biennial is a plant that requires two years from the germination of the seed to Maturity and production of fruit and seed (See Annual and perennial.). A good example would be the carrot. If you plant carrots in the spring and summer, you would be able to harvest them in the early fall and winter. But it must go into the next season to produce the flowers and seed. Carrots make a beautiful addition to the flower garden as well. The flowers resemble Queen Ann's Lace.

Budding: Budding is another method of propagation (see propagation). The bud of the plant is removed with a small piece if the wood underneath the bud. You use a compatible stock to attach it to, such as budding peach to a plum sprout, or peach to another peach. I prefer a seeding with the stock about one-half inch in diameter. Cut a "T" cut and carefully open it and place the bud into this, closing the bark of the receiving plant over it, then wrap with cloth strips and seal with wax. Cut the sprout you are budding to about an inch above the bud to force growth from this bud. (See Grafting)

Borax: This is sold in grocery stores as a laundry booster. For the gardener it can solve many problems as an aid in the use of other products. It also provides a source of boron, which is a minor nutrient plants need, and can be in short supply in some soils. It be an aid in controlling some insects, especially ants (see Addendum II for formulas).

Boric Acid: This can be use instead of Borax to supply boron, but the most important uses are controlling insects, especially roaches and ants.

Bulbs: Corms and bulbs (see corms) are closely related as to their function to produce plants. Both will produce a clone of the original plant. Some bulbs will last for many years, reproducing a plant and flowers for years, such as the lily. Bulbs have a short stem and leafy scales or layers around it. These scales can produce small bulblets that will take root and produce a large bulb.

Carbon Dioxide: This is a naturally occurring compound that is necessary for plants. Plants take in carbon dioxide in order that they may convert nutrients into energy for growth and production. Plants, in return, give off oxygen for us to breathe (see last paragraph in chapter 5).

Castor Oil: This can be used to repel rodents, especially moles, voles, mice, and other rodents. If you take it internally, it can also make you run to the bathroom.

Caterpillar: A caterpillar is the larva of the butterfly or moth. We may call the caterpillar a worm, but the true worm is not the larva of the butterfly or moth. The earthworm would be an example of a true worm. The caterpillar is in the stage of the developing butterfly, or moth, that feeds on plants. Good examples of some of the caterpillars are the cornear worm, cabbage worm, or the tomato hornworm

Compost: This is decayed plant and animal residue, which is produced by bacteria. It is full of nutrients for the plants to use. See *Chapter 4.*

Corms: These are the underground fleshy base of the stem of a plant such as the Gladiolus. Some refer to them as bulbs, but technically, there is a difference. Corms are solid.

Cornmeal: The common cornmeal you purchase for making cornbread is an excellent fungicide. Dust with it on any plants that have fungus diseases. Information on this is given in Chapter Five also.

James A. Eagle

Deciduous Deciduous plants are those that shed their leaves or foliage at the end of the growing season. (See Evergreen)

Diatomaceous Earth: Diatomaceous earth is shell of a tiny water plant known as the *diatom*. These shells are so small that it feels like fine powder. These tiny shells have very sharp edges that will cut the soft body of insects, causing them to lose their body fluids and die. There is one warning on using diatomaceous earth: do not use the diatomaceous earth that is used for swimming pool filters. It has been chemical treated, and the abrasiveness of it has been destroyed. Untreated diatomaceous earth is very abrasive to soft-bodied insects. Be sure your diatomaceous earth is for garden use. Diatomaceous earth can be used for dusting your garden and shrubs for aphids, whiteflies, snails, slugs and other soft bodied insects. Do not mix it with boric acid for this purpose. Boric acid is a mild acid, and can burn the foliage of plants. Always dust in the morning while the dew is still on the plants. It will hold to the foliage this way until the next rain.

Those of you that have poultry can use this diatomaceous earth to dust the nest boxes to control mites. You can make a slurry mixture by adding water and painting it on the roosts, or other places where mites are likely to hide.

For the dog and cat owners, here is an excellent control for fleas. If your pet lives in the home and has fleas, then you most likely have an infested home. Fleas lay eggs in the nap of carpets, so dusting the carpets with diatomaceous earth can kill fleas as they hatch out. You can also dust your pets with it. If the pets sleep outside, then dust with it outside where they sleep. Remember that a flea egg can stay in the carpet for many months before hatching. If you have an indoor infestation, then this powder must stay in the carpet for a year or more. When you vacuum, then dust the carpet again. Always work the powder into the nap of the carpet so it cannot be seen. The eggs will hatch whenever the moment is right for them. They can lie there a year or more before hatching.

Division of Plants: Some plants multiply by putting off-shoots (plants) that can be separated by the use of a shovel, sharp knife, or by pulling apart. These will grow as individual plants and also multiply. Some examples are: daylilies, hostas, and peace lilies

Drupe: The fleshy, soft fruit of plants, usually having a hard coated seed. A good example is the plum.

Emulsify: This means to blend or mix together, for instance, when using an oil spray with water, to mix the oil with the water by using an agent such as dishwashing detergent or Murphy's Oil Soap to emulsify them. Commercial horticulture oils already contain an agent so they will blend with water.

Epson Salts: Epson salts are a compound of magnesium and sulfur. Sometimes there may be a shortage of these minerals in the soil. The addition of Epson salts will quickly correct this deficiency. It can correct deficiencies in us as well.

Evergreens: Plants that have green foliage throughout the year. A good example is the pine, juniper, and camellia. Even these will shed old leaves eventually. Pines will usually shed after several years. In the fall, you will find the older needles falling until the arrival of spring, but always leaving the new leaves from the last year or two on the tree.

Fruit: When anyone mentions fruit, most of us think of items such as apples, peaches, oranges, or any fleshy-type fruit that we eat as a dessert . But the true definition is that it is the fertilized ovary of the flower of a plant that has matured to form a seed bearing container. It can be tomatoes, beans, vetch, apples, grass, or any plant that bears a seed carrying container (See vegetable).

Grafting: This is another method of reproducing a plant asexually. This is similar to budding, but in grafting you use a stem or cutting. There are several ways this can be done, but all require that the plant you are grafting to is "compatible". They must be of a type that will grow together. The scion you use to graft must use the roots of the plant you are grafting to. Be sure no sprouts come out of the stock below the graft, or they will be of the type of the stock plant.

Greensand: This is a sedimentary marine deposit and green in color, appearing like sand. It is sometimes referred to as *"glauconate"* but glauconate is only a substance found in greensand. Greensand is a good source of potassium, iron, magnesium, phosphorus, and calcium, plus more than thirty other trace minerals. It should be used with an organic source of nitrogen, such as alfalfa meal, soybean meal, cottonseed meal, or fish meal. Although greensand has the consistency of sand, it can absorb ten times more moisture than sand, making it an exceptional soil conditioner. When writing gardening columns for our local newspaper, their proof reader changed greensand to '...*greens and...*' This is when I started getting calls wanting to know what kind of greens.

Evolutionists claim greensand was formed over millions of years. I proclaim it was formed at the time of Noah's flood. See chapters seven and eight of Genesis. It tells us that the fountains of the deep erupted, as well as the rain from heaven. These eruptions were earthquakes and volcanic eruptions. Then came the receding waters with the quick washing of mineral segment of all kinds and the chemical reactions that took place at this time formed the greensand, plus coal, gold, petrified wood, oil, animals, etc. See www.answersingenesis.org for answers by scientists.

Hardy or Hardiness: Plant hardiness is the ability of the plant to withstand cold without killing it, and *not* its ability to ward off hardships or diseases. This ability is called stamina. The United States is divided into hardiness zones ranging from one to ten. Number one is the coldest and ten is the warmer or tropical areas. Most nursery and seed catalogs have a map showing the different zones. Many catalogs will list the zones the plant will do the best in.

Herbaceous: These are plants that are not woody, but have soft tissue stems and leaves. They can be annuals, biennials, or perennial plants.

Hydrogen Peroxide: Consists of two parts hydrogen to two parts oxygen. A 3 percent solution is the strength which is sold in stores. It is an antiseptic and bleach. It makes an excellent antibacterial agent to spray on your plants for disease control. A 32% hydrogen Peroxide is available, but this is not needed.

Kelp Meal: This is a natural fertilizer made from dry seaweed. Kelp is a variety of seaweed. There are other seaweeds, but this is the best and most plentiful. It contains just about all the elements God has created, and all are in the seas. It is an excellent source of potassium. It is best used with other organic fertilizers, such as fish-meal, soybean-meal, cottonseed-meal, and alfalfa meal, which provide a better nitrogen source. If your soil is lacking in any minor nutrients, such as zinc, magnesium, iron, etc., this is what you should use to replenish the minerals lacking. It is harvested and dried, then ground into a meal.

It not only provides nutrients, but acts as an activator and stimulator of microbes in the soil for them to break down organic matter, making it available to the plants. It also aids the breaking down of the materials you use to make compost. Kelp will break down all the material in your compost pile. I don't think you can say too much in praise of this product which God grows in the seas around the world.

Legume: A legume plant has the ability to draw nitrogen from the air and store it in its roots. There is a bacteria that lives in a nodule on the roots. A nodule is a knot-like growth. Some may mistake this knot for the damages inflected on the roots of plants cause by one species of nematode, but this nodule is much smaller then the nematode knot. Since a legume plant has this ability, it makes it a valuable plant for the gardener as a soil improvement crop. Some examples of a legume are *Alfalfa, Clover, Peas, and beans.* And all plants which belong to the *Pea Family* (See Plant Names).

Liquid Seaweed: This is a liquid form of seaweed. The kelp Meal listed above is dried seaweed. Both are excellent sources to provide the minor and trace minerals needed by plants. Use the liquid seaweed to soak seed in before planting. They will get a much faster start and be less likely to have any fungus or bacterial disease.

Lime: Lime has several purposes for the gardener. It provides calcium for plants, but we are interested in its ability to repel and control insects, especially when mixed with sulfur. Use either the ground limestone or hydrated lime.

Moats (Cotton Moats): These are the cleanings that are removed from cotton during the ginning process. I started using these in 1958, when no one was interested in them. At that time, they did not spray cotton with a defoliant before cotton was harvested. It was still harvested back then by hand. I hauled it by the pick-up loads and put over my garden and tilled it in. In a couple of weeks it would be broken down and I could plant.

Our postal letter carrier told me I would never be able to grow anything on that poor soil. That summer, I left in the mail box tomatoes as big as a pound or more and some other produce. The next Sunday at church, with a big grin on his face, he wanted to know where I bought them.

Moats themselves are an excellent source of nutrients. Twenty-four years ago when we moved back to South Carolina, I went to several gins around and no one was getting the moats, There were some places that earthworms were in them already working, so I started hauling again. I figured they could not be that bad if earth worms were in them. They decay very fast.

Molasses: This is good to add to sprays to control diseases. It feeds beneficial bacteria that destroys lots of the diseases we encounter. The bacteria increases faster when feeding on this. It is also loaded with nutrients.

Mulching: This is a natural method that God designed to return to the earth the nutrients the plants take from it. Observe a completely open field that has not been cultivated for several years. Weeds are the first thing that comes up. Then you will see seedlings of trees that have been distributed by wind, animals and birds. Within twenty years you will have a forest. Walk into this forest, and you discover leaves covering the earth, and decaying and refurnishing the soil with nutrients.

When you manually mulch your crops using vegetable matter, such as leaves, hay, straw, or grass clippings, you are replenishing the soil with nutrients. Not only that, but mulching preserves moisture, keeps plant roots cool, and improves the tilth of the soil.

Murphy's Oil Soap: This is sold in grocery stores where cleaning supplies are located. It is manufactured for the purpose of cleaning wood furniture, walls, and cabinets. We use it for a different purpose. We use it to emulsify oil sprays and mixes. It is a natural soap that breaks down and does not pollute our water supplies. Detergents are loaded with phosphates that pollute our streams and waterways. It also is a wonderful wetting agent, whereby the leaves, hay, straw, and other dry ingredients for the compost pile can absorb more water, allowing for quicker decomposing of the dry material. Use one teaspoon for each gallon of water for this purpose.

Neem: This is an extract from the *Neem Tree.* This tree is a native of the mid-east, especially India. Residents in India have been using all parts of the neem tree for diseases and sickness of many kinds. Also they use it for their plants to control disease and insects. There are commercial formulations that work very satisfactory in controlling insects. If any insect, of any developing stage, eats any part of a plant that contains it, or gets any on their body, they will stop eating immediately and die in time. It also interrupts the insects breeding also. It is safe for use.

Nematodes: Nematodes are very small worms. They are not an insect. Some feed on the roots of plants. There are others that feed on other larger worms and larva.

Node: A node on a plant is where a leaf is attached or where one was attached.

Oil of Wintergreen: This is available in most drug stores. It is a wonderful deterrent for insects and animals. It also has antibacterial qualities which help control some diseases.

Organic Gardening: My definition of organic is different from some people. Some seem to think that organic gardening is when you use only plant and animal waste. I believe if you use minerals or other substances in their natural state as God created them, then it is satisfactory and suitable to use them. Plants in their natural habitat , where they were placed by God, have all the substances and minerals they need for proper growth But when we try to grow the plant in another area, we may have to add ground limestone, magnesium, or some other substance that the plant may need, and is lacking in their new surroundings.

Ovary: This is the part of the pistil containing the future seeds. You can observe the ovary in some vegetables easily, such as a cucumber or squash. They appear as a small fruit before the flower blooms.

Parasite: This is an organism of a different species of the plant it inhabits, and from which it derives sustenance or food from. It can produce damage to its host plant. It can be vegetable or animal.

Perennial: A perennial is a plant that will last for three or longer years. Some plants may be a short-lived perennial, like the Aquilegia (Common name of Columbine), which lives for only four or five years. The trees are very long lived in comparison. There is an Olive tree near Jerusalem that some claim was standing there when Jesus Christ walked the earth. (See Annual and Biannual)

Perlite: This is a derivative, much lighter than sand, that is mixed with sand and peat moss for rooting cuttings and starting seed. It is available in most garden centers. It is not organic, nor a nutrient, but does improve the tilth of the soil and provide better drainage.

Peat Moss: There are many forms of peat moss. It depends on where it is dug or mined. The peat recovered in Florida looks and appears much different than the Canadian peat. There is peat that is recoved from many other areas. It is the partially decomposed plant materials such as sphagnum moss, or other plants which grow in a low moist area. They make an excellent mulch or added to potting mixes. They will continue to bread down adding nutrients.

PH: This is a rating method of determining the acidity or alkalinity of the soil. A rating of pH 7 is considered neutral. A rating lower than pH 7 is considered acid. One higher than pH 7 is considered alkaline. Most soils are slightly acid because most plants do better in slightly acid soil. Under rare conditions, there are some that requires alkaline soil. These are plants that the Creator made for areas that may be alkaline. (See Chapter Four). It goes into detail on why composting is the way to control the soil's condition.) If you want to test your soil's pH, use the method my dad used. He would pick up a handful of soil and smell it, then taste it. If it had a sour smell and taste, he would say it is too sour. If it had a bitter taste, it would be too alkaline. If it had a sweet taste and sweet smell, he would say it is just right. That meant it was between 6.0 to 7.0.

Pistil: This is the seed-bearing female sex organ of a flower consisting of the ovary, style, and stigma.

Plant Names: Plants have *botanical* names assigned by the American Horticulture Society in cooperation with the International Horticulture Society. The system used can get complicated for the novice. In fact, it can get complicated for me sometimes. I will try to make this as simple as possible. Botanical names of plants are assigned in the *Latin* language so there will not be the same name given to two different plants, or two or more plants having the same name. People give common names to plants, and they can vary in different parts of the country. Many times the same common name is given to two or more different plants. This is the reason botanical names are assigned in order to reduce the confusion in names.

Here an effort will be made to explain the scientific, or botanical names and classifications. First, plants are arranged in *'families',* such as the *"*Pea family," or the *"*Brassica family.*"* The scientific name does not indicate the class. The scientific name starts with the genus, such as "Ilex," which has the common name of holly. Then there are the cultivars, which we refer to as the variety. An example is the holly *Ilex opaca,* which has the common name of American Holly. Sometime botanical names are changed because it is realized that they may be in a different family or genus

Propagation: The propagation of a plant is to increase or reproduce it. This can be done in many ways. The most common one is by seed. Some plants can be separated from a crown formed underground and start another. Others that have bulbs or rhizomes produce others, and then we can multiply plants by. grafting, budding, and rooting. Usually, the tips of the plant are taken when grafting or rooting and they are referred to as cuttings.

Asexual reproduction is the ability to increase the plant without the union of male and female germ cells. We are producing a clone, a plant with the exact identity of the parent plant. When plants are started from seed, they will not produce an exact copy of one parent, but will have differences. By cross-pollinating plants of the same species we obtain differences that may be better or inferior to the parent or parents. Some plants produce both male and female flowers, which makes them able to pollinate themselves. Others have male and female plants, therefore requiring a male and female plant for it to produce seed. God established plant life different than animal. We cannot compare animal life with plant life. It is much different.

Pyrethrum: This is an extract from the roots of the pyrethrum plant, which is a species of the Chrysanthemum. Pyrethrum will kill insects instantly. It is fairly safe in that it dissipates within a short time, and the vegetable or fruit can be used for consumption within twenty-four to forty-eight hours after use. It is used in many commercial products today. It will also kill beneficial insects as well. Today they are manufacturing a synthetic pyrethrum that is not as safe. I do not recommend it. It will not dissipate as fast as natural pyrethrum, and it is more harmful to plant and animal life.

Rhizome: It is the enlarged stem of a root. Plants usually store food in them. The Iris is a good example of a plant that has rhizomes. You can plant the rhizome of a plant and it will produce you a plant. It is similar to planting a seed, but producing a clone instead of the original plant.

Row Covers or Plant Protectors: This is a porous material that lets the rain and sun through while protecting the plant from cold. Most garden shops offer only one thickness, but I have been able to purchase much heavier coverings wholesale. Most catalogs indicate that the plant will be protected about four degrees below

James A. Eagle

freezing. If you want to protect them from lower temperatures, double or triple the layers.

Rubbing Alcohol: This is an instant kill for many small insects, such as scale and mealy bugs. When these get on your house-plants, dip a cotton swab in the alcohol and touch it to the insect.

Scion: A scion is a small shoot, tip, or bud from a plant. They are used to asexually reproduce the plant by budding, grafting, or rooting. Usually the tips of plants are used for rooting or graft-ing. They are usually referred to as cuttings. The buds are used when budding the plant (See Asexually Reproduction, Budding, and Grafting).

Stamen: This is the pollen-bearing male organ of a flower.

Staminate: This is when a flower has stamens but no pistil, there-fore it cannot be pollinated.

Stigma: This is the part of the female pistil that receives the pol-len of a flower to pollinate it.

Stratification or Stratified: This is a process where the seeds of woody plants are harvested when well ripened, cleaned of all pulp, and left to dry for several days. They are then put in moist peat-moss or sand in a container. I use plastic food storage con-tainers. Zip-Lock bags can also be used. You then store in the refrigerator for approximately four months. This is required to break the dormancy of the seed. In nature, they get the treat-ment by being consumed by animals or birds. Their digestion system breaks the dormancy. Seed going through the winter and having freezing temperatures, then warming, then freezing again will break the dormancy. Some seed will require a second winter before breaking their dormancy. The seed is also stratified when eaten by a bird or animal. The digesting fluids will break the hard shell of these seed. God thought of it all.

Style: When we hear the word style we think of the style of fashions, or the method something is performed. But, in this case, we are thinking of the stem from the stigma of a flower that carries the pollen to the ovary.

Tabasco Sauce: This is especially useful when you want hot pepper for a spray formula, but have no hot peppers (see Addendum III for formulas).

Temperature Zones: The United States and Canada is divided into ten temperature zones, ranging from Zone Ten to Zone One. Zone Ten is the warmest area, being located in part of the southern part of Florida and Texas. Zone One is in the extreme northern part of Canada and Alaska. Some nursery catalogs will show a picture of the Zones.

Transpiration: The process whereby a plant gives off moisture through the pores of the leaves and stems. A large tree can give off as much as thirty gallons or more in a twenty-four-hour period on a hot summer day. This is a process that the Creator established to keep the plant cool. This is why it is necessary to provide a proper amount of water to a plant. An annual is the easiest plant to detect if it is not getting enough water. It will wilt. Shrubs and trees are harder to detect when there is an inadequate amount of water. Usually the tips of the leaves will start turning brown is one indication, but some will show signs of wilting. Some will start shedding their leaves.

Vegetable: Usually, we refer to vegetables as any herbaceous plant that is eaten raw or cooked (see herbaceous). It can be any part of the plant. The leaves, root, fruit, flowers, or the flower buds. You may think you don't eat flowers or buds, but if you have ever eaten cauliflower or broccoli, then you have eaten the buds of the flowers. There are many plants that the flowers of are delicious and very nutritious, such as the daylily and nasturtium. They can be eaten in soups, stir-fries, or salads.

James A. Eagle

Vegetable Cooking Oil: This is the oil you get in the grocery store. I use it instead of the horticulture oils, because it is cheaper and just as effective (see addendum II for formulas).

Vermiculite: Vermiculite is a mica-like mineral that is much lighter than sand. It has great moisture holding ability. Some use it in mixing with potting soil to improve its ability to hold more moisture, especially when potting soil is used for rooting cuttings. It also makes good mulch. It is not organic.

Vermiculture: Vermiculture is the system of using earthworms to convert vegetable waste into worm castings. The earthworm converts the waste into the most outstanding vermicompost known to mankind. Using vermicompost to make a tea to apply to your plants can prevent disease and insect damages.

Wall-O-Water: This is the trade name of a plastic unit with cells that are filled with water to protect individual plants from cold snaps. Many gardening stores and nurseries sell them. I have found that the easiest method to fill the individual cells is to place a large, five-gallon bucket over the plant up-side down, then place the unit around the bucket. Fill each cell, starting on one side and then going to the opposite side until all cells are full. Then pull the bucket out from the top of the unit. I think the patent on these has expired because some places are now calling them *Insulating Teepees.* These can last for several years when taken care of. Remove them as soon as the weather permits

Wood Ashes: Wood ashes are a good source of potash. They should not be exposed to rain or too much sun before they are used, because they can lose the nutrients very fast through exposure. They also are useful to raise the pH of your soil. Use them sparingly because excessive use can provide an extreme rise in the pH of your soil.

Worm: See caterpillar

Formulas for Insect and Disease Control and Nutrition

The formulas below can solve many gardening problems. Pick the ones that seem to work best for you. You may discover that just one formula may solve most of your gardening problems. Applying each week makes it more effective. *NOTE: Some of the formulas may burn some young and very tender plants. Before using try spraying on a leaf and wait twenty-four hours and observe if it did any damage.*

Formula No. 1
- 2 tablespoons of Castor oil
- 1 tablespoon Murphy's Oil soap
- 1 gallon of water

Mix all above ingredients and spray or apply with a sprinkling can to repel moles and voles in areas that show signs of their presence.

Formula No. 2
- 2 tablespoons Castor oil
- 1 tablespoon Oil of Wintergreen

- 2 tablespoons baking soda
- 1 tablespoon household ammonia
- 1 tablespoon Murphy's Oil soap
- 1 gallon of water

Mix all ingredients together. This is a multi-purpose spray. Use on plants for insect, disease, and animal control, especially the moles in your garden. Apply about every seven to ten days for best control.

Formula No. 3
- ½ cup dried peppermint leaves
- ½ cup dried chamomile flowers
- 1 gallon of water

Bring one quart of water to a boiling point and pour over the peppermint and chamomile. Let steep until cool. Strain and add an additional three quarts of water. This can be used as it is for fungal diseases and to repel some insects. Adding the ingredients in formula 3A without the extra water will make it a multipurpose spray for diseases to repel animals and to kill small soft bodied insects.

Formula No. 3A
- 2 tablespoons of vegetable oil
- 1 tablespoon wintergreen oil
- 1 tablespoon household ammonia
- 2 tablespoons Tabasco sauce (strained)
- 1 tablespoon baking soda
- 1 Gal. water

This is an excellent spray to control disease and insects, even those pesky rodents. If this is your choice of an all-purpose spray, then apply according to directions for formula No, 2.

Formula No 4
- ¼ cup blackstrap molasses or corn syrup
- 1 teaspoon borax or boric acid powder
- 1 tablespoon Epson salts
- 1 tablespoon baking soda

James A. Eagle

- 2 tablespoons of liquid kelp
- 1 cup skim milk (optional)
- 2 tablespoons liquid fish emulsion (Optional)
- 1 gallon of water

This is another general-purpose spray for controlling insects and disease. The molasses or corn syrup is an excellent way to increase the beneficial microorganisms in the soil that control disease, also microorganisms break down the nutrients in the soil so the plants can make use of them. If insects are attracted to the sweet substances, the borax will kill them. The molasses, kelp, and Epson salts will also act as a beneficial foliar spray to stimulate better growth. The milk is to provide calcium to the plants if they show signs of a calcium deficiency. If the young buds and leaves on the plant die back, then you probably have a calcium deficiency. Adding the fish emulsion makes it more effective as a foliar feed.

Formula No. 5
- 3 tablespoons Tabasco sauce
- 2 tablespoons vegetable oil
- 1 tablespoon baking soda
- 1 tablespoon Murphy's Oil soap
- 1 gallon of water

Strain the Tabasco sauce though a cloth or coffee filter. Mix all ingredients together. This is an excellent spray to control disease and insects. This also will repel rodents. This can also be used during the winter and early spring on shrubbery before it starts to put forth new growth to kill scale insects, aphids, and many other insects. This will also kill their eggs.

Formula No. 6
- 1 part lime
- 1 part sulfur powder

Sift these ingredients through a screen wire to remove any lumps. Mix ingredients thoroughly for dusting to control many kinds of insects. Dust corn ears just as you see the first silk starting to protrude from the ears. It will prevent the corn-ear worms from destroying your corn. This dust will also repel the squash vine borer. Apply as soon as the squash start blooming.

Formula No. 7
- 2 cups cider vinegar
- 1 cup molasses
- ¼ teaspoon ammonia
- 3 quarts water

Mix all ingredients together. Fill half-gallon milk jugs or any clear plastic container and fill one-third full of this liquid. Put the cap on the container. Cut holes on each side of the container about one-half to one inch above the liquid in the container. Punch or drill holes through the neck right under the cap to hang bottles. This is an excellent way to trap many destructive months and insects. Hang these in an orchard or around the garden. When it is loaded with insects, pour contents of the bottle into a hole and cover. Refill and use again. This can also be used for snails and slugs. If using it for this purpose, then insert the container into the soil up to about one inch below the openings on the side. They will fall into your mixture and drown.

Formula No. 8
- 1 teaspoon boric acid powder
- ½ cup corn syrup
- 1 pint water

Mix all ingredients well. Soak cotton balls in this solution. Place a few cotton balls in old margarine plastic containers or other containers with lids. Cut a small hole on each side so ants can enter. In two weeks, reduce the amount of boric acid to one-half. This will definitely keep the ants in your garden and home under control.

Formula No. 9
- 1 gallon of coffee
- 2 tablespoons blackstrap molasses
- 1 teaspoon liquid seaweed

James A. Eagle

- 1 tablespoon Epson salts
- ⅛ teaspoon boric acid powder or Borax
- 1 tablespoon Murphy's oil soap
- 2 tablespoons liquid fish emulsion (optional)
- 1 tablespoon baking soda (optional)

In one quart of warm coffee, add the next five ingredients, and mix well. Add the additional three quarts of coffee. Let cool and spray the upper and lower leaves of the plant. This solution will make a wonderful foliar spray that will correct most nutrient deficiencies, especially when adding the fish emulsion. To increase its fungicidal action, then add one tablespoon of baking soda.

Formula No. 10
- 8 pods of very hot pepper (preferably Habanero)
- 8 cloves of garlic
- 2 tablespoons of vegetable oil
- 1 tablespoon baking soda
- 1 tablespoon Murphy's oil soap

Blend the peppers and garlic in a blender with approximately one quart of water. Let set three days or more. Strain through a cloth, and then strain through a coffee filter. This is to insure all vegetable fibers are removed. Add additional water to make one gallon. To this add the other ingredients and mix well. This spray is an excellent spray for disease control when used at intervals of seven to ten days. It will repel or kill many insects and keep rodents and deer from your garden.

Formula No. 11
- 1 cup alfalfa meal
- 1 tablespoon of Murphy's oil soap
- 1 tablespoon baking soda
- 1 gallon of water

Add the alfalfa meal to a gallon of water and let soak for twenty-four hours. Strain through a cloth, then through a coffee filter. Add Murphy's oil soap and baking soda. An additional amount of water may be needed to make a gallon after straining. Spray plants with this mixture. The dry alfalfa meal is a good fertilizer, but making a foliar spray like this is a wonderful way to get nutrients to your plants in a hurry and give them a real boost, and help to prevent diseases, also. You can prevent many fungal diseases with this alfalfa meal spray by applying when plants are small and continuing about every ten days to two weeks until the plant starts blooming. Alfalfa hay may be substituted for the meal, but chop it into very small pieces before soaking.

Formula No. 12
- 3 cloves of garlic
- 2 tablespoons of olive oil
- 2 tablespoons of Tabasco sauce
- 2 tablespoons fish emulsion
- 2 tablespoons of household ammonia
- 1 teaspoon Murphy's oil soap

Blend the garlic and oil until it pureed. Let set for fourteen to seventy-two hours. Strain through coffee filter. Use a gallon, or larger, container and pour garlic oil, adding all other ingredients. Add enough water to make one gallon. This can be sprayed or sprinkled with a sprinkling can. This formula will repel just about any kind of animal, such as deer, rabbits, raccoons, squirrels, opossums, voles, and rats. The oil and Murphy's oil soap helps maintain the ingredients on the plant, making the foliage very distasteful to any animal.

Formula No. 13
- ¼ cup household ammonia
- ½ tablespoon of Murphy's oil soap
- ¼ cup castor oil
- ½ cup of dog, cat or human urine
- 1 gallon of water

This is another formula that will keep just about anything out of the garden, including yourself.

Mix all of the above ingredients with the one gallon of water and spray on the foliage of plants bothered by animals. *Do Not* use on vegetables that you plan on eating.

Formula 14
- 1 tablespoon fish emulsion
- 1 tablespoon liquid sea week
- 1 tablespoon natural apple cider vinegar
- 1 tablespoon black strap molasses
- 1 tablespoon Epson salts (optional)

This is an excellent spray for foliar feeding your plants at any time. It is a light spray, but I have found that is very effective when applying about every seven days on the plants. It seems to be more effective using it regular than one heavy spray. It keeps plants in a healthy and productive state. Use the Epson salts if you believe your soil may be deficient in magnesium or sulfur.

Formula 15
- 1 gallon of water
- 1 peel of one citrus fruit, this can be orange grapefruit, or lemon
- 2 tablespoons liquid seaweed (Kelp)
- 1 tablespoon Murphy's oil soap

This spray will help control insects, killing many, and provides nutrients for the plant as well. Blend citrus peel along with the seed in one cup of warm water. Let set for twenty-four hours and strain. Mix with other ingredients and one gallon of water. Spray on foliage of plants.

References

Acres USA Magazine from 1985 to 1997.

Wyman's Gardening Encyclopedia, New Expanded Edition by Donald Wyman, Copyright© MCMLXIV, MCMLXVII, New and Revised Addition MCMLXXII by The Greystone Press, 225Park Avenue South, New York, N. Y. 10003, Copyright© 1971, 1977, 1986 by Donald Wyman.

HORTUS THIRD, A Concise Dictionary of Plants Cultivated in the United States and Canada. Compiled by the staff of L.H. Bailey Hortorium, Cornell University, Copyright© 1976 by Cornell University for its L.H. Bailey Hortorium.

The New Illustrated Encyclopedia of Gardening. Edited by T.H. Everett. Assistant Director (Horticulture) and Curator of Education, New York Botanical Garden,

Publications of the American Rose Society.

Internet site www.answersingenesis.org. , and www.ins.org.

Organic Gardening Magazines from 1957 to 1987.

1998 Herb Quarterly Magazine.